"Every now and then a scholarly work so aptly meets a glaring need that one is tempted to cry out, 'Why wasn't this done before?' Once again, Francis Moloney has drawn upon his internationally renowned biblical expertise, vast knowledge of scholarly literature, and theological sensitivity to produce this timely resource for pastors and educators in the Christian tradition. It admirably achieves its aim of bridging the gap between technical biblical scholarship and scriptural literacy in the church."

—**Brendan Byrne, SJ**, University of Divinity (Melbourne)

"In this learned but pastoral guidebook, Moloney helps Catholics (and ecumenical readers) read Scripture both critically and with faith in Jesus, and in and for the church. Moloney immerses readers in early Christian beliefs in Jesus' death, resurrection, and living presence, vigorously rejecting the common academic distinction between the Jesus of history and the Christ of faith. I heartily recommend this introduction to reading the New Testament as an excellent textbook for seminaries and training programs for deacons and lay Catholic ministers."

—**William S. Kurz, SJ**, Marquette University

"Moloney's latest book is a gift for Catholics who want to read the New Testament as both serious Christians and intelligently critical citizens of the modern world. It will also serve as a comprehensive textbook for students who may read only one book on the subject. As always, Moloney's talent as a teacher is bolstered by his scholarship rather than encumbered by it."

—**Sandra M. Schneiders, IHM**, Jesuit School of Theology of Santa Clara University and Graduate Theological Union, Berkeley, California

"After many decades as a Catholic priest and a distinguished biblical scholar, Frank Moloney has written this important and reflective book to remind the modern church of the importance of its Scriptures. It guides readers through the New Testament documents with clarity and with the sure hands of an experienced exegete, pastor, and teacher. *Reading the New Testament in the Church* provides a timely reminder that the modern community of faith, both Catholic and non-Catholic, must read, appreciate, understand, and be informed by its ancient Scriptures."

—**David Sim**, Australian Catholic University

Reading the New Testament in the Church

A Primer for Pastors,
Religious Educators, and Believers

Francis J. Moloney, SDB

Baker Academic
a division of Baker Publishing Group
Grand Rapids, Michigan

© 2015 by Francis J. Moloney

Published by Baker Academic
a division of Baker Publishing Group
P.O. Box 6287, Grand Rapids, MI 49516-6287
www.bakeracademic.com

Printed and bound by CPI Group (UK) Ltd, Croydon, CR0 4YY

Library of Congress Cataloging-in-Publication Data

Moloney, Francis J.
    Reading the New Testament in the church : a primer for pastors, religious educators, and believers / Francis J. Moloney, SDB.
        pages cm
    Includes bibliographical references and index.
    ISBN 978-0-8010-4980-4 (pbk.)
    1. Bible. New Testament—Criticism, interpretation, etc. 2. Catholic Church—Doctrines.
I. Title.
    BS2361.3.M66 2015
    225.6′1—dc23   2014038725

Nihil Obstat: Reverend Peter J. Kenny, STD
            Diocesan Censor

Imprimatur: Monsignor Greg Bennet
            Vicar General

Date: July 28, 2014

The *Nihil Obstat* and *Imprimatur* are official declarations that a book or pamphlet is free of doctrinal or moral error. No implication is contained therein that those who have granted the *Nihil Obstat* and *Imprimatur* agree with the contents, opinions, or statements expressed. They do not necessarily signify that the work is approved as a basic text for catechetical instruction.

15   16   17   18   19   20   21   7   6   5   4   3   2   1

The relationship of Church, Scripture and scriptural interpretation has suddenly become a burning question in many circles. In my view we ought to be glad that an important theological theme of this kind is no longer the preserve of academic interests but has been taken up by local congregations.

—Ernst Käsemann, March 12, 1962

For my fellow Salesians, pastors,
religious educators, and believers
at Don Bosco Hall,
Berkeley, California, USA,
and Don Bosco House,
Clifton Hill, Victoria, Australia

Contents

Preface

First encounters can be fascinating. We like to know the ethnic and geographical origins of others, and we are interested in their occupations in life. I was born and bred in Australia. These origins are a good start. Many regard my far-flung homeland as a paradise, marked by a free and easy lifestyle, a sound economy, and a stable (if at times stormy) parliamentary government. Problems arise when a second question is asked: What do you do? My first response is that I am a Catholic priest, a member of a religious congregation. In today's increasingly secularized world, this can be something of a conversation stopper, but once people have this information, they generally ask which parish I serve.

However, my life and ministry have not been in a parish or a diocese. I have worked in education, and largely tertiary education, all my adult life. I am simultaneously a Catholic priest and a university professor. This information leads to a final question: What do you teach? My specialization is the Bible, with a particular interest and expertise in the more recent part of the Bible that was produced by the early Christian church in the second half of the first Christian century. It is generally known as the New Testament. In Australia, where universities with religious studies departments are rare, an academic career specializing in the New Testament is something of an anomaly. Most educated people are aware of the literary world with its many languages, literatures, numerous "classics" in different forms (poetry, narrative, critical essays, travel narratives, biographies, and so forth). Some are also aware of a solid body of critical theory that is used in assessing and appreciating these traditions. The discipline of biblical studies belongs to that area of academic interest. However, most biblical scholars, especially those who are ordained ministers in a Christian tradition, bring to their world and work a level of faith and commitment to Christianity. The interface between our professional careers and our day-to-day lives as believing Christians can become a problem.

My long experience as a priest, a religious, a teacher, and a published author tells me that there is still a need to build bridges between, on the one hand, those of us who devote our lives to the interpretation of the New Testament within the church and, on the other, the life of the church itself. The problem is not found so much in the situation described above—that is, the lack of awareness of thinking, teaching, and writing about the Bible. It runs deeper and is widespread, even in those places, such as the United States and Europe, where the study of the Bible and religions has long been part of university curricula. In most parts of the world, across all Christian traditions, tensions exist between ecclesial communities and biblical scholars. At worst, the suggestions of scholars are not trusted; they are regarded as a threat to the faith of believers. More common, however, is the lack of interest in what a small group of specialists are doing in their professional playpens, with their Hebrew, Greek, literary, and theological concerns. Pastors, religious educators, believers, and even theologians suffer from these tensions. It would be a blessing for all concerned if they could be eased.

No single contemporary figure better highlights this problem among Catholics than the prestigious German theologian Joseph Ratzinger, the retired Pope Benedict XVI. Professor Ratzinger was a leading expert at the Second Vatican Council. He had a special interest (and role) in the eventual proclamation of the groundbreaking document on Revelation from the council (*Dei Verbum*) in 1965.[1] In major contributions to a multivolume commentary on the conciliar documents, while still professor of systematic theology in the Catholic Faculty at the University of Tübingen, he wrote expertly of the relationship between the critical study of the Bible and the teaching authority of the Church. Commenting upon *Dei Verbum*, he wrote of the rich contribution of Vatican II to the relationship between Scripture and Tradition in paragraph 9:

> We shall have to acknowledge the truth of the criticism that there is, in fact, no explicit mention of the possibility of a distorting tradition and the place of Scripture as an element in the Church that is *also* critical of tradition, which means that a most important side of the problem of tradition, as shown by the history of the church—and perhaps the real crux of the *ecclesia semper*

1. All references and citations from the documents of the Second Vatican Council are taken from Austin Flannery, ed., *Vatican Council II: Constitutions, Decrees, Declarations; A Completely Revised Translation in Inclusive Language* (Northport, NY: Costello, 1995).

reformanda ["the church . . . always in need of being purified" (*Lumen Gentium* 8)]—has been overlooked. In particular a council that saw itself consciously as a council of reform and thus implicitly acknowledged the possibility and reality of distortion in tradition could have achieved here in its thinking a real achievement in theological examination, both of itself and of its own purpose. That this opportunity has been missed can only be regarded as an unfortunate omission.[2]

In a later reflection on *Dei Verbum* (*DV*), dedicated to the role of Scripture in the life of the Church, Ratzinger adds further food for thought: "A reference to the ecclesial nature of exegesis, on the one hand, and to its methodological correctness on the other [see *DV* 12], again expresses the inner tension of church exegesis, which can no longer be removed, *but must simply be accepted as tension.*"[3] These are fundamental and encouraging principles that should guide the work of the interpreter of the Word of God in the service of the Church. But the excitement and encouragement ushered in by Vatican II has waned, and many Catholic scholars, who hesitated a long time before joining the tradition of a critical approach exercised by many other Christian biblical scholars, find themselves in a period of lack of confidence, and even trust, in their service to the Church. Joseph Ratzinger's hope, in 1967, that this could serve as a life-giving tension within the Church needs to be restored.

Joseph Ratzinger's passion for the role of the Word of God in the life of the Christian Church remained vibrant as he exercised his papal ministry. This was especially evident in his exhortation on the Word of God in the life and mission of the Church that followed the Episcopal Synod of 2009, *Verbum Domini.*[4] However, it is also evident in his three-volume work on Jesus of Nazareth. Benedict XVI stated unequivocally that his voice was only one among many, and he did not wish to create the impression that his understanding of Jesus was the only one possible.[5]

The three volumes contain much that is helpful, and it is encouraging to see the Pope using critical scholarship, even though most of it is somewhat

2. Joseph Ratzinger, "The Transmission of Divine Revelation," in *Commentary on the Documents of Vatican II*, ed. Herbert Vorgrimler (London: Burns & Oates/Herder & Herder, 1969), 3:192–93.

3. Joseph Ratzinger, "Sacred Scripture in the Life of the Church," in *Commentary on the Documents of Vatican II*, 3:268. Emphasis added.

4. Pope Benedict XVI, *Verbum Domini: The Word of God in the Life and Mission of the Church*, Post-Synodal Apostolic Exhortation (Rome: Editrice Vaticana, 2010). For a commentary on this papal document, see James Chukwuma Okoye, *Scripture in the Church: The Synod on the Word of God and the Post-Synodal Exhortation* Verbum Domini (Collegeville, MN: Liturgical Press, 2011), 127–79.

5. See Joseph Ratzinger, *Jesus of Nazareth*, 3 vols. (New York/San Francisco: Doubleday/Image/Ignatius Press, 2007–12); here I refer to 1:xxiii–xxiv.

dated (reflecting his own time as a professional academic) or limited to a certain section of German scholarship (indicating his lack of time and space to conduct full-scale research). A careful reader senses Benedict's personal discomfort with critical biblical scholarship. He accepts the necessity of the historical-critical method but regards it as limited and suggests that there is not much more that it can offer. He claims that it no longer produces an "image" (*Gestalt*) of Jesus that nourishes the lives of the faithful.[6] His claim to be producing a study "to portray the Jesus of the Gospels as the real, 'historical' Jesus in the strict sense of the word" disappoints many who have a more critical, yet faith-filled, understanding of the Gospel texts analyzed by the Holy Father.[7]

Pope Benedict XVI writes to "be helpful to all believers who seek to encounter Jesus and to believe in him" and "to make possible a personal relationship with Jesus."[8] The Gospels are documents that come to us in a foreign language and were produced almost two thousand years ago. These two factors alone (an ancient language and a different time and culture) call for some critical skills. We, as Christian New Testament scholars who turn to the Gospels as part of a Christian revelation of the Word of God, wish to use our skills "to be helpful to all believers" and "to make possible a personal relationship with Jesus." The mission of the Christian New Testament scholar is to bridge the cultural, religious, and chronological gap that inevitably blocks direct access to the New Testament. This calls for the use of critical New Testament scholarship, on the one hand, and for a loyal articulation of one's Christian tradition, on the other. Ernst Käsemann, cited in the epigraph to this book, is a classic example of a passionate Lutheran scholar who recognizes that his service to his church as a New Testament scholar must follow the path of Martin Luther, for whom the Bible was "essentially an emergency aid, precisely because, in his view, God's Word is not susceptible of being confined in a book."[9] This has long been central to the Catholic Tradition, with its strong understanding of the role of Tradition as part of the Word of God, but most Protestant churches are also deeply concerned about the interpretation of the Bible within their tradition.

The study that follows attempts to open more widely the door that gives access to the New Testament, interpreted within the Christian and Catholic

---

6. See Ratzinger, *Jesus of Nazareth*, 1:xi–xiv; 2:xiii–xvii.

7. See Ratzinger, *Jesus of Nazareth*, 1:xxii.

8. See Ratzinger, *Jesus of Nazareth*, 2:xvii, xvi.

9. Ernst Käsemann, "Thoughts on the Present Controversy about Scriptural Interpretation," in *New Testament Questions of Today* (Philadelphia: Fortress, 1969), 274. The quotation in the epigraph of this book comes from p. 260 of Käsemann's essay.

Tradition. It is a faith-directed yet critical introduction to a reading of the New Testament in the Church, respecting the influence and limitations of the world that produced it, insisting that "just as the life of the Church grows through persistent participation in the Eucharistic mystery, so we may hope for a new surge of spiritual vitality from intensified veneration for God's word, which 'lasts forever' (Isa. 40:8; cf. 1 Pet. 1:23–25)" (*DV* 26).

This cannot be done without coming to grips with some fundamental elements that define the nature of the literature of the New Testament and the principles of interpretation that must come into play in reading this ancient document in our contemporary world. Only thus can we hope to acquire a creative and nourishing understanding of the New Testament that can then flow into and enrich our service of the Church and its faithful in our roles as pastors, religious educators, and theologians. Every book in the New Testament, from the simplest to the most complex, was born of passionate commitment to what God has done for us in and through Jesus Christ and was written to communicate and share that belief. This book attempts to capture that passionate communication of faith, hope, and love.

Like Benedict XVI, I have written the book that follows "to be helpful to all believers" and "to make possible a personal relationship with Jesus," as a Catholic response to Benedict's apostolic exhortation *Verbum Domini*, especially paragraphs 29–49, "The Interpretation of Sacred Scripture in the Church."[10] It is dedicated to the two communities of my religious congregation that housed and cared for me as I wrote it, one in Berkeley, California, and the other in Clifton Hill, Victoria, Australia. May we maintain and strengthen our commitment to live and proclaim the Word of God.

I express my gratitude to James Ernest, whose long-standing familiarity with my work on New Testament texts led him to suggest and supportively direct this more "hands-on" primer, raising the urgent question of how to read the New Testament in today's Church. To my objection that my main interest is not hermeneutics but texts, James responded, "Yes, but you know what you are doing when you work with texts. This is what you should share." I hope I have done so. I was privileged to have Pheme Perkins, an outstanding scholar from the Catholic tradition, read the entire manuscript in its original draft. Her scholarly acumen and awareness of what is both needed and useful for

10. See para. 45, "Dialogue between Pastors, Theologians and Exegetes." It closes: "Using appropriate techniques they should together set about examining and explaining the sacred texts in such a way that as many as possible of those who are ministers of God's Word may be able to dispense fruitfully the nourishment of the Scriptures to the people of God. This nourishment enlightens the mind, strengthens the will and fires the hearts of men and women with the love of God." On this section of the Pope's exhortation, see Okoye, *Scripture in the Church*, 147–57.

its proposed audience have made it a much better book. Author and readers are in her debt. I am also grateful to my editor, Tim West, whose careful attention to my writing has resulted in a quality production, as we have come to expect from the house of Baker Academic.

Francis J. Moloney, SDB, AM, FAHA
Institute for Religion and Critical Inquiry
Australian Catholic University, Melbourne, Victoria, Australia

1

Catholic and Critical

*The Challenge of Scripture
in the Catholic Tradition*

The Bible is known "by name." It can be seen in bookshops, in hotel rooms, at church services. Indeed, the Bible remains the best-selling book in the world. It contains passages that have become part of everyday use in English. Proverbial sayings such as "do unto others as you would have them do unto you" (see Luke 6:31), "go the extra mile" (see Matt. 5:41), "wash your hands" of something (see Pilate's action in Matt. 27:24), "eat, drink, and be merry" (see Luke 12:19), "it is more blessed to give than to receive" (see Acts 20:35), and "the powers that be" (see Rom. 13:1) are a tiny sample of the many well-known phrases that have their origins in the Bible.[1] Some will be familiar with a "family Bible," in which all the births, baptisms, marriages, and deaths have been recorded for several generations.

But once the book is opened and read, difficulties emerge. The language is archaic, and the world from which the various stories come is distant from

---

1. On how the Bible (especially the King James Version of 1611) has shaped English language and literature, see Northrop Frye, *The Great Code: The Bible and Literature* (London: Routledge & Kegan Paul, 1982). Harold Bloom, *The Shadow of a Great Rock: A Literary Appreciation of the King James Bible* (New Haven: Yale University Press, 2011), is less positive.

the one we inhabit. The experience becomes more critical when we seek answers to pressing contemporary issues in the pages of the Bible. It is helpful to know that one of the greatest figures from the Christian tradition, the young Augustine, found that the Bible "seemed to me unworthy in comparison with Cicero. My inflated conceit shunned the Bible's restraint, and my gaze never penetrated to its inwardness."[2] This "inwardness" is one of the reasons the Church regards the Bible as its Sacred Scripture.

Reading the Bible

The Bible is not *a book*. It is a collection of many books, starting from the book of Genesis on its first page and ending with the Apocalypse, or Revelation, on its last. The origin of the English word "bible" is a Greek word, *biblia*. It is a plural word that simply means "books." The *biblia* (Bible) is not *a* book but a *collection* of books. The older section of the Bible, most of which was established as the Sacred Scripture of Israel before the time of Jesus of Nazareth, is traditionally called "the Old Testament."[3] This name is sometimes challenged today, as calling the Christian Sacred Scriptures "the New Testament" can generate a distinction between what is old (and therefore outdated) and what is new (demanding more of our attention). Sometimes the names "First and Second Testament" or "the Hebrew Scriptures and the Christian Scriptures" are used to avoid the danger of that possible distinction. But that is not necessarily the case, and these alternatives also generate difficulties. For example, parts of the "Hebrew Bible" are in Aramaic, and the Greek version of the Hebrew, called the Septuagint (LXX), was for the majority of New Testament authors the text used as Scripture, and this continued to be the case in the early Church's use of "the Bible." In this book I will continue to use the traditional terminology, as the Old Testament is the older of the two testaments. This does not make it any less important. Indeed, it is impossible to understand Jesus, early Christianity, and the New Testament unless we see both Old and New Testament as one divinely revealed Word of God. They are both "testament," a precious "gift," and one is older than the other.[4]

2. Saint Augustine, *Confessions*, trans. Henry Chadwick (Oxford: Oxford University Press, 1991), 6.10 (p. 40).

3. It is not clear when the whole of the Old Testament as we know it was regarded by the Jews as Sacred Scripture, but the process was nearing completion in the first Christian century.

4. On this, see the wise remarks of Gerhard Lohfink, *Jesus of Nazareth: What He Wanted, Who He Was*, trans. Linda M. Maloney (Collegeville, MN: Liturgical Press, 2012), 188–89.

Within these "books" we find stories that look like narrative *history*. Some texts in the Old Testament are called "the historical books." This expression is applied especially, but not only, to the two books of Samuel and the two books of Kings. There are also books in the New Testament that look like narrative *history*: the Gospels of Matthew, Mark, Luke, and John and the Acts of the Apostles tell the story of Jesus' birth, his life and teaching, his death and resurrection (Gospels), and the subsequent spread of the Christian community from Jerusalem to Rome (Acts). They look like "history books" to a reader living in the third Christian millennium, and most churchgoers understand them as such. But these impressions can be deceiving. There is also a great deal of poetry in the Old Testament, especially, but not only, in the book of Psalms. Poetry is also found in the New Testament. Two well-known "poems," most likely early Christian hymns, can be found in the Prologue to the Gospel of John (John 1:1–18) and Paul's Letter to the Philippians (Phil. 2:5–11), the latter of which describes Jesus' descent from equality with God, through death on a cross, to an ascent into exaltation at the right hand of God, where every knee will bow at his name. There are other such "hymns" scattered across the New Testament, especially in the Apocalypse.

The prophets wrote oracles that accuse, cajole, encourage, condemn, and punish. There is also a lot of "teaching" in the Old Testament, including in the great law books of Israel—Genesis, Exodus, Leviticus, Numbers, Deuteronomy—and in the Prophets and books that come from what we call the Wisdom tradition—Ben Sirach (also called Ecclesiasticus and found only in Catholic Bibles), Qoheleth (Ecclesiastes in Protestant Bibles), the book of Wisdom of Solomon (also only found in Catholic Bibles), and Proverbs. There is even a very beautiful love song, the Canticle of Canticles (also called Song of Songs or Song of Solomon), that affirms the beauty and importance of sexual love in an interpretation that runs side by side with a long Catholic tradition that this song is about the soul's desire for union with God. A challenging form of literature called "apocalyptic" also appears from time to time, especially in the book of Daniel. It seeks to explain current suffering and the apparent lack of any possible human resolution of that suffering as part of God's design, pointing to God's intervention as the Lord of all history.

The same variety is found in the New Testament. Paul's letters contain the earliest written "teaching" of the Christian Church. But in these letters, side by side with letters from other figures from the early Church, one can also find accusing oracles, cajoling, condemnation, and the threat of punishment. One can also find indications of affection and close fellowship. The teaching tradition continues in the practice of writing theological tracts (Letter to the

Hebrews). The practice of apocalyptic writing brings the New Testament and the Bible to an end (the Apocalypse).

These many "books" come from very different times; have their own historical, religious, and social background; and were written to address different issues across those centuries. The oldest of the literary traditions in the Old Testament probably reaches back to about 1000 BCE (Before the Common Era). Although we can only speculate about dates, about the antiquity of the traditions, and about whether they came from family or tribal origins, these ancient traditions may have had their origins in a very ancient culture that told its "stories" in familiar family and tribal settings, and these stories were eventually committed to writing. From that earliest period, almost every period of Israel's history until 165–70 BCE (the book of Daniel) is represented by a book or section of a book in the Old Testament.

The time span behind the New Testament is much briefer. We cannot be certain, but Jesus of Nazareth lived from about 4 BCE until the early 30s of the Common Era (CE). The earliest subsequent document that we have (Paul's First Letter to the Thessalonians) was written about 50 CE. The most recent of the Gospels probably appeared about 100 CE (John), but later documents that continued the Pauline traditions appeared early in the second Christian century (1–2 Timothy, Titus). While the Old Testament reflects almost one thousand years of Israel's history and response to God's initiative, the New Testament appeared across less than one hundred years. In itself this says something about the explosive nature of the story of Jesus of Nazareth's life, teaching, death, and resurrection and the subsequent emergence of a powerful group of believers who wanted to tell that story and reflect upon its meaning. But it does not take away from the majesty of a national story of a God-chosen people and the record of its problematic relationship with its God across a thousand years, found in the pages of the Old Testament. One of the reasons the early Christians began to think of a "Sacred Scripture" associated with the life, death, resurrection, and subsequent heritage of Jesus was that they already accepted the Old Testament, the Sacred Scripture of Israel, as part of their heritage. The New Testament continued that heritage in the light of the event of Jesus Christ.

The variety of types of literature and the great span of historical and socio-religious settings within which the books of the New Testament were eventually produced are significant challenges to any interpreter. Added to these is the fact that all the books were written in a popular late form of Greek known as koinē. As outsiders looking into the world of Greek-speaking authors, we will always be limited in what we can catch of the original sense of those foreign words, even if we know some Greek.

Necessary or Not?

Week by week we listen to biblical texts read in church services. Bible-study groups and prayer groups that rely on the Bible as the Word of God for their inspiration and guidance are found all over the world. Some Catholics claim that one only needs to hear *what they think* the Pope, bishops, and priests have to say.[5] They claim that there is no need for the interpretation of the New Testament in the Church. It is irrelevant at best or damaging to the Christian and Catholic Church at worst. Another approach to reading the New Testament is "fundamentalism." These believers claim that no "mediation" is required between the Word of God articulated in the biblical text and the reader or hearer of that text. All one needs to do is hear or read the biblical Word proclaimed or read in an English translation. This must be taken as an infallible Word of God. Rigid groups found across all Christian confessions follow this interpretative practice. They run the danger of yielding to fanaticism and often lack tolerance of any point of view other than their own. This approach to the Word of God and to others is hard to accept within a more universal understanding of Jesus Christ and those who follow him.

Nevertheless, Catholic interpretation wears its presuppositions on its sleeve. It is part of an interpretative tradition that has gone on for almost two thousand years. God's word is available to us in other places, not only in the holy book of the Bible. It must be so, as no book can hope to contain all that God has made known in the past, continues to communicate today, and will reveal in the future. Interpreting the New Testament in the Church calls for openness to the guidance provided to the interpreter by the Tradition to which she or he belongs. This process is not a restrictive imposition or a loss of academic freedom. It often proves to be a way into unexpected and exciting developments of the Tradition itself.

Catholics and the Bible: A Brief History

Beginnings

Prior to the Protestant Reformation in the sixteenth century, the Christian Church, although divided within itself among Eastern churches and thus

5. The indication that some Catholics follow "what they think" various Church authorities are saying reflects a further step in the process of interpretation. Quite complex issues are faced by Church leadership, and those listening to their decisions listen with their prejudices and prior judgments in place. It is impossible not to do so. It is true of reading the Bible and also true for an understanding of Church teaching.

not without its sinfulness, always regarded the Gospels and the Epistles as the "apostolic preaching," the foundation of Christian faith. In the earliest Church the authors of the New Testament books looked back to the Old Testament as their Scripture, as they began to articulate what the God of Israel had done for humankind through the life, teaching, death, and resurrection of Jesus. In the time of the so-called apostolic fathers, Christian authors continued to use the Old Testament as their Scripture and steadily began to recognize many early Christian writings as authoritative. As we will see later, the eventual acceptance of the New Testament as part of the Church's Scripture emerged in the third century. The apostolic fathers of the second century strained to articulate the message of the Bible, and especially the message of Jesus Christ, in a new world that had little or no understanding of either the Jewish matrix that had given birth to Jesus or the subsequent early reflection on what God had done in and through him. This task was undertaken, in different ways, by all these early interpreters, especially Clement of Alexandria (150–215), who bridged from the apostolic fathers and apologists of the second century to the patristic tradition of the third and later centuries.

The great fathers of the Church constantly used the Scriptures to develop and understand the Christian mysteries and the life and practice of the Church. There was *no single interpretation* of the Bible. Different methods of interpretation were used in the West and in the East, and in the East between Antioch and Alexandria. The great councils that determined the Christian community's teaching and practice (Nicaea [325], Constantinople I [381], Ephesus [431], Chalcedon [451], Constantinople II [553]) are awash with reflections on the Word of God. Indeed, debate over the many possible meanings of the one text was at the heart of the heated conciliar disputes and generated "parties," schisms, and even persecutions among Christian peoples. The results of this widespread, contested, and varied interpretation of the Bible can still be traced in the richness of that heritage. It is found in the writings of such figures in the West as Tertullian (ca. 160–ca. 225), Saint Ambrose (340–97), Saint Jerome (347–420), Saint Augustine (354–430), Leo the Great (ca. 391–461), and Saint Gregory the Great (540–604), and in the East, Origen (184–254), Saint Athanasius (ca. 296–373), Saint John Chrysostom (347–407), Saint Basil (329–79), and Saint Gregory of Nyssa (335–95), to mention only a few of the giants from that era.

Many of these biblically inspired traditions were forced into the background in the eleventh century as papal authority struggled with the secular princes. A more juridical and less biblical, theological, and sacramental self-understanding of Christianity began to develop.[6] In the medieval period significant women emerged, such as Margaret of Scotland (1045–93), Hildegard of Bingen (1098–1179), Elizabeth of Hungary (1207–31), and Julian of Norwich (1342–ca. 1419). The great theological synthesis of Thomas Aquinas (1225–74) appeared. He had been preceded by Saint Anselm (1033–1109) and Peter Lombard (1096–1164), who wrote, along with his famous *Four Books of Sentences*, commentaries on the Psalms and the letters of Saint Paul. Thomas Aquinas had been taught by Saint Albert the Great (1193–1280). The essential point of reference in the differing approaches and critical questioning of *all these figures* was the Bible, despite a Church leadership that focused more closely on its legal authority over secular powers.

A similar richness can be heard in the splendor of the musical rendering of biblical texts in Gregorian chant and in the more delicate music of Hildegard of Bingen. It can be seen in the glass windows of the great medieval churches in Europe. Thomas Aquinas, whose theological synthesis brought the philosophy of Aristotle into the thought of the Church and was the high point of medieval Catholic thought, depended heavily on the Bible. He produced commentaries on the Psalms, Job, Lamentations, the Gospel of John, Romans, Galatians, 1 and 2 Corinthians, 1 Thessalonians, Philippians, Philemon, Colossians, Ephesians, and Hebrews, and an amazing collection of *different* patristic readings of the four Gospels in his famous *Catena Aurea* (Golden Chain). He also looked upon Augustine, and his biblically based writings, as the greatest of the fathers of the Church.

The Council of Trent and Vatican I

A narrowing of the Catholic Church's earlier rich practice of interpreting the Bible reaches back to the Council of Trent, which met intermittently from 1545 to 1563. This great ecumenical council was called to guide the Roman tradition in its struggle to respond to the Protestant Reformation. Briefly, the Council of Trent insisted that the interpretation of the Word of God as it is found in the Bible had to be directed by the teaching of the Church. By this stage in the history of the Catholic Church there were many doctrines and practices that could not be found in the New Testament. The Reformers

---

6. The development of a more juridically structured Church goes back to the reforms of Pope Gregory VII (1073–85). The authority of the Pope over the secular princes was dramatically acted out in the submission of Henry VII (Holy Roman Emperor) to Gregory VII at Canossa in 1077. For a brief summary of this period and its effects upon the Catholic Church's self-understanding, see Richard Gaillardetz, *The Church in the Making*, Rediscovering Vatican II (Mahwah, NJ: Paulist Press, 2006), 145–47.

seized upon that, rejecting such beliefs and practices as the institution of the priesthood, many of the Marian teachings, the seven Sacraments, the papacy, and the real presence of the crucified and risen Jesus in the celebration of the Eucharist, to name some of the most critical points of division. These doctrines were not found in the Word of God, regarded by the Protestant tradition as found only in the Bible.

The council responded by teaching that there were two sources of Revelation: Tradition and Scripture. It was true that many doctrines and practices of the Catholic Church could not be found in the New Testament, but they could be found in the Tradition. If a belief or a practice of the Catholic Church could not be found in the New Testament, only one of the sources of Revelation, then the authentic Tradition of the Church could be called upon as the other source of Revelation. Never explicitly stated, there was a presupposition that the Revelation found in the Catholic Tradition was superior to the Revelation found in the Bible. It certainly appeared to have more authority. This same assessment of Tradition and Scripture as different sources of Revelation was repeated in 1870, in the Constitution *Dei Filius*, when Vatican I reexamined the Church's doctrine of Revelation. In the face of emerging radical, and sometimes anti-Christian, critical biblical scholarship, the authority of the Tradition was reaffirmed.

Another major decision made at Trent was the virtual "canonization" of the Latin Vulgate Bible. This Latin translation of the original Hebrew, Aramaic, and Greek, which was largely (but not only) the work of Saint Jerome, was declared the text to be used by Catholics. The Church moved away from the original languages of Hebrew and Greek. For five centuries there was a neglect of the original biblical texts by laypeople and clergy. Those few who developed a biblical culture did so on the basis of the Latin text.[7]

Most Catholics are unaware of the richness of the Catholic practice of interpreting the Bible critically but within—and never against—the authentic Tradition, practiced in the Church for the greater part of fourteen hundred years. Passing "traditions," generated by a given time and place, are dearer to many Catholics than the Word of God. The acceptance and observance of these "traditions" can become the touchstone of Catholic orthodoxy, as a critical reading of the Bible is less common in Catholic practice.[8] This has

---

7. Some care is needed in assessing the Council of Trent. Crucial biblical issues were faced in the council's fourth session in April 1546, but the bishops, at that stage still hoping for the presence of some of the Reformers in Trent, nuanced what it taught. See John W. O'Malley, *Trent: What Happened at the Council* (Cambridge, MA: Harvard University Press, 2013), 89–102. However, these nuanced positions *at the council* were applied more rigidly *after the council*. See ibid., 260–75.

8. The use of the two forms of the same word, "Tradition" and "traditions," is common in Roman Catholic discussions. Within the Tradition one finds the long-standing and permanent

led to a decreased practice of reading and interpreting the New Testament in the Church.

Vatican II, in its all-determining agenda of returning to the sources of the faith (using the French word *ressourcement*), has asked all Catholics to rediscover the original "sources" of their faith and practice. This necessarily summons the whole of the Catholic Church to return to the Scriptures, but the process did not start with Vatican II. It had its beginnings in an encyclical of Leo XIII in 1893, *Providentissimus Deus* (PD), and a further biblical encyclical from Pius XII, *Divino Afflante Spiritu* (DAS), written in 1943 to commemorate the fiftieth anniversary of *Providentissimus Deus*.[9]

Leo XIII and Pius XII

Providentissimus Deus comes from an era when the negative results of emerging—and sometimes stridently anti-Christian—critical biblical scholarship had to be countered (PD 2, 10). Great attention is given to the long Catholic tradition of studying the Word of God (PD 7–8) and the need to explain the Scriptures within that tradition (PD 15–17). According to *Providentissimus Deus*, the Word of God is authentically transmitted in the Latin Vulgate (PD 13) and is the result of divine authorship (PD 1: "a Letter written by our Heavenly Father, and transmitted by the sacred writers"), a theory that leads to a very restrictive notion of inerrancy (PD 21). The proper formation of Catholic teachers, and the course of studies that should be taught in the seminaries, up until this time was somewhat dependent on local decisions (PD 11–14). Everything must proceed under "the watchful care of the Church" (PD 6). Given the hostile context and the fact that Vatican I had spoken on this matter as recently as 1870 (*Dei Filius*), *Providentissimus Deus* is, on the whole, understandably defensive. However, something new was in the air, as Leo XIII explicitly stated: "Most desirable is it, and most

beliefs that lie at the heart of Catholic life and practice, many of which are not found in the Bible (e.g., the Trinity, the human and the divine in Jesus, the seven Sacraments [including marriage], the papacy, the priesthood). One the other hand, "traditions" are beliefs and practices that come and go, often the result of given ecclesial, social, and civil situations (e.g., devotion to the Sacred Heart, devotion to Divine Mercy and its liturgical celebration, the many Marian devotions, Benediction and Adoration, the practice of the nine First Fridays and the five First Saturdays, clerical celibacy). However important they may be to some Catholics, traditions do not form part of the Tradition. See the further discussion of this matter below, pp. 199–201.

9. For another useful history of Catholic biblical scholarship in this period, see Okoye, *Scripture in the Church*, 69–91. The English translations of the two encyclicals cited here are Pope Leo XIII, *Holy Scripture (Providentissimus Deus)* (New York: Paulist Press, 1951), and Pope Pius XII, *Foundations of Renewal: Four Great Encyclicals of Pope Pius XII*, Deus Books (New York: Paulist Press, 1961), 64–87.

essential, that the whole teaching of theology should be pervaded and ani-
mated by the use of the divine Word of God. This is what the Fathers and
the greatest theologians of all ages have desired and reduced to practice"
(*PD* 16). In the midst of his careful defense of the theological agenda of
the time, Leo XIII paved the way for the breakthrough of Pius XII's *Divino
Afflante Spiritu* in 1943. However tentatively, in a number of areas creative
biblical research is advocated. In a memorable affirmation Leo XIII makes
clear:

> But he [the Catholic biblical scholar] must not on that account consider that
> it is forbidden, when just cause exists, to push enquiry and exposition beyond
> what the Fathers have done; provided he carefully observes the rule so wisely laid
> down by St Augustine—not to depart from the literal and obvious sense, except
> only where reason makes it untenable or necessity requires. (*PD* 15, referring to
> Augustine, *De Genesi ad litteram* 1.8.7:13)

Breaking from the dominance of the Latin text that had been in place since the
time of the Council of Trent, the Pope instructs: "Hence it is most proper that
professors of sacred Scripture and theologians should master those tongues
in which the sacred books were originally written; and it would be well that
Church students should also cultivate them, more especially those who aspire
to academic degrees" (*PD* 17).

In 1890 Leo XIII had authorized the establishment of the École Biblique et
Archéologique de Jérusalem by Marie-Joseph Lagrange, OP, and the Pontifical Biblical Commission was formed in 1902, the last year of his life. In his
wake Pius X founded the Pontifical Biblical Institute in Rome in 1909. This
new openness, however, was tempered by Pius X's decree *Lamentabili sane*
(1907) and his encyclical *Pascendi dominici gregis* (1907). Pius X sensed that
the "modern world" was alien to the Catholic Church and its traditions, and
he strove to protect the integrity of Catholic faith and practice. Defensively,
he spoke of a new heresy called "modernism" or even "Americanism." It was
difficult, even in those days, to understand what the elements of this "heresy"
were, except for a general sense of any attachment to the allure of the modern
world. Despite its subsequent outstanding contribution to Catholic biblical
studies, the Pontifical Biblical Institute (with a small sister-house in Jerusalem)
was founded by Pius X partly to "keep an eye on" what was emerging from
the École Biblique. But something had been set loose in the Catholic Church,
and the subsequent history of the Pontifical Biblical Institute, to this day one
of the finest centers for critical biblical studies in the world, is an excellent
indication of that truth.

Across the turn of the twentieth century there was an increasing sense of the importance of the Word of God for the life of the Church, only to be sidelined by concern over so-called modernism in the Catholic communion and, more important, two world wars and the arrogance, inhumanity, and slaughter that marked the first fifty years of the twentieth century (1914–19; 1940–45). Astonishingly, during a period of widespread conflict during the latter part of the Second World War, as the Allies struck back on all fronts, including in the Pacific, Pius XII produced *Divino Afflante Spiritu*. The situation of 1943 is appropriately described in *Divino Afflante Spiritu* 56:

> If these things which We have said, venerable brothers and beloved sons, are necessary in every age, much more urgently are they needed in our sorrowful times, when almost all peoples and nations are plunged in a sea of calamities, when a cruel war heaps ruins upon ruins and slaughter upon slaughter, when, owing to the most bitter hatred stirred up among the nations, We perceive with greatest sorrow that in not a few has been extinguished the sense not only of Christian moderation and charity, but also of humanity itself.

This document was a watershed for Catholic biblical scholarship, and its influence is ongoing. The Holy Father exhibits exquisite awareness of the importance of critical scholarship. He insists that great advancements had taken place since 1893 (*DAS* 11–13). He asks for a return to the ancient languages as the source for all correct interpretation (*DAS* 14–18), and also that due respect be given to the other historical sciences: archaeology, philology, comparative religions, and other allied sciences (*DAS* 24, 33, 35–40). *DAS* 16 is memorable: "In like manner therefore ought we to explain the original text which, having been written by the inspired author himself, has more authority and greater weight than even the very best translation, whether ancient or modern." The Holy Father states elsewhere: "For all human knowledge, even the non-sacred, has indeed its own proper dignity and excellence, being a finite participation of the infinite knowledge of God, but it acquires a new and higher dignity and, as it were, a consecration, when it is employed to cast a brighter light upon the things of God" (*DAS* 41).

Pius XII asks that Greek and Hebrew texts, in addition to the Latin Vulgate, "be published for the benefit of the Holy Church of God" (*DAS* 20). With great astuteness, the Holy Father defends the Vulgate and its role in the Catholic Tradition but points out that it was not established "particularly for critical reasons, but rather on account of its lawful use in the Church through so many centuries." He rightly notes that "authenticity of this sort is called not primarily critical but juridical" (*DAS* 21). Although couched in a different way, the role of the Word of God in theology is again found in *Divino Afflante Spiritu*. Speaking directly to Catholic exegetes, Pius XII insists:

> With special zeal should they apply themselves, not only by expounding exclusively these matters which belong to the historical, archaeological, philological and other auxiliary sciences . . . but, having duly referred to these, in so far as they may aid the exegesis, they should set forth in particular the theological doctrine in faith and morals of the individual books or texts so that their exposition may not only aid the professors of theology in their explanations and proofs of the dogmas of faith, but may also be of assistance to priests in their presentation of Christian doctrine to the people, and finally may help all the faithful to lead a life that is holy and worthy of a Christian. (*DAS* 24)

Pius XII instructs Catholic scholars to use the same "scientific arms" as those used by all who study the Bible (*DAS* 42) and thus "endeavor to determine the peculiar character and circumstances of the sacred writer, the age in which he lived, the sources written or oral to which he had recourse and the forms of expression he employed" (*DAS* 33). Embracing this mandate, hardworking Catholic biblical scholars turned their minds, hearts, and lives to the service of the Christian and Catholic Church.[10] In a very brief time Catholic scholarship, especially in Europe and the United States, was regarded by scholars from all faiths as equal to the best in the world. Among the luminaries of this period were Joseph Coppens and Lucien Cerfaux in Belgium; Roland de Vaux, Pierre Benoit, and Marie-Émile Boismard at the French-speaking École Biblique; Rudolph Schnackenburg and Heinz Schürmann in Germany; Stanislaus Lyonnet and Maximilian Zerwick in Rome; and Carrol Steinmuller, Barnabas Ahern, and David Stanley in the United States and Canada. But old habits die hard, and these brave scholars and committed Roman Catholics often suffered from misunderstanding and rejection. Their integrity was often questioned, despite their loyalty to the Catholic Church and its authentic Tradition. The position of the Catholic Church had to be further spelled out; that took place at Vatican II.

Vatican II

The texts that came from Vatican II (1962–65) are very different from the documents from earlier ecumenical councils. Part of the reason for this difference

10. These scholars took the Pope's challenge seriously: "A biblical scholar who closes off to himself access to the original texts by the willful neglect of these cannot possibly escape the tag of superficiality and laziness" (*DAS* 15).

was the request of Pope John XXIII that this council not be one of great doctrinal debates but one that gave life to the Church in the contemporary world through reflection on the biblical, patristic, and liturgical traditions of Christianity.[11] The most important reason, however, was the practice of *ressourcement*. The fathers of the council wanted to go back to the *sources* of the Church's life, the Word of God as it is found in the Bible and in the patristic and liturgical life of the Catholic Tradition, and to express themselves in the language and style of those sources. The first document that appeared from the work of the council was *Sacrosanctum Concilium* (Constitution on the Sacred Liturgy), and one of the last was *Dei Verbum* (Dogmatic Constitution on Divine Revelation). Vatican II began and ended in a way that signaled the return of the Word of God to its rightful place at the center of the life and practice of the Catholic Church.

Sacrosanctum Concilium

Sacrosanctum Concilium (*SC*) was promulgated at the end of the council's second session on December 4, 1963. Ideological struggles within the council had begun to appear during the first session in 1962. A feature of this conflict between what has been called the conservative and the progressive elements in the council was the rejection of the Preparatory Commission's schemes *De Ecclesia* (On the Church) and *De Fontibus Revelationis* (On the Sources of Revelation) in the first session (November 1962). The council's maturing thought on the Word of God is found in *Dei Verbum*, promulgated as the council came to an end after the fourth session, on November 18, 1965. A process of theological and pastoral maturation took place between the promulgation of *Sacrosanctum Concilium* (1963) and *Dei Verbum* (1965), something that can be sensed in the sketch that follows.

When *Sacrosanctum Concilium* was formally approved in late 1963, the entire Catholic Church was amazed by its boldness. Principles stated in the document promised to make the liturgy, so crucial to Catholic faith and practice (see *SC* 1–2), understandable to all peoples and cultures. These truths were couched in a biblical and theological language that was unheard of in earlier conciliar documents.

- It is the liturgy through which, especially in the divine sacrifice of the Eucharist, "the work of our redemption takes place," and it is through the liturgy, especially, that the faithful are enabled to express in their lives and manifest to others the mystery of Christ and the real nature of the Church (*SC* 2).

11. On the calling of Vatican II by Pope John XXIII and his hopes for the council, see John W. O'Malley, *What Happened at Vatican II* (Cambridge, MA: Harvard University Press, 2008), 15–18.

- Christ Our Lord achieved his task principally by the paschal mystery of his blessed passion, resurrection from the dead, and glorious ascension, whereby "dying, he destroyed our death and rising, restored our life." For it was from the side of Christ as he slept the sleep of death upon the cross that there came forth "the wondrous sacrament of the whole Church" (SC 5).

- To accomplish so great a work Christ is always present in his Church, especially in her liturgical celebrations. He is present in the sacrifice of the Mass, not only in the person of his minister, "the same now offering, through the ministry of priests, who formerly offered himself on the cross," but especially in the eucharistic species. By his power he is present in the sacraments so that when anyone baptizes it is really Christ himself who baptizes. He is present in his Word since it is he himself who speaks when the Holy Scriptures are read in the Church (SC 7).

These and similar biblically and theologically rich affirmations opening *Sacrosanctum Concilium* enabled the council to announce that "the liturgy is the summit toward which the activity of the Church is directed; it is also the source from which all its power flows" (SC 10) and to articulate the purpose of *Sacrosanctum Concilium* in paragraph 14: "In the restoration and promotion of the sacred liturgy the full and active participation by all the people is the paramount concern, for it is the primary, indeed the indispensable source from which the faithful are to derive the true Christian spirit."

As is carefully stated in the conciliar document, practices such as the introduction of the vernacular into liturgical celebrations; the renewal of the liturgical year; renewal of the use of liturgical books, including the lectionary; permission for clergy to concelebrate; respect for local cultures, their music, and their rites; and an increased respect for differing forms of art and architecture all flow logically from the theological and biblical basis upon which the document is founded. These practices were a dream for only a handful of Catholics who had looked back to the biblical, patristic, liturgical, and sacramental part of the Church Catholic in the preconciliar period. These Catholics were very few. For the rest of us, it all came as a surprise. As the first conciliar document to appear, *Sacrosanctum Concilium* protects many earlier traditions, including the primacy of the Latin Mass, the single celebrant, control of the Holy See, and the control of a "competent territorial ecclesiastical authority" or a local Ordinary over all change, no matter how insignificant some of these things may appear to us today.

But this first Constitution developed a new "literary form," never seen before Vatican II. Almost every affirmation, either theological or pastoral, is inspired or supported by the use of biblical texts. This characteristic is an indication of the decision of the fathers of the council, responding to the desires of Pope John XXIII for the council. This practice continued and strengthened as the council unfolded. It demonstrates what happens when the riches of the biblical text are well used in theological and pastoral discourse.

No space in *Sacrosanctum Concilium* is specifically dedicated to the role of the Word of God in the liturgy, but the demand for a renewal of the liturgical life of the Church brought with it a plea for an increase of awareness of the importance of Scripture in the life of the Church. *Sacrosanctum Concilium* carried the seed that would produce further fruit in *Dei Verbum* and beyond. Although sometimes stated in passing, as attention is devoted to some other aspect of the liturgical renewal, some important new guidelines were established:

- In the "general norms" for the renewal of the liturgy, the council states: "Sacred Scripture is of the greatest importance in the celebration of the liturgy" (*SC* 24). It then lists the elements that depend upon the Word of God: the readings, the homily, the psalms, the eucharistic prayers, the collects, the hymns (see also *SC* 51). Typical of Roman documents, it goes on to say that this is nothing new but reflects "that warm and living love for scripture to which the venerable tradition of both eastern and western rites gives testimony." My contemporaries have no memory of a "warm and living love for scripture" across that period. The "norm" that the proper use of the Word of God be the guiding principle for readings, homilies, eucharistic prayers, the prayers of the Mass, and hymns was new.

- In *Sacrosanctum Concilium* 33, in the norms devoted to the educative nature of the liturgy, an oft-neglected element in the liturgy emerges: the instruction of the faithful. "For in the liturgy God speaks to his people, Christ is still proclaiming his Gospel, and the people reply to God both in song and in prayer." The liturgy is not simply the action of God; it is essentially dialogical, with the celebrant, no matter the rite, facilitating that dialogue.

- Consequently, in paragraph 35 from the same section of the document, the council gives a number of directives about the use of Sacred Scripture, including

  · a richer selection of texts;

  · preaching that is more biblical; and

  · Bible services as vigils for important feasts, especially in those places where a priest is unavailable.

A shadow of what will later be said (explicitly in *Dei Verbum*) appears several times in chapter 2 of *Sacrosanctum Concilium*, dedicated to the Most Sacred

Mystery of the Eucharist. The dynamic relationship that exists between the Word of God and the Sacrament of the Eucharist is clearly stated, first in *Sacrosanctum Concilium* 48: "They [the faithful] should be formed by God's word, and be nourished at the table of the Lord's body." A similar thought is found among the "norms" that appear in this chapter: the liturgy of the Word and the eucharistic ministry are so closely connected with each other "that they form but one single act of worship" (*SC* 56).

Much of the document legislates who will be responsible for the new initiatives, many of which have subsequently developed beyond what the council had in mind. *Sacrosanctum Concilium* gives more space to the liturgical year (102–11), to sacred music (112–21), and to sacred art and furnishings (122–29) than to the use of Scripture in the life and liturgy of the Church. But within its pages are the first steps that began the intense renewal in interest in the Scriptures in the life of the Church that was the logical consequence of *Providentissimus Deus* and *Divino Afflante Spiritu*. It was further enhanced in one of the council's final documents, *Dei Verbum*.

Dei Verbum

Dei Verbum, the Dogmatic Constitution on Divine Revelation, was one of the great battlefields of the council. The rejection of the Preparatory Commission's document on the sources of Revelation in 1962 led to the writing and rewriting of a potential conciliar statement across three years. This long gestation process produced a final text in 1965 that is an epoch-making statement on the communication that takes place between God and the human condition by means of Scripture and Tradition. The preface to the document states unequivocally that the council, citing Augustine, wishes "to set forth authentic teaching on divine Revelation and its transmission. For it wants the whole world to hear summons to salvation, so that through hearing it may believe, through belief it may hope, through hope it may come to love" (*DV* 1). The intimate link between Revelation and the Christian commitment to faith, hope, and love is established in a way unheard of in earlier teaching on Revelation. It is not something that responds to human needs but is rather the result of the loving initiative of God. Through a unique revealing initiative, God invites human beings into a relationship with the Father, through Christ, the Word made flesh, in the Holy Spirit. Revelation is a gratuitous call to a personal intimacy with the Trinity (*DV* 2).

Despite opposition from conservative members of the council, throughout the document Scripture and Tradition are intimately linked. Both contribute "to make the people of God live their lives in holiness and increase their faith" and "converse with the spouse of His beloved Son" (*DV* 8). The two different sources for Revelation are now regarded as one. The theological principle is stated unequivocally in *Dei Verbum* 9: "Sacred tradition and sacred scripture, then, are bound closely together, and communicate one with the other. Flowing from the same divine wellspring, both of them merge, in a sense, and move towards the same goal." This is a major contribution to the history of Roman Catholic thought. Despite a long tradition, running from Trent to Vatican I, a healthy tension is found in the words "both of them merge, in a sense [Latin: *in unum quodammodo coalescunt*], and move towards the same goal." This statement comes as a result of serious debate at the council. Some sought a restatement of "two sources," which they regarded as an already-established teaching of the Church (Trent and Vatican I), while others insisted that God's dialogue with humans came from "the same divine wellspring," nourished by both Scripture and Tradition. The fathers of the council wisely decided not to attempt a description of *how* the two merge into one. This is providential. We are dealing with divine communication with the human. The initiative in this communicative act lies with God, and thus we do not know *how* this functions, but the highest form of the Church's Magisterium stated in *Dei Verbum* 9 *that* it happens.

Chapters dealing with Scripture, its inspiration and interpretation (*DV* 11–13), the Old Testament (*DV* 14–16), and the New Testament (*DV* 17–20) follow. The council follows Pius XII's *Divino Afflante Spiritu* 35–42, endorsing the use of critical methods to interpret the Scriptures (*DV* 12). It insists on the essential historicity of the Gospels and their apostolic origins (*DV* 18–19). Between the lines one senses an understandable concern with European and American New Testament scholarship, especially in the period of the early 1960s, still under the fascination of Rudolf Bultmann's brilliant existentialist reading of the New Testament, where "what actually happened" played a very minor (if any) role in the act of interpretation.

Reaching beyond these narrow academic concerns, the council asks for interpretation of the biblical text in the light of the fathers of the West and East and the Sacred Liturgy (*DV* 23). The council fathers correctly insist that "the living tradition of the whole Church must be taken into account along with the harmony which exists between elements of the faith" (*DV* 12). These elements of *Dei Verbum* have led many to insist that the Catholic scholar should never push at the boundaries of interpretation but should work only under the guidance of the teaching office of the Church. But *Dei Verbum* 10 indicates:

> The task of giving an authentic interpretation of the Word of God, whether in its written form or in the form of tradition, has been entrusted to the living teaching office of the Church alone. Its authority in this matter is exercised in

the name of Jesus Christ. *The Magisterium is not superior to the Word of God, but is rather its servant. It teaches only what has been handed on to it. At the divine command and with the help of the holy Spirit, it listens to this devoutly, guards it reverently and expounds it faithfully.* (emphasis added)

This passage needs careful exegesis and depends a great deal upon the distinction made between "the Word of God" and "the Magisterium." The teaching office of the Church has come to be known (relatively recently) as the Magisterium. It is important to be aware that what is said in *Dei Verbum* 10 does not disrupt the unity that exists between the Word of God in the Scriptures and the Word of God in the Tradition, affirmed in paragraph 9. The Magisterium is a *third element*: the interpretative ministry of the Church's leadership, "exercised in the name of Jesus Christ." This is evident in the structure of the text of *Dei Verbum* itself when it deals with the issue of the transmission of Revelation. It first presents Scripture (*DV* 7), then the role of Tradition in both forming Scripture and handing it on (*DV* 8), then the union between Scripture and Tradition in a Revelation that flows "from the same divine wellspring" (*DV* 9).[12] Finally, the relationship between Revelation (found in Scripture and Tradition) and the teaching office of the Church is stated (*DV* 10). The Magisterium must always listen humbly to the Word of God that comes to it in *both* Scripture and Tradition. The Magisterium is *not* Revelation but humbly serves God's self-revelation.

The final chapter of *Dei Verbum* is devoted to "Sacred Scripture in the Life of the Church" (*DV* 21–26). This section of the document opens with one of the most memorable statements from Vatican II: "The Church has always venerated the divine Scriptures as it has venerated the Body of the Lord, in that it never ceases, above all in the sacred liturgy, to partake of the bread of life and to offer it to the faithful from the one table of the word of God and the Body of Christ" (*DV* 21). The parallel between the reception of the Eucharist and the reception of God's Word from the same table strikes the Catholic mind and heart forcibly. There may have been a time when the Scriptures and the Eucharist were equally "venerated," but this was not the case for Catholics all over the world in the preconciliar period. The Mass stood at the heart of what it meant to be Catholic, and Scripture played a very minor role.

Dei Verbum asked that a series of initiatives and practices be implemented to see that the Scriptures be restored to their place of veneration, side by side with traditional Catholic veneration of the Eucharist:

12. The word "wellspring," approved by the council fathers, uses a rare but beautiful Latin word, *scaturigo*. It indicates a source that produces a flow of gifts.

- Provide access to the biblical text through accurate and correct translations (*DV* 22).
- Come to a deeper understanding of the Scriptures by reading them in the light of the patristic interpretations and the liturgy (*DV* 23).
- Make the Scriptures a source for theological reflection, not just a tool: "The study of the sacred page should be the very soul of sacred theology" (*DV* 24).
- Form all clergy in an adequate understanding of the Scriptures to enrich their preaching and pastoral ministry (*DV* 25a).
- Commission the bishops to ensure that these norms are put into place (*DV* 25b).

This rich section of *Dei Verbum* closes in paragraph 26 in a way that parallels its opening: "Just as from constant attendance at the eucharistic mystery the life of the Church draws increase, so a new impulse of spiritual life may be expected from increased veneration of the word of God, which 'stands forever' (Isa. 40:8; see 1 Pet. 1:23–25)."

Conclusion

A commentary on the intimate link between the Word of God and the Eucharist can be found in Benedict XVI's postsynodal exhortation of 2010. In *Verbum Domini* 56, he cites the striking words of Saint Jerome: "When we approach the Mystery, if a crumb falls to the ground we are troubled. Yet when we are listening to the Word of God, and God's Word and Christ's flesh are being poured into our ears yet we pay no heed, what great peril should we not feel?" The long process of gestation that ran from the council's beginnings in 1962 until its closing moments in 1965 enabled the fathers of the council to come to a greater awareness of the centrality of the Sacred Scriptures. To repeat other, more famous words of Saint Jerome, much loved by Saint Therese of Lisieux, cited in her autobiography as she struggled to learn Hebrew and Greek: "Ignorance of the Scriptures is ignorance of Christ" (*DV* 25, citing the prologue of Jerome's *Commentary on Isaiah*).

Dei Verbum, hand in hand with the liturgical renewal initiated by *Sacrosanctum Concilium*, set in motion a renewal of Catholic focus on the Word of God. The council's document on the liturgy initiated an important exposure to the Word of God. The gradual introduction of English into the celebration of the Eucharist and the Sacraments, and especially the eventual production of the postconciliar lectionary, stirred the minds and imaginations of many.

The first twenty years after the council were marked by great excitement and by a growth of interest in the Scriptures. Practicing Catholics began to hear, for the first time, from the historical, wisdom, and legislative texts of the Old Testament. Who were the prophets? When did they live, and what was their role in the life and faith of Israel? What is the difference between Matthew, Mark, Luke, and John? Who was Paul and why is he so important? The idea that "going to Mass" was now a privileged moment when the Church "never ceases . . . to partake of the bread of life and to offer it to the faithful from the one table of the word of God and the Body of Christ" (*DV* 21) led to an enthusiastic and excited response from the bulk of practicing Catholics but was fiercely opposed by a vocal minority.

This initial fervor has run into hard times, as Christian practice has run into hard times in the developed world. It is difficult to pinpoint just when and where this enthusiasm ran out of steam. It was not a dramatic process but the result of gradual cultural changes that have touched all aspects of life. Nevertheless, an ecumenical council is the highest level of the Church's teaching and cannot be ignored. Two significant publications from the Holy See show that the council's teaching on the centrality of the Scriptures in the life of the Church remains firmly at the heart of the Church's agenda. The first of these is the 1993 document of the Pontifical Biblical Commission, *The Interpretation of the Bible in the Church*.[13] Second, Benedict XVI entrusted the 2008 Synod of Bishops with the theme of the Word of God in the life and mission of the Church. He subsequently released the postsynodal exhortation *Verbum Domini*. These documents are very different in scope and content, but both respond to the agenda initiated by *Dei Verbum*, paragraphs 21–26. The *need* for Benedict XVI to state his aim of pointing out "fundamental approaches to a rediscovery of God's word in the life of the Church as a wellspring of constant renewal" (*Verbum Domini*, 1) indicates that fifty years after the promulgation of *Sacrosanctum Concilium* this rediscovery and renewal are yet to be realized.

In the second decade of Christianity's third millennium, bishops, priests, Catholic religious, and active Catholics are worried by matters they consider more urgent for the ongoing life of the Church than the Scriptures, but all Christian churches can be distracted from the need to rediscover the Scriptures as an essential element in God's dialogue with humankind. Most Christian traditions now recognize that biblical interpretation within their Church must respect their Tradition. Although articulated at an ecumenical council of the Catholic Church, it could be said of all Christians that their search for an encounter with God takes place by means of a Revelation that contains both

13. Rome: Editrice Vaticana, 1993.

Scripture and Tradition, flowing from the same divine wellspring, merging into a unity and tending toward the same end (see *DV* 9). "God's word is not susceptible of being contained in a book."[14]

The American Protestant scholar Frederick C. Grant, commenting on *Dei Verbum*, wrote almost fifty years ago: "What I wish is that we could all go back to the days of Erasmus and work together in harmony, especially in biblical studies, and forget about the intervening four centuries of confusion, distrust and antagonism. But history is irreversible. We must go on from where we are. Thank God, a brighter path is now opening up before us than any our fathers were compelled to tread."[15] That "brighter path" is under threat as a secular and sometimes very hostile Western society questions the relevance of the Christian tradition and as Christians live lives that reflect poorly upon that tradition. But the dreams of *Dei Verbum* (1965) and the subsequent exhortations from the Pontifical Biblical Commission (*The Word of God in the Life and Mission of the Church* [1993]) and Pope Benedict XVI (*Verbum Domini* [2010]) remain part of our agenda. The primer that follows is a response to the request of the highest teaching office of the Catholic Church: an ecumenical council. The Church has repeatedly asked us to rediscover the richness that a critical reading of the New Testament offers to the life and practice of the Christian faith, especially in the Catholic tradition. This should be not an option but rather an essential element in "the life and mission of the Church."

14. Käsemann, "Thoughts on the Present Controversy," 274.
15. Frederick C. Grant, "A Response," in *The Documents of Vatican II*, ed. Walter M. Abbott (New York: Herder & Herder, 1966), 132.

2

Historical Context

*The New Testament World
and Our World*

The books of the New Testament were written in the world of the Roman Empire, which inherited centuries of Greek cultural and religious dominance. They have their origins, however, in the life of a Jew, Jesus of Nazareth. His first followers and interpreters were also Jews. The roots of Christianity and its sacred book, the New Testament, are found in Judaism. But very rapidly the story of Jesus and the subsequent interpretation of that story as a saving action of God were told and preached in the wider world, which was politically dominated by Rome but heavily dependent upon a culture and language that had its roots in the glory that had been Greece. That culture and language were now marked by new social and religious currents and movements, some of which came from Rome, some from Greek traditions, while others came from the East, having been drawn into the Mediterranean world by the armies of Alexander the Great (356–323 BCE).

Unlike Judaism, which retained a single-mindedness about God's dealings with humankind, what is known as the Greco-Roman world contained many differing cultures and religions. In accord with the request from Pius XII that readers of the Bible "endeavour to determine the peculiar character and circumstances of the sacred writer, the age in which he lived, the sources written or oral to which he had recourse and the forms of expression he employed" (*DAS* 33; see *DV* 12 [1965]; *The Word of God in the Life and Mission of the Church* [1993]; Benedict XVI, *Verbum Domini* [2010]), an appreciation of the Jewish and the Greco-Roman worlds in which (and for which) the books of the New Testament were written is essential for a faith-filled reading of the New Testament.[1] No matter how much goodwill readers may have, reading the New Testament is difficult, as much of it seems "foreign" to us. It was written at a time (almost two thousand years ago), in places (the Mediterranean world and the Roman Empire), and in a language (Greek) that are foreign to us.

The name "Jesus Christ," familiar to us as if it were his family name, is really the very early Christian confession of belief that the man named Jesus who came from Nazareth (see Matt. 2:23) and whose mother and father were recognized as Mary and Joseph (see Mark 6:3; Matt. 13:55) was the expected Messiah of Israel (see 2 Sam. 7:12–15; Ps. 89:3–4; Luke 7:20; Mark 1:1; 8:29; John 20:30–31). The Hebrew/Aramaic word *messiah* and the Greek word *christos* both mean "anointed one" (see John 1:41; 4:25). The expectation of a Messiah, which was by no means uniform or even universal among Jews at the time of Jesus,[2] was a reflection of the troubled era of what we now call the first Christian century (AD) or the first century of the Common Era (CE).[3]

1. What follows describes for a nonexpert some elements that are essential for an understanding of the religious and cultural background to the New Testament. For a fuller introduction, see Joel B. Green and Lee Martin McDonald, eds., *The World of the New Testament: Cultural, Social, and Historical Contexts* (Grand Rapids: Baker Academic, 2013). For the Jewish world, the Greco-Roman world, and the Jewish people within the context of Roman Hellenism, see pp. 23–341. There are many fine introductions to the New Testament. I will consistently use what I regard as the three best. On what follows, see Raymond E. Brown, *An Introduction to the New Testament*, Anchor Bible Reference Library (New York: Doubleday, 1996), 55–96; Mark Allan Powell, *Introducing the New Testament: A Historical, Literary, and Theological Survey* (Grand Rapids: Baker Academic, 2009), 15–45; Robert A. Spivey, D. Moody Smith, and C. Clifton Black, *Anatomy of the New Testament*, 7th ed. (Minneapolis: Fortress, 2013), 11–48. Powell and Spivey, Smith, and Black provide helpful maps, timelines, photographs of artifacts, and geographical locations.

2. A good survey of the variety of expressions of Jewish messianic hope is found in John J. Collins, *The Scepter and the Star: Messianism in Light of the Dead Sea Scrolls*, 2nd ed. (Grand Rapids: Eerdmans, 2010).

3. Two eras of history are often referred to as "before Christ" (BC) and "in the year of the Lord" (AD, *anno Domini*). The multireligious and secular nature of contemporary society has led to the use of BCE (Before the Common Era) and CE (Common Era), adopted here. The numbering system was first mistakenly calculated by a Christian monk, Dionysius Exiguus. He calculated the year 1 CE as the year of the birth of Jesus, but in the light of the data given in the New Testament (esp. Matt. 2:1–23; Luke 1:5; 2:1–2), Jesus must have been born at least four years before that date. Herod died in 4 BCE. Jesus' life must have roughly spanned the years 4 BCE–30 CE. In Dionysius' calculations, there is no zero; 1 BCE passes immediately to 1 CE.

The Political Situation of the Jewish People

From the time of the Babylonian conquest of Judea in 587 BCE until the time
of the Roman destruction of Jerusalem and its temple in 70 CE, the Jews in
Palestine lived mostly under foreign domination.[4] Thanks to the destruction
of the Babylonian Empire by the Persians in 538 BCE and the grace of the
victorious emperor, Cyrus the Great, ruler and emperor from 559 to 530 BCE,
the exiles had returned to the land of Palestine[5] to join those who had never left
the land.[6] Cyrus is always mentioned with praise in the Old Testament, and he
is the first named person to be called "the Messiah" in the biblical literature
(Isa. 45:1: "Thus says the LORD to his anointed [*messiah*], to Cyrus, whose
right hand I have grasped"). He is seen as an agent of the Lord, "anointed" for
the delivery of Israel. The Jewish people were allowed to rebuild the temple
in Jerusalem and to resume Jewish piety and practices. But they were part
of the Persian Empire until it was destroyed by the military campaigns of
Alexander the Great. After the early death of Alexander (he was only thirty-
three), his empire was divided among his generals. Thus began a tumultuous
period when these generals and their successors struggled, militarily and
politically, to overthrow one another to broaden their hold on the different
parts of what is now called the Hellenistic world. The word "Hellenism"
(*hellēnismos*) comes from the word for "a Greek." An essential part of Alexander's conquest, and that of his successors, was the imposition of Hellenistic
religion and culture on "the whole world."[7] The uniqueness of traditional
Greek religion and culture had been lost by the time of Jesus. Hellenism was

4. On this period, see the essays in Green and McDonald, *World of the New Testament*,
25–84.

5. The expression "Palestine" was not used until the early second century CE and is thus
anachronistic, but it is used here in a geographical sense. The expression "Israel" carries with
it many political and religious issues. At the time that we are considering, what I have called
"Palestine" was part of the Roman region of Syria.

6. The biblical books, especially 2 Kings 25:1–30; Isa. 40:1–55:13; Jer. 50:1–52:34; Lamentations; and Ezek. 25:1–48:35, create the impression that all Jews were led off into exile. This was
not the case. Some were left in a conquered land, vassals in the Babylonian Empire. Others had
fled to Egypt and other surrounding Mediterranean lands (see Jer. 43:1–13). The flight from
Israel generated by the Babylonian victory in 587 BCE played a major role in the migration of
many Jews to different parts of the Mediterranean world, commonly called "the Diaspora,"
an expression that means "the dispersion." However, even before this time Jews were already a
widespread presence around the Mediterranean.

7. Today we might distinguish "religion" and "culture," but they were one and the same for
Jews, Greeks, and Romans. A similar identity is found, for example, in contemporary Islam and
in some currents of contemporary Christianity. For the Hellenists "the whole world" referred
to the largely Mediterranean world that had been conquered by Alexander, but also penetrated
eastward as far as the west of modern India.

a continuation of classical Greek tradition, but it had become more hybrid, strongly influenced by new traditions that came from the expansion into the East.

Perched between Egypt (much of today's eastern Africa), which was ruled by the Ptolemies, and Syria (today's Turkey and Syria), which was ruled by the Seleucids, the tiny land of Palestine became something of a battleground between the two warring Hellenistic powers in the post-Alexandrian period. One of the most successful Seleucid kings, especially victorious in struggles with the Ptolemies, was Antiochus IV, also called Epiphanes ("[God] manifest"), who ruled in Syria from 175 BCE until his death in 164 BCE. He set about a determined program to impose Hellenism on the Jews living in Palestine, accompanying the program with fierce and bloody persecution (see 1 Macc. 1:41–56). Many Jews succumbed to the temptation to leave their traditional faith for the Hellenistic way of life. They hid their circumcision and assembled in Hellenistic gymnasiums and baths, even in the holy city of Jerusalem (see 1 Macc. 1:10–15; 2 Macc. 6:1–6).

There were various responses to this desperate situation. One was theological, and it produced one of the most fascinating books in the Old Testament: the book of Daniel. In the face of impossible odds Daniel promised the ultimate victory of God to those who remain "holy," faithful to the traditions of Israel (see esp. Dan. 7:1–28). This period also saw the beginnings of another Jewish response that had far-reaching results: passive resistance and martyrdom inspired by a new belief in resurrection (see 2 Macc. 12:41–45). This tradition also played an important role in early Christianity. Another response was military, initiated and led by the Maccabean family. Due to a series of remarkable circumstances, initially caused by the Syrians' false sense of the weakness of Jewish resistance, this revolt was victorious, especially under the leadership of Judas Maccabeus (167–160 BCE). These feats are recorded in 1 Maccabees and are partly told again, from a different perspective, in 2 Maccabees.[8] Although we have no original Hebrew text of either of these books, and for that reason both Jewish and Protestant traditions do not regard them as part of the Bible, the Catholic tradition has always accepted the Greek translation of the Septuagint as inspired. This leads to the presence of a number of books

8. Second Maccabees does not continue the story of 1 Maccabees in the way that 1 and 2 Samuel and 1 and 2 Kings tell the earlier story of Israel's royal tradition. Second Maccabees repeats and fills in much of the material found in 1 Maccabees. First Maccabees (somewhat breathlessly) describes events from the reign of Antiochus IV (175 BCE) to the ascent of John Hyrcanus (135 BCE), while 2 Maccabees (more solemnly) begins with a description of the Syrian king Seleucus IV (c. 180 BCE) and reports events through to the defeat of the Syrian army by Judas in 161 BCE. The purpose of 2 Maccabees was to dwell theologically on the revolt against Syria, rather than detailing the events.

and sections of books in a Catholic Bible that are not found in other Bibles.[9] First Maccabees records the heroic and victorious struggles of Mattathias of the Maccabee family, the founder of the revolt (2:1–70); his sons, Judas (3:1–9:22), Jonathan (9:23–12:53), and Simon (13:1–16:17); and the emergence of John Hyrcanus (16:18–24), the son of Simon (thus Mattathias' grandson), as the first of the Hasmonean kings.

The successful military response to the Syrian presence resulted in the restoration and reconsecration of the temple, as well as political and religious independence under the rule of Hyrcanus and his family, called the Hasmonean period. But struggles between different Jewish groups and surrounding parties continued. The independence of Palestine was always under threat because of the hovering presence of the Romans, with whom Judas, Jonathan, and Simon made treaties (1 Macc. 8:1–32; 12:1–4; 14:16–19, 24). The Romans recognized the Hasmonean dynasty as a ruling class in 139 BCE. The Hasmonean rulers willingly accepted the support of Roman and surrounding Hellenistic powers. From the time of Simon (who ruled from 142 to 135 BCE), they occasionally took upon themselves the role of high priest, even though they did not belong to the priestly descendants of Zadok. Nor were they true kings, as they did not belong to the line of David. Weakened by corruption and internal conflict, seen by many pious Jews as illegitimate bearers of the titles "high priest" and "king," they were despised by many.[10]

The Hasmonean family eventually tore itself apart with corruption and internal factions until the Roman general Pompey invaded Palestine and took control of the nation in 63 BCE, after a three-month siege of Jerusalem. At that stage two brothers, Hyrcanus II (who supported the emerging Pharisees) and Aristobulus II (who supported the more traditional Sadducees), were in bitter dispute over the throne. Hyrcanus had asked for Roman intervention. Aristobulus resisted fiercely, but eventually Jerusalem fell and Aristobulus was taken as a prisoner to Rome. The arrival of the Roman army and its authority brought the brief and trouble-filled independence of the Jewish people to an

9. These books are Tobit, Judith, Baruch, Ben Sirach, Wisdom, sections of Esther and Daniel, and the two books of Maccabees.

10. It is widely accepted that at this time sectarian Jews called Essenes deliberately withdrew from the corrupt Israel of the Hasmonean kings and settled in communities in various places to live as commanded by God. It is also widely but not universally accepted that the community at Qumran was Essene. For a good summary discussion, see Geza Vermes, *The Complete Dead Sea Scrolls in English*, 7th ed., Penguin Classics (Harmondsworth, UK: Penguin, 2012), 10–21. There are a number of references in the Qumran documents to "the wicked Priest," most likely referring to one of the Hasmonean kings who assumed the priesthood. Scholars debate which king is intended, but the animosity toward the Hasmoneans can be sensed in these and other texts. See the summary in ibid., 54–66. We will discuss the Essenes later in this chapter.

end. Pompey appointed Hyrcanus as ethnarch and high priest, but his presence was both scandalous and ineffectual. Jewish independence lasted only seventy-seven years (140–63 BCE), during which time no fewer than seven figures claimed sovereign and sometimes priestly authority.[11] Palestine now became part of the Roman Empire, belonging to the province of Syria.

One of the players in the Roman invasion of Palestine was Antipater of Idumea, a master of political intrigue. He convinced the Romans to declare his son Herod king of the Jews. To distinguish him from lesser "Herods" who followed him, he is known as Herod the Great. Herod ruled, effectively and with extreme cruelty, from 37 to 4 BCE. Continuing the political cunning of his father, he did all he could to build and support Jewish institutions in Jewish centers while also constructing magnificent Hellenistic stadiums, gymnasiums, theaters, and pagan temples in non-Jewish areas.[12] Not Jewish, he married a Hasmonean princess, Mariamne, in the hope that he would be accepted by his subjects. He was deeply resented by the Jewish people. As his rule lengthened, he became more violent and erratic. He murdered two of his sons and his wife out of fear and jealousy. We have no extrabiblical evidence that Herod slew the young boys in Bethlehem (Matt. 2:16–18), but such an action, after the suggestion that a king had been born (Matt. 2:2–3), is entirely in character. The Jewish historian Josephus reports that as Herod approached death he jailed many of the best-loved Jewish leaders.[13] His soldiers had been instructed to slay them all at his death so that there would be tears in Palestine despite the hatred the Jews had for him (*Jewish Antiquities* 17.174–79).

Herod the Great had always been a puppet in the hands of the Romans. After his death they split his kingdom into three regions and allocated the regions to three of his remaining sons. They ruled as tetrarchs.[14] All of them

11. After Simon Maccabeus (142–135 BCE), the following "kings" and one "queen" made up the Hasmonean dynasty: John Hyrcanus (134–104 BCE), Aristobulus I (104–103 BCE), Alexander Jannaeus (103–76 BCE), Salome Alexandra (76–67 BCE), Hyrcanus II (67–66 BCE), and Aristobulus II (66–63 BCE).

12. Some of the most magnificent archaeological remains in today's Israel indicate Herod's commitment to a remarkable building program: the temple in Jerusalem; the city of Caesarea, with its aqueducts, port, and theater; and the well-known fortress of Masada, by the Dead Sea.

13. Josephus (37–ca. 100 CE), a former Pharisee who had initially taken part in the revolt against Rome, changed sides. Under Roman patronage he produced an account of Israel's history (*Jewish Antiquities*) and a moving, if prejudiced, firsthand account of the war that led up to the destruction of Jerusalem and its aftermath (*Jewish War*). The best Greek-English edition of these works is *Josephus in Nine Volumes*, ed. and trans. Henry St. John Thackeray, Ralph Marcus, and Louis Feldman, Loeb Classical Library (London: William Heinemann; Cambridge, MA: Harvard University Press, 1927–65). Readers can easily approach Josephus' fascinating contribution by reading *The Jewish War*, trans. Geoffrey A. Williamson, ed. E. Mary Smallwood, Penguin Classics (London: Penguin Books, 1981).

14. The word "tetrarch" simply means that the rule was divided among the three of them.

appear in the New Testament: Philip in the northeast (4 BCE–34 CE; see Mark 6:17), Herod Antipas in Galilee and other parts of the north (4 BCE–39 CE; see Luke 23:6–12), and Archelaus in the south (4 BCE–6 CE; see Matt. 2:22). They were entirely in the service of Rome, and after the Romans exiled Archelaus from his rule in Judea (6 CE), Roman procurators were appointed. There was a brief time when Herod Agrippa's closeness to Rome gained him the role of king—initially in Galilee and Perea (37–44 CE, northern regions), but eventually also in Samaria and Judea (39–44 CE, southern regions)—but in real terms Palestine was governed by Roman procurators. The most famous of them, Pontius Pilate (26–36 CE), was the fifth procurator and was not liked by the people.[15] He is known to have taken money from the temple. Supposedly he wished to build an aqueduct for public welfare, but the only way he could raise the money without major disturbance was to insist that the Jewish authorities give it to him. He brought banners with images of the emperor into Jerusalem and slew some innocent Samaritans who were listening to a prophet.[16] As a Roman soldier, he had little allegiance or sensitivity to Jewish laws and practices.

On the whole, as was usual across the Roman Empire, where local tradition and religions were respected, the procurators administered the province of Judea well. They lived not in Jerusalem but in the more comfortable Hellenistic city of Caesarea. Much of the day-to-day administration of the lives of the Jews was managed by a group of about seventy distinguished Jewish elders, known as the Sanhedrin, made up of priests, scribes, and laypeople. The high priest was the head of this body; real power lay with him and his associates. In the villages the synagogue served as a law court where the scribes interpreted and applied the law, known as the Torah, a word that means "instruction" and is used in reference to the first five books of the Bible: Genesis, Exodus, Leviticus, Numbers, and Deuteronomy. But tensions grew, and as the decades under the Roman procurators passed, the administration became increasingly callous, and Jewish sensitivities were less and less respected. Eventually, in the midst of growing tension, a Jewish revolt against the Romans broke out in 66 CE. After some initial Jewish victories, the might of Rome prevailed. The Roman armies conducted a long siege of the city of Jerusalem and laid

---

15. The procurators were generally chosen from Romans of senior military rank (known as "equestrians") and were answerable only to the emperor. Prior to Pilate, the procurators had been Coponius (6–10 CE), Ambivius (10–13 CE), Annius Rufus (13–15 CE), and Valerius Gratus (15–26 CE). As can be inferred from some of the brief periods of office, administering Palestine was not a simple task.

16. Much of this information can be found in Josephus, and some of it also appears in the New Testament (see Luke 13:1–3). See, for example, Josephus, *Jewish War* 2.169–77; *Antiquities* 18.35, 55–59, 62.

it waste, desecrating and destroying the temple in 70 CE. The Essene outpost at Qumran had been destroyed in 68 CE, and eventually the Roman general and future emperor Titus took the last line of resistance, a fortress poised on a hill overlooking the Dead Sea: Masada.

Opposition continued, and there were ongoing skirmishes between determined Jews and the resilient Romans. The emperor Hadrian (117–38 CE) planned to completely destroy Jerusalem and build a Roman city on the site, called Aelia Capitolina, with a temple to the god Jupiter on the site of the now-destroyed Jewish temple. Many Jews again rose in revolt, this time around a figure regarded by some as the Messiah. He was even given the name Bar Kochba ("Son of the Star") by the revered Rabbi Akiba. But this second Jewish revolt (132–35 CE), under the leadership of Bar Kochba and often referred to as the Bar Kochba Revolt, was ultimately put down, the plan for the building of Aelia Capitolina went ahead, and Jews were forbidden entry to the former Jerusalem under pain of death. Despite the presence of many Jewish people in Palestine over the centuries, no Jewish homeland existed from that time until the decision of the United Nations in 1948 to allow the establishment of the modern state of Israel.

The political turmoil that marked the life of the Jewish people in Palestine from the exile to the total destruction of Jerusalem, and the consequent Diaspora, was not simply a manifestation of a people who would not be subdued for *political* reasons. The continued unhappiness with their situation of subjugation and their equally profound unhappiness with the years of independence under the Hasmoneans were driven by belief and by an undying and courageous commitment to God's law that was to be observed in God's land. The Jews believed that their land had been given to them by the God who had called Abraham out of Ur of the Chaldees, guided the growing Abrahamic tribes through the time of the great patriarchs (Abraham, Isaac, and Jacob), and eventually liberated them, under the guidance of Moses, from slavery in Egypt. God raised up Moses, and he led them into their promised land.

They had told this story repeatedly, as we continue to tell it today, especially in the reading of the first five books of the Bible, the "Torah." They had led a mixed history of faithfulness and sin in that land, a history that is found in the "Writings" of the Bible, but God had raised up "Prophets" to warn, chastise, cajole, encourage, and promise them.[17] God had also given them

---

17. The words "Torah," "Prophets," and "Writings" are in quotation marks because they form the Hebrew Scriptures, known by the Jews as the Law, the Prophets, and the Writings. These three words in Hebrew are *Torah*, *Nevi'im*, and *Khetuvim*, the initial letters of which form an acronym that is the Hebrew title for the whole collection of books we know as the Old Testament: the Tanakh.

the Davidic monarchy, with a promise that the Jews were his people and that he was their God. The Torah was "the word of God," instructing people in God's law; the Writings called the people to faithfulness and courage in the light of God's guidance and presence, even during times of failure and punishment; and the Prophets announced "the word of the Lord." Although the fierce loyalty of the Jewish people in Palestine manifested itself in political and revolutionary activity, it was motivated by what they regarded as God's word to them, God's chosen people. God's saving action recorded across all the vicissitudes of a chosen people in the Old Testament remains the Word of God, telling of God's patient and unfolding action across time, success, failure, grace, and sinfulness. It is an essential part of the life and belief of the Christian churches (see *DV* 14–16).

Judaism at the Time of Jesus

The Jewish people maintained their singular adhesion to God and the Torah across many centuries. Central to their faith and practice were the temple in Jerusalem and its priests. The Lord was present to the people in the temple, and the priests ministered there. Every pious Jew hoped to be able to go to the temple ceremonies that accompanied the great pilgrim festivals (Pentecost, Passover, and Tabernacles). Despite the loss of the temple, Jewish people remain a Torah-centered people. This reflects a way of life, now known as rabbinic Judaism, that came into existence later than the time of Jesus. Not focused on the Jerusalem temple, its rituals, or priesthood, so-called rabbinic Judaism, based on instruction and commentary upon the Torah, can be found throughout the world.[18] The Prophets and the Writings, even though eventually established as part of Israel's Sacred Scriptures, were the first commentary

18. Rabbinic "commentary" is one of the richest literatures of the world. It had its beginnings in the Aramaic translations of the Scriptures (known as Targums), first used to translate and comment upon the Hebrew Bible for Jews who no longer understood Hebrew but spoke Aramaic. Very early further "commentary" (known as midrash) led to a magisterial collection of legal and moral rabbinic commentary, citing rabbis from pre-Christian times through the end of the Jewish state, in the Mishnah (ca. 220 CE), lest they be forgotten. Midrashic commentary continued, and what are called "great midrashim" were written as midrashic commentary on many books of the Bible over the centuries. The Mishnah was further expanded by the commentary of the two great Talmuds, the Babylonian Talmud (ca. 300 CE) and the somewhat later Jerusalem Talmud (ca. 400 CE). Commentary continued to flow from the European rabbis of late antiquity and the medieval period (e.g., in Europe, in what is called the Ashkenazi tradition, Rashi [1040–1140], and in Spain and North Africa, in what is called the Sephardic tradition, Maimonides [1135–1204 CE]). These Jewish scholars commented in very creative ways upon the Tanakh and the subsequent commentary of the midrashim and the Talmuds. It continues

upon the Torah. They, in their own time, have been subject to later extensive rabbinic commentary. At the time of Jesus, however, Judaism and its practice had a number of quite different expressions.[19] Their difference depended upon a variety of ways in which obedience to Torah was understood and taught.

The Pharisees

The Pharisees are the most significant Jewish group mentioned in the New Testament.[20] Despite the regularly negative presentation of Pharisees as characters in the Gospel stories, they were perhaps the most positive, dynamic, and pastoral Jewish group in first-century Judaism. It is difficult to trace their origins, but they were already a force to be reckoned with in the Hasmonean period. They may have had earlier origins, but they certainly began to become an influential current in Jewish thought and practice at that time. There is a dynamism in their interpretation of Torah and its application to everyday Jewish life that is not found among other first-century groups, perhaps with the exception of early Jewish Christians. At the center of Pharisaic life and practice was an unconditional commitment to Torah, as was the case for all practicing Jews. Although we cannot be sure of the origins of the name "Pharisee," it is likely that it comes from a Hebrew verb that means "to separate." There appears to be a sense among the Pharisees that they alone were living as righteous Jews should be living, "separated" from the rest of the Jewish people. The root of this movement to separate themselves from others was unhappiness with the current situation of the temple and the lack of observance of purity there. They developed another interpretation of being pure and holy and of how they should worship God.

But they looked not only to the written word of Torah. According to the Pharisees, a great deal of instruction on Jewish life and practice was to be found in "oral Torah," traditions that may not be present in the written word of Torah but that have been handed down over the centuries, from the time of Moses, in the teaching of the rabbis. This understanding of ancient oral traditions generates the Pharisees' capacity to interpret and apply the Mosaic tradition to changing times and situations in life. In the Gospel of John,

---

today, as rabbis read the Scriptures, guided by centuries of rabbinic tradition, in the light of contemporary events and issues.

19. This could also be said of contemporary Judaism, but it is ultimately based on a rabbinic interpretation of the biblical tradition. That was not the case in the time of Jesus.

20. For a detailed study of the Pharisees, see John P. Meier, *A Marginal Jew: Rethinking the Historical Jesus*, Anchor Yale Bible Reference Library (New Haven: Yale University Press, 2001), 3:289–388. On the Pharisees, scribes, and Essenes, see Michelle Lee-Barnewall, "Pharisees, Scribes, and Essenes," in Green and McDonald, *World of the New Testament*, 217–27.

as Jesus teaches authoritatively during the celebration of Tabernacles, "the Jews" marvel, and ask the question: "How is it that this man has learning, when he has never studied?" (John 7:15). A rabbi must learn from an earlier rabbi, and that chain of teaching must reach back to Moses. On another occasion the Pharisees accuse Jesus of not following the traditions of the elders (Mark 7:5), but Jesus replies that they are placing human traditions before the commandment of God (7:8, 13). Paul, a former Pharisee (Phil. 3:5), claims that he had progressed greatly in understanding the traditions of his Jewish forefathers (Gal. 1:14).

The pastoral outreach of the Pharisees was also heightened by their being free from a priestly cult. Their focus was on the Torah and its interpretation. This meant that wherever there were Jews, even in the Diaspora, the Pharisees were able to reach out to them, establishing synagogues (a Greek word meaning "a place where people gather"), bringing Torah to the people. This could not be the case for the priestly Sadducees, as they expected the people to gather at the Jerusalem temple. There are remains of ancient Jewish synagogues in many far-flung locations, in Syria and beyond.

The negative portrayal of the Pharisees in the New Testament does not reflect the reality of Pharisaism in the first century. After the fall of Jerusalem in 70 CE, as we will see, the main representatives of prewar Judaism that remained substantially intact were the Pharisees, along with the followers of Jesus (later to be called Christians [see Acts 11:26; 26:28; 1 Pet. 4:16]), although the other groups no doubt continued their independent approach for some time. Both Jews and Christians were searching for their identity in a world without the land of Israel, its temple, or its cult in Jerusalem. Understandable conflict emerged between the Pharisees, who turned more vigorously to Torah, and the followers of Jesus, who looked to the person of Jesus of Nazareth as the Christ. The heated debates between Jesus and the Pharisees in the Gospels, especially Matthew and John, reflect this tension that—after a long period of time and in different ways in different places—eventually led to the separation of Jews and Christians.

The survival of the Pharisees after the Jewish War of 66–70 CE was crucial for the future of a Jewish way of life. After a skillful escape from the siege of Jerusalem, and with permission from the Romans, Rabbi Johanan Ben Zakkai (ca. 30–90 CE) established a synagogue at Jamnia (Hebrew: *Javne*) and was among those, known as the Tannaim, who originated some of the oldest Jewish midrashim. After the destruction of Jerusalem he and his followers played a part in the long and difficult process of establishing a Jewish identity and way of life amid the disaster and destruction of the land of Israel. The origins of rabbinic Judaism might be found among the Pharisees. It emerged as the dominant form of Jewish life and practice only in the second century and took on a life and practice of its own. The basic document of rabbinic Judaism is the Mishnah, a collection of the interpretations and sayings of the rabbis that reaches back to pre-Christian times. The documents of later rabbinic Judaism seem to distance themselves from the Pharisees, whom they associate with the Sadducees (see below), but they regard themselves as continuing traditions that had their origins in the rabbis of the Pharisaic period.

The New Testament often associates scribes with the Pharisees, and this is historically correct. However, not all scribes were Pharisees, nor were scribes a specific religious party in first-century Judaism.[21] They were the experts in the interpretation of Torah and were consulted by the Pharisees in the process of developing their teachings on any issue. Like today's lawyers or attorneys, however, they were available for consultation on legal matters by any stream within Judaism. There would have also been scribes in the service of the Sadducees. However, because of the Pharisees' intense focus on the law, they are often closely associated with scribes in the New Testament.

The Sadducees

As with the Pharisees, the history of the Sadducees and the origin of the name are hard to trace with certainty.[22] Most accept that the name comes from the high priest Zadok, who anointed Solomon king (1 Kings 1:39). By New Testament times the Sadducees were closely associated with the priestly aristocracy. In Acts 5:17 the high priest and the Sadducees are linked, and in Acts 4:1 the priests, the captain of the temple, and the Sadducees appear together. They are separate entities but are all associated with temple worship. This made them key figures during the period leading up to the destruction of Jerusalem and its temple in 70 CE. Ideally, all Jews would come to the temple in Jerusalem to celebrate the high feasts and to participate in the sacrifices that were offered there each day. This was a ritual form of communication with God, and the yearly ritual of the Day of Atonement was central to this relationship. Only the high priest approached the Holy of Holies (the inner sanctum of the temple area) and came into the presence of the Holy One. He entered and was met and not destroyed by the God of Israel. This action signified that the sins of the Jewish people were no longer held against them.

This priestly caste was perpetuated by birth into a priestly family, in the line of Levi. They exercised a sacred ministry, preserved the cultic rites, and

---

21. For more detail on the scribes, see Meier, *Marginal Jew*, 3:549–60.
22. For more detail on the Sadducees, see ibid., 3:389–487.

were generally (although not always) wealthy and traditional. They held fast to the teachings of the Torah but rejected the suggestion that, beyond the written Torah, the righteous Jew also had to follow the traditions of the oral Torah. They accepted only the written word of Israel's Scriptures and thus could be considered as more conservative than the Pharisees. It is from this understanding of the beliefs of the Sadducees that the New Testament claims they did not believe in angels, the resurrection, or the afterlife (see Mark 12:18). In this they differed from the Pharisees, Jesus, and his followers (see Mark 12:24–27; John 11:25–27). They did not believe in armed struggle and tended to cooperate with Roman authorities. Once the cultic center of the Jerusalem temple was desecrated and destroyed in 70 CE, they had lost the focus of their life and no longer retained a place of religious significance among the postwar Jewish people. Many would have perished at the hands of the Romans, especially as there appears to have been a close association between the priests and the Zealots (see below) during the Jewish revolt against Rome. However strongly Sadducee survivors may have held their views in the postwar period, they eventually either died out or joined the Pharisaic remnant that was struggling to reconstruct a Jewish way of life and faith in that disastrous period.

The Essenes

The Essenes, who practiced a form of Jewish observance of Torah that is not mentioned in the New Testament, have become very important in the past sixty years for our understanding of the world that produced the New Testament.[23] They are described by the Hellenistic Jewish philosopher Philo (ca. 20 BCE–50 CE) and by the Jewish historian Josephus. From this evidence, they were a closely united sectarian group that was dedicated to extreme asceticism and to living in community. Their significance for our understanding of the world of first-century Judaism exploded onto the scene in 1948 after the discovery of what have come to be known as the Dead Sea Scrolls. On the basis of this archaeological discovery, a long-recognized ruin at Qumran, beside the northwestern end of the Dead Sea, has widely been identified as a place where a community of Essenes had lived, perhaps for 150 years before the community was destroyed by the Romans. It is generally thought (but has not been proven) that the many documents that have been found in surrounding caves were hurriedly placed there by the members of the Qumran

---

23. See further Meier, *Marginal Jew*, 3:488–532. Like most, Meier accepts that the Qumran community was Essene.

community as the danger of Roman destruction became imminent. There are many biblical texts in these scrolls,[24] along with some important documents that describe their life together and their understanding of righteous Judaism, sometimes called the sectarian documents. It appears that they were founded as a form of protest during the period of the Hasmoneans' corrupt royal and priestly claims, including the establishment of an erroneous festival calendar. Variously identified, the corrupt figure thought to be responsible for these digressions is described as the "wicked priest." The founder of the Qumran community is called the "teacher of righteousness."

On the whole, the community lived an ascetical life marked by many ritual and ethical obligations. They did this because they recognized the initiative of God's love as central to the community and saw their punctilious lifestyle as rendering a more acceptable obedience to God. But there were also Essene families, who focused on relationships with others in the sect, not with outsiders. The Essene belief was that God has a special love for the spirit of light found in the community and takes pleasure in its works. The community responds by loving God and one another. In this way they preserve the holy community. Only those who love God can be admitted to the community. They must detest the sons of darkness. While God's love remains strongly in place, absence of a command to love people *outside* the community indicates the sectarian nature of the community.[25] Members of the Qumran community looked forward to the future vindication of Israel, or at least the vindication of their community as the true remnant of Israel. The language they use to describe this final apocalyptic battle, in which the forces of God will be victorious, is very dualistic. The forces of light battle against the forces of darkness, and the elect, "the children of truth," will be victorious over "the children of falsehood." The former "spring from a fountain of light," while the latter "are

---

24. These biblical texts are extremely important. Prior to their discovery, the only complete copy of the Hebrew Bible was the Leningrad Codex, which dates from 1008–9 CE. (A partial text, the Aleppo Codex, is dated earlier, in the tenth century.) The Qumran caves provided Hebrew texts that were more than one thousand years older than the biblical text used for scholarship and translation until recent times.

25. These features of the life and thought of the Essene community at Qumran are found in many of their documents, especially in what are known as the *Damascus Document* (CD), the *Community Rule* (1QS), and the *Hymns* (1QH). Each document from Qumran is referred to by a number (e.g., 1) that indicates the cave in which it was found (there are many caves in the Qumran region where scrolls and artifacts have been found) and Q, indicating that it is a Qumran document (as other documents were also found during the excavations). The second letter indicates the precise document (e.g., S = rule; H = hymns). The *Damascus Document* has a special abbreviation (CD) because it was found earlier in Egypt, as well as in other places. Its discovery at Qumran established it as a sectarian document of the Essenes. The most widely available translation of these documents is from Vermes, *Complete Dead Sea Scrolls.*

ruled by the angel of darkness and walk in the ways of darkness."[26] These hopes of restoration were not realized, and the Qumran sectarians, as an identifiable group within Judaism, also came to an end in 73–74 CE.[27]

The Qumran documents are of inestimable value to a student of the New Testament.[28] They provide a vivid portrait of the way of life of a Jewish community that existed at the same time the Jesus movement existed. Many elements that were previously thought to have come to Christianity from a Greco-Roman background, such as the dualism mentioned above, are now thought to have been commonplace in a first-century Jewish sect. Some ascetical practices found among early Christians are also found at Qumran. Not only can direct correlation between ideas be found, but there is also evidence of parallel ways of interpreting Israel's biblical tradition between the Qumran sectarians and the early Christians. Earliest Christianity was also a Jewish sect. However, never do the followers of Jesus ask that the community members hate their enemies. The rigid sectarianism of the Qumran documents is not found in the New Testament.

The Zealots

A further group is even harder to identify.[29] When Josephus discusses the various "philosophies" that can be found within Jewish society, he speaks of Sadducees, Pharisees, and Essenes (*Jewish War* 2.119, 164). He then speaks of the "fourth philosophy." They are clearly the group that he blames for the disaster of the Jewish revolt and subsequent war against Rome. In modern scholarship they are identified as the Zealots, even though Josephus does not give them that name. They do not play an active role in the New Testament, apart from the fact that one of the disciples is called Simon the Zealot (Luke 6:15; Acts 1:13). We are again not sure of their origins or their influence in Jewish religion and society. The difficulty is created by the fact that Josephus blames them for all the trouble that descended upon Israel, including its eventual destruction. For Josephus, salvation was possible, and this is what the Romans

26. The description of this final conflict is found in the *War Scroll* (1QM). It can be found in Vermes, *Complete Dead Sea Scrolls*, 163–85.

27. Josephus describes this end spectacularly: the last of the sectarians fled to the protection of the fortress of Masada, south of Qumran. According to Josephus, when the Romans penetrated the fortress, all who were at Masada, including some Essenes, committed suicide so as not to fall into the hands of the agents of darkness.

28. For a general discussion, see C. D. Elledge, "The Dead Sea Scrolls," in Green and McDonald, *World of the New Testament*, 228–41.

29. See further James D. G. Dunn, "Prophetic Movements and Zealots," in Green and McDonald, *World of the New Testament*, 242–51.

really sought, but the Zealots continued an increasingly fanatic anti-Roman stance that led to destruction.

No doubt, however, a certain group of people within Jewish society regarded their mission as the restoration of the land of Israel to its God-appointed people and was prepared to stop at nothing to see this happen. It is possible that the description of Barabbas as a violent revolutionary (see Mark 15:6–15 and John 18:38b–40, where Barabbas is called a *lēstēs*, the Greek word used by Josephus to speak of the Zealots) lists him among their number. For the New Testament, this way of violence was a false messianic hope. Like the Sadducees and the Essenes, the Zealots (who were, according to Josephus, the group that conducted the war to its very end) became increasingly insignificant after 70 CE. Obviously, remnants may have still existed and may have played a role in the emergence of postwar Judaism, but they were no longer a force in the religion and politics of the period.

The Followers of Jesus

From other sources we are aware that there were other ways in which Jewish people lived their life of love and obedience under Torah. But the Pharisees, Sadducees, Essenes (if that is the correct identity of the Qumran sectarians), and Zealots were key players. Also present was the small group of people who regarded themselves as Jews but were convinced that Jesus of Nazareth was the Messiah. This book is an introduction to the story of Jesus and what several generations of his first followers thought of him. The earliest written witnesses to Jesus from Christian authors come from the 50s of the first Christian century (Paul), and the first Gospel (Mark) most likely appeared about the time of the destruction of Jerusalem (70 CE). From these earliest documents in the New Testament, and from others that were written later, even into the early decades of the second century, we can sense who these followers of Jesus were and how they related to the God of Israel in and through Jesus. The stories of Jesus and the other documents (letters, theological tracts, apocalyptic) that they produced are best understood against the political and religious background outlined above.

The development, life, and thought of the earliest Christians will be more fully developed later in this book. But one further introductory point should be made. With the exception of the Pauline letters, all the New Testament documents, and especially the Gospels, were written after 70 CE. At this stage of Jewish history, after the Jewish War, which led to the decreasing significance of the Sadducees, Zealots, and Essenes, there were basically two ways of being a Jew. Going by the evidence we have, most became followers of the emerging form of Jewish life later known as rabbinic Judaism. Although generated by other factors, the gathering at Jamnia to restore a broken people by means of a more assiduous observance of the Torah, guided by rabbinic teaching (the oral Torah), played an important part in this development. Some, however, became followers of Jesus. This group had its origins within Judaism, but by the time the New Testament was written it was already reaching into the Mediterranean world, preaching that Jesus of Nazareth was the Messiah.

Originally both groups regarded themselves as continuing the religious tradition and faith of Israel, but their estimation of what God had done in and through Jesus divided them even before the Jewish revolt.[30] As already mentioned, this situation necessarily led to the many conflicts between the Pharisees and Jesus and his disciples that we find reported in the Gospels, especially in the Gospel of John, often regarded as the most anti-Jewish document in the New Testament (see esp. John 8:31–59). The historical background that generated these heated encounters, however, was not so much the life and times of Jesus but the life and times of the postwar parting of the ways between Judaism and Christianity.[31] There is some continuation with the past, however, as we can see from the treatment meted out to prophetic figures earlier in the century, especially John the Baptist.

The Greco-Roman World

Jesus was a Jew, and Christianity came into existence in a Jewish world, but that world existed within the larger context of the Roman Empire. In a remarkably short time this new religion was being taught, lived, and even died for within the empire. But the Roman Empire, which certainly had many unique characteristics, was itself a product of late Hellenism. Thus we speak of the Greco-Roman world. There had already been considerable penetration of Hellenism into Judaism before the time of Jesus.[32] The most obvious sign of this penetration was the translation of the Hebrew Scriptures into Greek late in the second century BCE. This translation is known as the Septuagint

30. If the Gospel of Mark appeared about 70 CE, we already find stories of Jesus and the Jewish leaders in conflict (see esp. Mark 11:27–12:40).

31. Interested readers might follow this further in the fine recent study of Peter Schäfer, *The Jewish Jesus: How Judaism and Christianity Shaped Each Other* (Princeton: Princeton University Press, 2012).

32. The definitive work on this is Martin Hengel, *Judaism and Hellenism: Studies in Their Encounter in Palestine during the Hellenistic Period*, trans. John Bowden, 2 vols. (Philadelphia: Fortress, 1974).

and is represented by the Roman numerals for seventy: LXX.[33] Even though Alexander the Great's empire disintegrated rapidly after his death because of the internecine strife of his successors and the eventual military and political dominance of Rome, his dream of a world unified by a common language and a common religion met considerable success. The classical Greek of Sophocles and Plato and the Greek of the great dramatists of the fifth century BCE was no longer in use, but the simpler dialect called "common" (*koinē*) Greek was the accepted language of the ancient world for three centuries before Jesus Christ. The New Testament is written in this form of Greek. Greek religion had likewise departed from its Athenian roots. Alexander's openness to the world of the East introduced many new currents of thought, and the Romans adopted and adapted these religious traditions. For example, the three prominent Greek gods—Zeus, Hera, and Athena—were identified with the Roman gods Jupiter, Juno, and Minerva, respectively.[34] In many ways, the Roman dominance of the Mediterranean world brought many benefits, including widespread peace and active trade throughout the empire.

In addition to the Roman use of the Greek gods and their associated myths and cults, other influences from the East, now part of the Hellenistic-Roman world, destabilized religious thought and practice. A number of major philosophical schools developed across this period, and each of them sought to bring stability and systematic thinking into the increasingly diverse forms of religious practice of the time.[35]

- *Stoicism* was founded in Athens by Zeno (332–260 BCE) and introduced in Rome in 161 BCE. Seneca (ca. 4 BCE–65 CE) was its outstanding representative, insisting that virtue is the only good. The wise person is superior to pain, pleasure, wealth and poverty, or success and misfortune. Self-control is the hallmark of such a person.

- *Epicureanism* is linked to the name of Epicurus (341–269 BCE), who advocated the higher pleasures of the mind, associated with an emphasis

33. According to a Jewish legend (found in a document called the *Letter of Aristeas*), the LXX was the product of a simultaneous translation made by seventy-two Jewish elders working in Egypt for the royal library. However, it was most likely the work of various Diaspora Jews who were no longer familiar with Hebrew.

34. See Nancy Evans, "Embedding Rome in Athens," in *Rome and Religion: A Cross-Disciplinary Dialogue on the Imperial Cult*, ed. Jeffrey Brodd and Jonathan L. Reed, Writings from the Greco-Roman World Supplement Series 5 (Atlanta: SBL, 2011), 83–97.

35. For fuller descriptions of major philosophical schools and their possible influence on the New Testament writings, see W. Randolph Tate, *Biblical Interpretation: An Integrated Approach*, 3rd ed. (Grand Rapids: Baker Academic, 2008), 54–63. See the studies of John T. Fitzgerald, "Greco-Roman Philosophical Schools," in Green and McDonald, *World of the New Testament*, 135–48, and Moyer V. Hubbard, "Greek Religion," in ibid., 105–23.

on friendship and happiness. We know most about Epicureanism through Lucretius (94–55 BCE). Epicureanism had no concerns about a future life and thus insisted that one must focus on what could be attained and enjoyed in this life. As the Hellenistic hope for a unified community across the whole known world faded, Epicureanism fostered the generation of communities or circles of close friends to compensate for this loss. The soul finds pleasure in friendship in a world where everyone is a stranger.

- *Neopythagoreanism* marked a return in the first century BCE to the ideas of Pythagoras (570–494 BCE). It is best known through the figure of Apollonius of Tyana (15–100 CE). Philostratus (ca. 170–ca. 245 CE) wrote a prejudiced and highly fanciful biography of this wandering charismatic. There are many parallels between Philostratus' life of Apollonius and the life of Jesus (miraculous birth, disciples, miracles), but the major element in Neopythagorean thought is a negative view of the material world. It must be evil since it is so far from a transcendent God. This view was shared by gnosticism.

Perhaps even more popular than the philosophical schools were two further so-called religions that are harder to describe: the mystery religions and gnosticism. The traditional gods and the legends and cults that surrounded them did not affect the lives of ordinary people, and these two "popular" forms of religion emerged from a search for meaning and belonging. People were searching for some form of salvation. They were subject to moral and physical evil, and many lived in great poverty. They seemed to be dominated by a destiny they could not determine, and they wished to free themselves from the corruption that appeared to be an essential part of the material side of life.

There were many mystery religions, and the secrecy that surrounded both the religions themselves and their rites makes it difficult to be sure about each one of them. On the whole, people sought help by becoming members of a secret and well-organized group through initiation rites and participation in meetings where certain rites, often orgiastic, were practiced. Through these rites they were put into contact with the divine (e.g., the physical self-loss that accompanies sexual experience). All members had to maintain the secrets that were part of the life and practice of the cult, give unconditional obedience to the cult leaders, and be loyal to those who shared the mysteries with them. A sense of community and release from the limitations of the material world (however transient in the cultic act) led to the widespread popularity of these cults.[36]

36. See Tate, *Biblical Interpretation*, 60–63.

Gnosticism as it eventually emerged in the second century in a number of different religious systems was not present in the first century. But the seeds of speculative theories from the East that suggested the possibility of salvation from chaos by knowledge were most likely "in the air." In various ways, through a great number of gnostic "myths," the gnostics taught that God was now beyond reach. Emanations from God had fought and entered into wicked relationships, generating evil and chaos that went on and on self-propagating. Between the unreachable God and human beings, only chaos existed. The world that humans inhabit is caught up in evil matter, part of the chaos. Yet within every human dwells a spark that reflects divine origins, and this generates an anxiety about the true meaning of life and ultimate destiny. Existence as "matter" and in "matter" is ultimately unsatisfying. Salvation was only possible for a few "illuminated" people who heard the story of the generation of the chaotic situation and learned how salvation was possible. In some gnostic systems, this "knowledge" (Greek: *gnōsis*) was made known to them in a myth that told of a saving figure who came down from the divine, penetrated the chaos, and revealed the truth to them. The divine spark bursts into flame, and salvation is made possible through this "knowledge."[37]

Finally, the New Testament was written in the Roman Empire. No one could avoid the presence of Roman authority.[38] The emperor Augustus (27 BCE–14 CE) tried to impose traditional Roman religion, deriving from the Greek religions. Temples to the traditional gods were erected across the empire, and they were very popular in many of the Roman provinces. But a new god was appearing on the scene. Already in the time of Alexander the Great there had been a tendency to regard the emperor as a god. Augustus spurned divine honors during his life, but he did associate the custom of uniting kingship and priesthood in himself. After his death he was accorded a divine status, and successive emperors further developed the tendency to insist that the emperor was a divine figure even while still alive. This insistence was by no means uniform, and it was often used to unify the empire rather than insist on the worldwide worship of the emperor as a god. As early as the emperor Nero (54–68 CE), Christians were singled out for special treatment (persecution after they were blamed for the destruction of much of Rome by fire). They were already an identifiable group in the empire. Early Christianity grew in this world of Roman religion and different forms and practices of the imperial

37. For a lucid study of the complex systems of gnosticism, see David Brakke, *The Gnostics: Myth, Ritual and Diversity in Early Christianity* (Cambridge, MA: Harvard University Press, 2010).

38. See Nicholas Perrin, "The Imperial Cult," in Green and McDonald, *World of the New Testament*, 124–34.

cult, and there is much in the New Testament that shows how early Christians "negotiated" their presence in that world.[39] The same could be said for the attitude of the leaders of the Greco-Roman world toward other religions, as long as they did not seek to claim exclusive worship. For example, the Jews were tolerated and were granted exemptions that would allow them to follow their ancestral religion: they did not have to attend court on the Sabbath and were allowed to send contributions to the temple.

Conclusion

The words of Jesus to the Samaritan woman in the Gospel of John affirm an undeniable historical fact, as far as Christians are concerned: "Salvation is from the Jews" (John 4:22). The Old Testament told the story of God's presence in the history and religion of the Jews. Jesus was a Jew, the disciples were Jews, and most likely all the authors of the writings that we call the New Testament were Jews. An understanding of the general situation in Palestine and within the various representatives of Jewish faith and practice, before and after the Jewish War of 70 CE, is clearly integral to a more meaningful reading of the New Testament. Who were the various "Herods"? Why do we hear of Pharisees, Sadducees, scribes, and Zealots? Are they all Jewish? Whom did they represent? What was the Jerusalem temple, and how different was the synagogue? What was the Sanhedrin? Why is there so much bitterness between Jesus and the Pharisees, or between Jesus and "the Jews"? Indeed, especially in the Gospel of John, are those called "the Jews" in the story to be identified as the forefathers of the Jews of our own day?

An informed awareness of the Jewish background to the life of Jesus and to the emergence of the early Church and its writings should be seen as essential to a coherent and faith-filled reading of the New Testament. There is no need to be an expert, but we must appreciate that profoundly religious world, driven by a certain understanding of God and by a hope that God would never abandon his people. This is essential for an acceptance of the ongoing relevance of the Jewish messianic understanding of Jesus of Nazareth as the

---

39. It has long been held that there was fierce opposition between the emerging Church and the imposition of the imperial cult and other Roman religious practices, generating an understanding of the New Testament that was isolated from the empire. Recent scholarship questions this and shows that there may have been some obvious "rejection" (e.g., the Apocalypse) but also a great deal of "negotiation." On this, see the helpful studies in Brodd and Reed, *Rome and Religion*, especially the important essays of the classicist Karl Galinsky, "The Cult of the Roman Emperor: Uniter or Divider?," 1–21, and "In the Shadow (or Not) of the Imperial Cult: A Cooperative Agenda," 215–25.

Davidic son of God and the Messiah. But more than that, if we are armed with this knowledge, the pages of the New Testament can leap into life for us and can take on the color of the world that produced them. As we will see in the following chapter, which considers how the New Testament came into existence, it is only when we are able to understand why certain Christian documents made sense when they were first written, heard, and read that we can begin to grasp why later generations accepted them as inspired Sacred Scripture and why they continue to speak to us as the Word of God read, heard, and lived in the life of the Church.

The same must be said for the Greco-Roman background. In the rapid overview of formative elements of that complex and multilayered religious and social world, some crucial points of contact between that world and the New Testament can be sensed. The understanding of Jesus Christ as Savior in a world hungry for an answer to the deepest needs of humankind was very welcome. It is worth noting that, even though E. R. Dodds was referring to a period later than the first Christian century (160–330 CE) and has been widely questioned by contemporary classical scholars, he described the era in which Christianity emerged in the midst of the dominant Greco-Roman tradition as "the age of anxiety."[40] Epicurus was called "savior" by his followers, and both the mystery religions and gnosticism sought some form of salvation. Stoicism and Neopythagoreanism sought to transcend the limitations of the material world, as did gnosticism and the mystery religions. Epicureanism sought to create communities of friendship, goodwill, and mutual pleasure, offering comfort to strangers in this world.

None of this is foreign to the Gospel stories or the teaching of Jesus found there, nor is it foreign to the Pauline gospel. This had to be the case, as early Christianity shaped its understanding and preaching of what God had done for humankind in and through Jesus in a world that was shot through with these ideas, longings, and hopes. Jesus, the Christian community, and the New Testament were *born* in a Jewish world, but Christianity quickly grew and developed into a world religion within a context where Greco-Roman religions and other newer religions were rife. It had to be *preached* and *lived* in a world dominated by the Roman Empire.

---

40. Eric Robertson Dodds, *Pagans and Christians in an Age of Anxiety: Some Aspects of Religious Experience from Marcus Aurelius to Constantine* (Cambridge: Cambridge University Press, 1965). Dodds was the Regius Professor of Greek at the University of Oxford. Earlier, while at the University of Birmingham (1924–35), he met W. H. Auden. In 1947 Auden published a memorable four-part poem with the title "The Age of Anxiety." Auden's poem reflected human instability during the period of industrialization. It generated a symphony (by Leonard Bernstein) and a ballet (by Jerome Robbins). Dodds' later study, using the same title to describe an earlier age of instability, is the published version of the Wiles Lectures, given at Queen's University, Belfast, in 1963.

The remarkable growth of the religious teaching and practice of Christianity, which became the imperial religion by the time of Constantine, less than three hundred years after the death of Jesus, indicates that among many factors, the Sacred Scriptures of the Christians spoke to people of that era.[41] They were *born* in a Jewish world but, although there are pages that are anti-Roman (e.g., the Apocalypse), they carried a universal message that "negotiated" the Greco-Roman world that *received* them and made sense to many. As we shall see in the following chapter, if that had not been the case, a New Testament would never have come into existence.

41. The growth of Christianity cannot be credited simply to the relevance of its Sacred Scriptures. Indeed, many educated people (famously, the young Augustine) thought these writings were unsophisticated. There were many elements that influenced this growth, including the witness of the martyrs, the sacramental life, Eucharist, saintly leadership, the community experience, and the teaching of resurrection from the dead (based on belief in Jesus' resurrection from death). A recent valuable study by a sociologist has cogently argued that it was the care the Christians had for one another, especially for women, the sick, and the marginalized, that generated this growth, especially in Rome. See Rodney Stark, *The Rise of Christianity: A Sociologist Reconsiders History* (Princeton: Princeton University Press, 1996).

3

The Origins
of the New Testament

Its Creation and Reception

Faith in Jesus of Nazareth as the Christ and the Son of God (see Mark 1:1; John 20:30–31) generated the books that we now regard as our New Testament. Jesus was a man like us who lived in the first thirty years of the Christian era. Along with Christian sources and stories, even non-Christian authors (the Jewish historian Josephus and the Roman historian Tacitus [56–117 CE]) tell us something of his life, ministry, and death. Jesus told his immediate disciples that he was bringing in a new era, a time when God would reign in their hearts, minds, and lives as their king. They became aware that in his teaching, in his life-giving ministry, and indeed in his personality, there were clear signs that the kingdom of God was at hand.[1] In the words of Jesus: "If it is by the finger of God that I cast out demons, then the kingdom of God has come upon you" (Luke 11:20; see also Matt. 12:28).[2]

1. The well-known New Testament expression "the kingdom of God" is difficult to render in English. It is not a geographical "kingdom," and God is not a "political king" as we understand kings. In Jesus' original Aramaic preaching the notion was more dynamic than "space" and "authority."
2. Matthew has "If it is by the Spirit of God that I cast out demons." Luke is most likely transmitting words closer to what Jesus actually said. We will see below that this is what is called a passage from "Q," a source common to Luke and Matthew.

But not everyone was convinced. In the end, the Romans and the Jewish leadership joined in an alliance that led to Jesus' crucifixion as a blasphemer (according to the Jewish leaders) and a political threat (according to the Roman authority).[3] One thing is certain about Jesus of Nazareth: he was crucified. Non-Christian sources of the time (Josephus and Tacitus) record that event.[4] There was nothing attractive about the historical event of the crucifixion of Jesus; he was cruelly and violently executed by the Romans in a fashion used only for the worst criminals.[5] Strange as it may seem, this horrific event must be seen as one of the major elements that led to the eventual writing of what we know as the New Testament. The earliest Christians, no doubt because of the experience they had had with Jesus during his ministry and the impact that his teaching had made upon them, believed that he was the expected Messiah (see Mark 8:29; Matt. 16:15–16; Luke 9:20). For a few decades their "memories" of Jesus remained unwritten. The early Christians encouraged one another in difficulty: they gathered for prayer and remembered things that Jesus had said and done. They celebrated a meal together, "in memory" of him, as he had instructed (see 1 Cor. 11:23–26). At the beginning there was no need for a "story of Jesus." They knew it. They had either been with Jesus (a small minority: the Twelve and probably some other followers, including significant women, among them his mother) or had at least known him (the majority of people whose villages and homes he visited).[6] One thing they all knew was that he had been crucified.

3. The responsibility for the death of Jesus has long been debated, especially in the light of European Christian persecution of the Jews as those responsible for the slaying of Jesus Christ. A critical reading of the Gospels indicates that there was an understandable collusion between Jewish leaders, who would not accept his teaching on the kingdom of God, and Roman authorities, who saw him as a threat to Roman political stability.

4. Josephus tells of Jesus' execution under Pontius Pilate in *Jewish Antiquities* 18.63–64, a passage known as the *Testimonium Flavianum*. No doubt it has been expanded into its present form by Christian editors through the centuries, but most scholars claim that reference to Pilate's execution of Jesus is original. The same can be said for the witness of Tacitus in his *Annals* 15.44.3. For evaluations of the witness of Josephus and Tacitus, see John P. Meier, *Marginal Jew*, 1:56–111; Gerd Theissen and Annette Merz, *The Historical Jesus: A Comprehensive Guide*, trans. John Bowden (Minneapolis: Fortress, 1998), 63–89.

5. Because of the centrality of the crucifixion in Christian theology, the horrific nature of this form of Roman execution is often forgotten in the midst of theological speculation about its meaning and in the use of the cross in art and decoration. Readers would do well to consult Martin Hengel, *The Crucifixion in the Ancient World and the Folly of the Message of the Cross*, trans. John Bowden (Philadelphia: Fortress, 1977).

6. See the most helpful analysis of the social setting of these earliest "followers" in Gerd Theissen, *Sociology of Early Palestinian Christianity*, trans. John Bowden (Philadelphia: Fortress, 1978). See also the somewhat larger presentation of different social groups that were "called," in Lohfink, *Jesus of Nazareth*, 86–99.

Their hopes, focused on Jesus during his ministry, could have been destroyed by the fact that he ended his life among them with an ignominious death. Not only did the earliest Christians have to face their own doubts and confusion over Jesus' apparent failure; very soon after his death they set out on a mission to proclaim a crucified criminal as the Messiah. The words of the disciples on their way to Emmaus tell of their disappointment: "We had hoped that he was the one to redeem Israel" (Luke 24:21), and Paul instructs the Corinthians on the apparent stupidity of their belief in a crucified Messiah: "For Jews demand signs and Greeks seek wisdom, but we preach Christ crucified, a stumbling block to Jews and folly to Gentiles" (1 Cor. 1:22–23). In the world that produced the New Testament, for both Jew and gentile, a Messiah could not possibly have been crucified!

A Story That Begins with an Ending

The earliest Christians believed that the crucified Jesus had been raised by God from the dead. The crucifixion and God's action in the resurrection are the bedrock upon which the documents that eventually formed the New Testament were built. Christians quickly began to "tell the story" of the crucifixion of Jesus in the light of the resurrection. The earliest coherent narratives that they told were the narratives of Jesus' death and resurrection. We have no firsthand sources that provide us with this early account, but behind all four Gospels there appears to be a traditional story. Elsewhere in the Gospel narratives of Jesus' life and teaching, the sequence of events is often strikingly different. This is already the case when one compares the story lines of the so-called Synoptic Gospels, Mark, Matthew, and Luke.[7] But striking differences are found in the Gospel of John, where the timeline of Mark, Matthew, and Luke is not apparent.[8] However, once Mark, Matthew, Luke, and John come to the end of Jesus' life, the sequence of events is the same: a final evening together, Gethsemane, arrest, a Jewish hearing, a Roman trial, crucifixion,

---

7. Mark, Matthew, and Luke are called the Synoptic Gospels because they can be put side by side and compared with one glance of the eye (Greek: *syn*, "with"; *opsis*, "the eye"). There are useful books that provide this "glance." See, e.g., Burton H. Throckmorton Jr., *Gospel Parallels: A Comparison of the Synoptic Gospels* (Nashville: Thomas Nelson, 1992).

8. Scholars have long debated whether John used the Synoptic Gospels. He may have known them, but he uses his own strong traditions, whose origins are independent of the Synoptic Gospels. For this position, see the classic work of Charles H. Dodd, *Historical Tradition in the Fourth Gospel* (Cambridge: Cambridge University Press, 1965), and the more recent study of D. Moody Smith, *John among the Gospels*, 2nd ed. (Columbia: University of South Carolina Press, 2001).

death, burial, and the discovery of an empty tomb.[9] Each evangelist develops an individual and rich interpretation of that sequence of events by telling it in a different way and by introducing elements in the story that are unique to each narrative, but they all go back to the same primitive story.[10] But the writing of the Gospels came later. The first Christian that we know of who courageously faced the scandal of Jesus' crucifixion and God's action in the resurrection was Saul/Paul of Tarsus.[11]

Paul was born around 6–8 BCE into a Jewish family in the city of Tarsus, a cultural center in Asia Minor, near the Mediterranean coast in present-day Turkey. He was a product of both the Jewish world and the Greco-Roman world outlined in chapter 2. No Jew could accept that the expected Christ would be crucified. Like any believing Jew, Saul initially discounted the idea that Jesus of Nazareth could have been the Christ. After all, he had been hung upon a tree, and this had already been described in the Old Testament as a curse (Deut. 21:23; see Gal. 3:13). The message was also abroad that Jesus had been raised from the dead. Saul was the product of a thousand years of Israelite religious history, and he had been expertly further trained, possibly to "the strict manner" of the Pharisees in Jerusalem at the feet of Gamaliel (Acts 22:3; see Gal. 1:14; 2 Cor. 11:22). It is not difficult to understand why Saul originally joined the opposition to this new form of Judaism, based on a message that the man who had been crucified by the Romans had been raised and was in some way "alive" among those who followed his teaching. Saul's passion for the God of Israel could not tolerate this betrayal, and he actively persecuted Christians from 33 to 35 CE (see Acts 8:1; 9:1–2; 22:1–5; Gal. 1:13–14; Phil. 3:3–6).

9. Only Luke has a slight variation on this sequence. He divides the Jewish hearing into two parts, one in the night (Luke 22:54–65 [in the high priest's house]) and one at daybreak (22:66–71). He also inserts a presence before Herod into the Roman trial (23:6–12). As we will see, Luke is a very creative author, but the hearing in the morning may more closely reflect what actually happened.

10. On the primitive passion narrative, see Marion Soards, "The Question of a PreMarcan Passion Narrative," appendix 9 in *The Death of the Messiah: A Commentary on the Passion Narratives in the Four Gospels*, by Raymond E. Brown, Anchor Bible Reference Library (New York: Doubleday, 1993), 2:1429–1524. On the uniqueness of each Gospel story of Jesus' death and resurrection, see Francis J. Moloney, *The Resurrection of the Messiah: A Narrative Commentary on the Resurrection Accounts in the Four Gospels* (Mahwah, NJ: Paulist Press, 2013).

11. The two names, Saul and Paul, have often been taken as an indication of the Jew (Saul) becoming a Christian (Paul). This is most likely not the case. They were a Jewish version (Saul) and a Roman version (Latin: Paul) of the same name, although Acts of the Apostles generally uses "Saul" to speak of him during his period of anti-Christian persecution and "Paul" to speak of him as the apostle (largely "Saul" until Acts 13:9 and "Paul" after that). On this, see David G. Horrell, *An Introduction to the Study of Paul*, 2nd ed., T&T Clark Approaches to Biblical Studies (London: T&T Clark, 2006), 28.

After his "Damascus road" experience, which probably took place in 35 CE, his passion for the God of Israel did not lessen, but he came to see that this God had acted decisively for the whole of humankind, indeed the whole of creation, in and through the death and resurrection of Jesus. If we had only the letters of Paul from that first century, we would have very little contemporary evidence about Jesus of Nazareth. We would hear from Paul that he was born of a woman in the fullness of time (Gal. 4:4); that the night before he died he celebrated a meal with his disciples, described as the establishment of a new covenant (1 Cor. 11:23–26); and that he was crucified and buried yet subsequently seen by many (1 Cor. 15:3–8). Paul took the two passages in 1 Corinthians from traditions that were older than him. He says in both places that he is passing on to them what he also received (1 Cor. 11:23; 15:3). If Paul is writing to the Corinthians in 54 CE, then these traditions about the life of Jesus are very old indeed.

But for our purposes we need to focus on the fact that Paul's message, in all his letters, depends entirely upon what God has done for the whole of creation through the death and resurrection of Jesus. As we will see, there is a great deal to Paul's thought. But his Christology, his understanding of Christian life, of grace, of sin, and of the end of time (so-called eschatology), to mention some important issues, all depend upon his interpretation of what God did in and through the death and resurrection of Jesus. This was Paul's response to the problem of a crucified Messiah as a Jewish stumbling block and a Greek scandal (1 Cor. 1:23–25): "but to those who are the called, both Jews and Greeks, Christ the power of God and the wisdom of God. For God's foolishness is wiser than human wisdom, and God's weakness is stronger than human strength" (vv. 24–25 NRSV).

Paul is the author of the earliest documents of the New Testament. The letters that certainly come from him (1 Thessalonians, Galatians, 1 and 2 Corinthians, Philippians, Philemon, and Romans) were all written between 50 and 60 CE. Paul may have also been the author of Colossians. We will consider these details later, but if that was the case, the Letter to the Colossians would have been written in the early 60s of the first century. This means that the earliest Christian writings that we have *began with profound and necessary reflection upon the end of Jesus' story*. The scandal of the cross and the intervention of God in the resurrection lay at the origins of Christian thought and practice, expressing unconditional confidence that Jesus' obedience unto death and God's intervention into the world of the dead transformed human history. Paul responds to the scandal of the cross with a deep and inspired insight into what God has done for us in and through the resurrection. According to sound Christian tradition, Paul was executed in Rome during the reign of the emperor Nero (54–68 CE) around 64 CE.

Paul's presentation of the significance of the death and resurrection of Jesus, articulated only some twenty years after the death of Jesus, in the midst of a passionate missionary life, has never been surpassed. Paul is a powerful representative of the earliest Christian response to the scandal of the cross. There may have been others, but his writings are the ones that have endured as part of the New Testament, a life-giving "Word of God," for two thousand years. His message endures as one of hope for all as we live in the "new creation" (Gal. 6:15; 2 Cor. 5:17). By focusing his attention on the dramatic and shocking *end* of the story of Jesus, he provided Christianity with an essential part of its life-giving Sacred Scriptures: the Christian life makes sense because of the way the life of its founder *ended*, in death and resurrection.[12]

The Stories Begin: The Gospels

Nevertheless, the early Christians told stories about Jesus' life and teaching. Although they were written later, we can gather from the Gospels that these stories always formed part of "what they talked about." In the earliest days, to the best of our knowledge, nothing was *written*, but the Gospels make it clear that Mark, Matthew, Luke, and John (and no doubt others) had recourse to widely known oral traditions when they eventually came to write what was regarded as "the good news."[13] These stories recalled his words and his teaching as well as what he did and what had been done to him. They also generated a life of prayer. Chief among such prayers was the "Our Father" (see Matt. 6:9–15; Luke 11:1–4), still known to us as the Lord's Prayer. The memory of what he had said and done on the night before he died was recalled and enacted in the celebrations of the Lord's Supper (see 1 Cor. 11:23–26; Mark 14:22–25; Matt. 26:26–29; Luke 22:15–20). Paul instructs the Corinthians on the central importance of this prayerful action,

12. Although Paul does not describe the physical ascension of Jesus (his going up into heaven, as it is found in Luke 24:51 and Acts 1:9–10 [see also John 20:17]), he takes a return to God for granted in his message of "exaltation." This is most clearly spelled out in the famous hymn in Phil. 2:6–11. After telling of Jesus' emptying of himself and humiliation unto death, even death on a cross, Paul writes: "Therefore God has highly exalted him and bestowed on him the name which is above every name" (v. 9). Once the early Christians begin to tell Jesus' life story, this "exaltation" will be described in the stories of the life of Jesus as his "ascension" by Luke and John.

13. The expression "good news" is a literal translation of the Greek word *euangelion*. The English expression comes from the Old English "god-spel," also best rendered as "good news." The Greek had long been used to speak of the announcement of a gracious and joy-filled moment. Paul had already written of the "good news" of the death and resurrection of Jesus. But the "Gospels" take the use of the word one step further: a Gospel is a narrative that announces the "good news" of what God did for us by telling the story of the life, teaching, death, and resurrection of Jesus of Nazareth.

which today we call "liturgy": "For as often as you eat this bread and drink the cup, you proclaim the Lord's death until he comes" (1 Cor. 11:26).[14]

In the New Testament we also find hymns and fragments of hymns that would have been sung or proclaimed in the communities before they were written down in documents. The most famous of these are the Prologue to the Gospel of John (1:1–18) and the hymn to Jesus in the Letter to the Philippians (2:6–11), but there are many others. Memories of Jesus' life and teaching were alive well before the Gospels appeared. The best indication of this has already been hinted at in the fact that the Lord's Prayer appears only in Matthew and Luke. There are many words of Jesus that are found in Matthew and Luke but nowhere else. Another famous example is Jesus' sermon, delivered on a mountain in Matthew (5:1–7:29) and on a plain in Luke (6:17–45).[15] It is widely accepted that these traditions came to Matthew and Luke from a source, most likely written, that they had in common. New Testament scholars have collected these sayings, which are known as "Q," the first letter of the German word for "source": *Quelle*.[16] We no longer have Q, but we do have other collections of Jesus' sayings that may come from a later period yet indicate that the practice of recalling and writing down the words of Jesus was not uncommon. The most famous of these is the *Gospel of Thomas*, which probably dates from the second century CE.[17]

The Gospels were not written "out of thin air." They are not the imaginative reconstructions of early Christian writers. They developed from stories about Jesus that were told and retold in the communities (oral tradition), from prayers and liturgies celebrated there (liturgical tradition), and probably from some written documents that the evangelists had at their disposal, even though they are now lost to us (e.g., Q).[18] Although the inspired creativity of

14. Reading the words of the Lord's Prayer in Matthew and Luke, and the account of the Lord's Supper in Paul, Mark, Matthew, Luke, and John, reveals that each writer shapes Jesus' words differently. There seem to have been at least two different traditions for the Lord's Supper (Paul and Luke, sometimes called the Antioch tradition; and Mark and Matthew, sometimes called the Jerusalem tradition). The words of Jesus in John 6:51 may reflect another tradition, unique to John's community. This is important, as it shows that there was no *uniformity* in the way the early Church recalled Jesus, told others about him, and celebrated what he had done for us.

15. We have already had occasion to see the Q-saying of Jesus relating his exorcisms with the arrival of the kingdom of God in Luke 11:20 and Matthew 12:28.

16. For an introduction to Q, see John S. Kloppenborg, *Q, the Earliest Gospel: An Introduction to the Original Stories and Sayings of Jesus* (Louisville: Westminster John Knox, 2008); see 123–44 for a reconstructed Q.

17. For an excellent presentation of the *Gospel of Thomas*, see Christopher S. Skinner, *What Are They Saying about the Gospel of Thomas?* (Mahwah, NJ: Paulist Press, 2012).

18. Since we no longer have them, it is important not to insist that Luke and Matthew had a *written* text that today we call Q. While that is most likely, these common traditions may be the

each author must be recognized and taken into account as part of the ongoing revelation of God in the unfolding history of humankind, these stories have their roots in authentic memories of and witness to the person of Jesus of Nazareth (see *DV* 19).

As the first generation of Christians came to an end, the need to "tell the story of Jesus" for a newer generation must have emerged. The timing of the appearance of the Gospel of Mark at about 70 CE makes this motive likely.[19] It was not the only motive, nor even the most important one, but the Christian community's focus on the significance of the death and resurrection of Jesus, outstandingly and profoundly portrayed in the Pauline letters, generated questions for a newer generation that was now some distance from the life and times, and even the Jewish background, of Jesus. If Jesus is the crucified Christ, why did the Jewish leadership and the Romans collude to crucify him? How did he live his life and what did he say that produced his death by crucifixion, his resurrection, and his exaltation as *the end of the story*? This information was not immediately available to them. The first generation of Christians that had experienced Jesus firsthand was passing away. A newer generation had to be told of his life and the meaning of that life as well as the meaning of the death, resurrection, and exaltation that brought it to an end.

As Luke opens his Gospel (1:1–4), he tells Theophilus, to whom he dedicates both his Gospel and his Acts of the Apostles (Acts 1:1; see Luke 1:4), the stages through which the stories of Jesus have passed. What Jesus had done among us has been told in narratives (Luke 1:1) that had been passed on by those who "from the beginning were eyewitnesses and ministers of the word" (v. 2). In verses 1–2 Luke has described two generations: the eyewitnesses and first ministers of the Word (v. 2) and those who received from them the account of things that Jesus accomplished (v. 1). He then locates himself as a member of a third generation: "It seemed good to me also, having followed all things closely for some time past, to write an orderly account for you" (v. 3).[20]

---

result of the ongoing presence of a powerful set of shared oral traditions that were not present to Mark. I do not think that this is the case, but some do.

19. It is not unanimously agreed that Mark was the first Gospel to appear; however, that is the opinion of the vast majority of scholars. Neither is it always dated to 70 CE; however, all would associate it with the Jewish War of 66–70 CE. Some would date it before, and some after, the fall of Jerusalem in 70 CE.

20. We cannot be sure of the names of the historical authors of the four Gospels. Only the Fourth Gospel mentions its author as "the Beloved Disciple" (see John 21:24), but it does not identify him as "John." All the names were attached to manuscripts by the end of the second century CE in order to identify them. This book will refer to the authors as Mark, Matthew,

Each of the Gospels can claim to be an "orderly account," but they differ in what they understand as the appropriate "order," in terms of both the timeline and the message of what God has done for us in and through Jesus. We will sense the richness that this difference has created for the Christian Tradition when we consider each of the Gospels in a little more detail. For the moment, it is interesting how the time span of the story of Jesus is different across the four Gospels.

The earliest of the Gospels, Mark, begins with Jesus as an adult. He is introduced to the readers by John the Baptist, baptized in the Jordan, tempted, and begins his ministry, all within the first fifteen verses of chapter 1. Mark's ending is also very brief in comparison with the other three Gospels. Three women find an empty tomb, and they hear the Easter proclamation: "He has been raised" (16:6 AT). They are instructed to return to the disciples and to Peter in order to tell them that the risen Jesus is going before them into Galilee. There they will see him. They are so frightened that they run away, saying nothing to anyone (v. 8). The Gospel of Mark ends with this story of the risen Jesus and frightened women. There are no stories in the Gospel of Mark about Jesus' infancy, his resurrection appearances, or his ascension.[21]

The Gospels of Matthew and Luke appeared in the mid to late 80s CE. A further development is found *at the beginning* of these two accounts. Both have stories of Jesus' annunciation and birth (Matt. 1–2; Luke 1–2). The question of *origins* was becoming more important for the people to whom the Gospels were first directed. In many ways, although this was most likely not the only motivation, an interest in origins propelled the spread of the Christian mission into the Hellenistic world, where such questions were very important. Newer Christians in the world outside Judaism needed to know not only *what he said and did* (Mark) but also *where he came from* (Matthew and Luke). Although the infancy stories of Matthew and Luke are different, they agree that Jesus has his origins in God and that he appeared in the human story through a virgin birth. This is no ordinary beginning! The Gospels of Matthew and

Luke, and John out of respect for the tradition, while not deciding one way or the other on their historical identities. The wise decision of the second-century Church to add names to the Gospels to indicate the *different* stories of the *same* Jesus must be maintained. There is not one story of Jesus but four: those of Mark, Matthew, Luke, and John, whoever the historical authors may have been. We are enriched by this fourfold witness.

21. Most Bibles will print a longer ending (Mark 16:9–20) but indicate that this ending is not found in the earliest manuscripts. Indeed there is also a shorter ending (often printed in Bibles), as well as a third ending, containing vv. 9–20 along with some extra verses. The Gospel of Mark must be interpreted in the light of its conclusion in 16:8. For more detail, see Moloney, *Resurrection of the Messiah*, 13–18.

Luke also extend *the end* of Jesus' life story. Both have accounts of the empty tomb (Matt. 28:1–10; Luke 24:1–12), but they add stories of the appearances of Jesus to the disciples, the disciples' commissioning for a future mission, and Jesus' promises that he will remain with the Christian community (Matt. 28:16–20; Luke 24:13–49). They do this differently. Matthew states that the risen Jesus will be with them until the end of all time (Matt. 28:20), while Luke has Jesus ascend to heaven, so that he can send the power from on high (the Spirit) upon them (Luke 24:44–53). The tradition is expanding both backward and forward in time: into the past, to his wonderful birth from God, and into the future, to his return to heaven (Luke) and his never-failing presence to the Church as its risen Lord (Matthew).[22]

The final development in the inspired telling of Jesus' story emerges in the Gospel of John, where there is no infancy narrative but rather a prologue that announces that the Word of God existed before all time, in oneness with God (John 1:1–2). This preexistent Word has become flesh and has dwelt among us (v. 14). His name is Jesus Christ (v. 17), and he is the unique revelation of God and God's ways among us (vv. 4–5, 14, 16–18). As the Gospel tradition reaches further into the Greco-Roman world, the response to the question of origins became even more radical. His presence begins not in a virginal conception that assures his beginnings with God but before all time, in a union with God. Because of this oneness with God, his revelation of God guarantees his message of the divine design for humankind. No one else has ever seen God (1:18; 3:13; 6:46), but Jesus comes from God and is thus able to make God known in a way unparalleled by any other person or religious tradition. For John, like Luke, the ascension is important, as the Son of God must go back to the place and the glory that was his before the world was made (17:4–5; 20:17). For John, Jesus is the Word who begins in God and ends in God, sending the Spirit Paraclete to support, guide, and instruct the Christian community until he returns again (14:16–17, 25–26; 15:26–27; 16:7–15).[23]

---

22. These different ways of telling of the presence of the risen Christ again reflect the worlds into which the Gospels were written. Matthew, writing for a Jewish community, uses the Old Testament expression "Emmanuel" ("God with us" [see Matt. 1:23; 28:20; Isa. 7:14]), to indicate the risen Jesus' presence to that early Christian community. Luke's more dynamic presentation of Jesus' departure from this world and sending of the Spirit upon the Christian community (see Luke 24:48–49; Acts 1:6–11; 2:1–13) addresses a community in a gentile world.

23. The word "Paraclete" (regularly translated as "Counselor" in the RSV) has its origins in the language of the law court. It refers to someone who speaks in defense of another. In the Gospel of John this meaning is still present, but it has been expanded to refer to the ongoing role of the Spirit of God in the community after the departure of Jesus. The Spirit Paraclete strengthens, teaches, and reminds the community of Jesus' person and teaching. The Paraclete

The Spirit-filled Christian community grows in its understanding of what God has done for humankind in and through Jesus of Nazareth. We can follow that growth by tracing the growth in the written traditions that come from those first decades. Paul focused his attention on *the end* (50–60 CE). Mark's attention is completely devoted to the ministry of the adult Jesus, *from the beginning of his ministry to an empty tomb* (70 CE). Matthew and Luke reach further behind the mystery of Jesus. They report the early Christian traditions of his origins in God in *the infancy stories* and his ongoing presence to the Christian community *after his death and resurrection*, being "with" them in Matthew and in the gift of the Holy Spirit in Luke. John brings this development to a close by drawing the origins and the goal of Jesus' life outside time. He has no beginning. *He has existed with God from before all time* and has come among us to make that God known (John 1:1–18). While we think of the story of Jesus as beginning in God; leading to a birth, infancy and adolescence, silence about his young life, his powerful ministry of word and deed; and ending in death, resurrection, and ascension, *the storytelling tradition developed in the other direction.* An understanding of God's saving action in the cross and resurrection is the bedrock of the Christian tradition. Everything in the story develops either backward (death and resurrection, life and ministry, youth, infancy, conception, preexistence) or forward (empty tomb, appearances, commissioning, permanent presence with the community, return to God by ascension, return to where he was before all time), driven by faith in Jesus' death and resurrection. Without the death and resurrection, nothing in the story of the Gospels would have made sense. Everything in the Gospels swivels around that intervention of God into human history in and through Jesus of Nazareth.

This seemingly simple tracing of the way the Christian message grew historically, from Paul's teaching on Jesus' death and resurrection, *backward* to virgin birth and preexistence (Matthew, Luke, and John), *forward* to ascension (Luke and John) and permanent presence with the community as risen Lord (Matthew), and both *backward and forward* to the preexistent Logos returning to the glory he had before the foundation of the world (John). An appreciation of the growth of the early Church's understanding and articulation of these truths is fundamental to a faith-filled reading of the New Testament. *Everything is written in the light of Jesus' death and resurrection.* There is not a letter, a word, a phrase, a sentence, a paragraph, a document, that does

---

also judges the world's opposition to Jesus and the disciples (again, see John 14:15–17, 25–26; 15:26–27; 16:7–15).

not come from belief that the crucified Jesus has been raised by God. Because of his death and resurrection, the New Testament authors eventually wrote of his preexistence, his virgin birth, the wonders of his ministry, his victory over death, his never-failing presence to the Church, and his return to his Father. This fact shapes how and why the New Testament emerged and became Christianity's Sacred Scripture.

The New Testament is not a history book about Jesus or moral instruction from Paul and the other New Testament writers. It is at all times an attempt to draw readers or listeners into a shared faith in Jesus of Nazareth as the crucified and risen Lord. This faith, however, is something that is "shared" across the centuries. Not only do we share it among ourselves in a believing community, but we must reach back to the original articulation of that faith in order to read and hear what the inspired founders of the Christian tradition attempted to communicate through their faith-filled writings. We belong to a believing community that exists because of our foundational Sacred Scriptures and the Tradition that has communicated those Scriptures to us across almost two thousand years. This is the importance of the Christian insistence upon the relationship between Scripture and Tradition: "Sacred scripture is the utterance of God put down as it is in writing under the inspiration of the Holy Spirit. And Tradition transmits in its entirety the word of God which has been entrusted to the apostles by Christ the Lord and the Holy Spirit" (DV 9).

We Christians belong to a long history that had its beginnings in the saving intervention of God in and through the death and resurrection of Jesus of Nazareth. So that we might better understand this, we have privileged access to the inspired Word of God in the New Testament. Our New Testament Scriptures tell what God has done for us through the gift of his Son, Jesus Christ. When we read the Gospels and the letters of Paul as history books or as a summons to better moral performance, we miss the revelation of God that comes to us from the inspired word about Jesus Christ, found in the New Testament. In a privileged way, these inspired texts call us to accept what God has done for us in and through Jesus of Nazareth, who is our risen Lord. The New Testament is the Word of God communicated by the time-conditioned, limited, and frail words of men and women, writing in Greek almost two thousand years ago. We must do what we can to better equip ourselves to enter that world so that we might be captured by the literature and the rhetoric generated by those first-century Christians. Only thus can we join them in that inspired revelation. "The word of God, which to everyone who has faith contains God's saving power (see Rom. 1:16), is set forth and marvelously displays its power in the writings of the New Testament" (DV 17). However difficult they may appear to be, "the most intimate truth thus revealed by God and human salvation shines forth for us in Christ, who is himself both the mediator and the sum total of revelation" (*DV* 2).

The Church Receives Its Sacred Book

The collection of twenty-seven documents from the beginnings of the Christian movement that we now know as the New Testament took some time to emerge. The early Christians had already received Sacred Scriptures from their origins in Judaism. We know this because the authors of the New Testament regularly cite or name Old Testament passages as "Scripture" (Greek: *graphē*; see, for some examples, Mark 12:24; Matt. 21:42; Luke 4:21; John 19:24; Rom. 4:3; 1 Tim. 5:18; James 2:8; 1 Pet. 2:6). As we have already seen, Paul was writing letters to his communities as early as 50 CE, and by the final decades of the first Christian century written documents were multiplying, among them the four Gospels. The author of 2 Peter makes clear that by the time he was writing (probably in the first decades of the second Christian century), the letters of Paul were being collected. He writes: "So also our beloved brother Paul wrote to you according to the wisdom given him, speaking of this as he does in all his letters. There are some things in them hard to understand, which the ignorant and unstable twist to their own destruction, as they do the *other scriptures*" (2 Pet. 3:15–16, emphasis added). He draws a parallel between the collection of Paul's letters and the "other scriptures" (Greek: *graphas*) that are being wrongly interpreted.

As Christianity developed across the second century, a steady flow of early Christian literature appeared. The Christians began to develop a sense of having their own Sacred Scripture, a literature that depended on the person and message of Jesus of Nazareth, now the risen, ascended, and exalted Christ. Out of a large collection of early Christian literature, the New Testament emerged. It was a slow process. By means of his widely read novel *The Da Vinci Code*, Dan Brown has convinced millions that the books that formed the New Testament were imposed on the Christian Church under the authority of the emperor Constantine in order to maintain good order and ensure that some of the more original, and perhaps shocking, evidence (e.g., that Jesus and Mary Magdalene were lovers and had children) was suppressed.[24] *It simply did not happen that way!*

The tendency to form a collection of Christian Scriptures began very early. A document found in the Ambrosian Library in Milan and published by Ludovico Antonio Muratori in 1740 contains a list of books regarded by Christians

24. Dan Brown, *The Da Vinci Code* (New York: Random House, 2003).

sometime between the end of the second century and the third century as Sacred Scripture. Named after the man who discovered and published it, the Muratorian Fragment lists the four Gospels, Acts, and the Pauline letters.[25] There is no sign of other books that eventually came into what is known as the Christian canon.[26] Interestingly it lists other works important for the early Christians: the Wisdom of Solomon and the *Apocalypse of Peter*. It mentions with respect, but not final approval, the *Shepherd of Hermas*. The *Shepherd of Hermas* said many good things but was not to be read aloud in public. An attempt to establish a Christian canon was under way.

Two major figures, the theologian Origen (ca. 185–ca. 254) and the historian Eusebius of Caesarea (260–ca. 340), clarified the matter further. They classified some books as certainly canonical, others as still debated, and a third group as to be rejected. For Origen, whose authority was very great, 1 Peter and 1 John already belonged to the "certain," but 2 Peter, 2 and 3 John, James, and Jude were still "debated." However, none of them were "rejected." At the time of Origen, however, there was still flexibility, as he regarded the *Epistle of Barnabas* as part of the Christian Scriptures, while the *Shepherd of Hermas* and the *Didache*, although called "writings," were not included.[27] Eusebius also admits that 1 Peter, 2 and 3 John, James, and Jude were in the "debated" category but claims that by his time (a generation after Origen), they were uncontested by the majority of authorities.

Well before Constantine the Christian canon was taking shape as a list of books, but there was still fluidity, evidenced by the collections found in the great manuscripts that we have from the fourth century.[28] In them the *Epistle*

25. The Muratorian Fragment is, as the name suggests, a fragmented document likely written in the seventh or eighth century CE in very bad Latin and is probably the translation of a Greek document that scholars date anywhere from 170 to 400 CE.

26. The word "canon" in Greek has a very positive meaning, aptly described by Elaine Pagels as "a carpenter's term meaning 'guideline'—often a string with a weight attached—to check that a wall is straight" (*Beyond Belief: The Secret Gospel of Thomas* [New York: Random House, 2003], 148). The Christian canon, which we now call the Old and New Testaments, was developed to include those documents that indicated "the wall was straight." See also Bruce M. Metzger, *The Canon of the New Testament: Its Origin, Development, and Significance* (Oxford: Clarendon, 1987), 289–93.

27. These documents, and others mentioned below (*1–2 Clement*), are early Christian writings from late in the first century and early in the second century. There is no need for us to investigate them further. They addressed issues faced in those early decades, and they were esteemed by many. As such, they were candidates for an eventual New Testament.

28. We have many papyrus manuscripts containing New Testament texts that predate the fourth century, but it was at that time that large "books" (codices) were written on skin in beautiful capital letters (known as "uncials" because of the capital letters), containing what was regarded by their scribes as the books of the New Testament. The most important early uncials are known as Sinaiticus (found in Saint Catherine's Monastery at the foot of Mount Sinai), Vaticanus (in

of Barnabas and the *Shepherd of Hermas* and *1–2 Clement* appear after the Apocalypse. The Apocalypse itself was not always accepted into canonical lists. The final statement on books of the New Testament, as we have it, came for the Church in the East through the authority of Saint Athanasius (ca. 296–373). In his thirty-ninth Easter letter, in 367, which is preserved for us almost completely in Greek, Syriac, and Coptic, he designated the twenty-seven books of our present New Testament as the only canonical books. The existence of this letter in three versions is an indication of the authority of Athanasius and the widespread acceptance of his list. He includes the four Gospels, followed by Acts and the Catholic Epistles (James, 1–2 Peter, 1–3 John, and Jude), then fourteen Pauline epistles (Hebrews is listed after 2 Thessalonians, before the Pastorals and Philemon). In the Latin tradition in the West, Pope Innocent I (pope from 401 to 417), in response to a question from the Gallic bishops concerning the canon, named in 405 the list of Athanasius. He was most likely under the influence of the authority of the great fathers of the Latin-speaking Church, Jerome and Augustine, who had already accepted the Athanasian canon.[29]

For many people it comes as a surprise to learn that it was not until the much-troubled Council of Florence,[30] as East and West debated their divisions and sought reunion, that the Athanasian list was formally defined by the Roman Church as the canon of the New Testament.[31] This happened for the first time in a document called *Cantate Domino* ("Sing to the Lord"), written in 1442 to mark the union between the Coptic and Ethiopian churches. Part of the reason for that union was that both churches shared the identical inspired Word of God, found in the twenty-seven books of the New Testament.

---

the possession of the Vatican Library), and Alexandrinus (found in Alexandria, Egypt, but given to James I of England in 1629 and now housed in the British Library). Excellent examples of these manuscripts can be viewed online by searching for "images of New Testament codices."

29. Questions can be asked about the inclusion of 3 John (fifteen verses) and Jude (twenty-five verses). The former was accepted very early as it was part of the influential correspondence initiated by 1 John. The latter was included because of its closeness to 2 Peter, traditionally attached to the first bishop of Rome.

30. This ecumenical council was troubled from its beginning in Basel in 1438, when it had to be abandoned because of military threat. From Basel it moved to Ferrara and then to Florence as plague ran through Ferrara. It met in Florence from 1439 to 1445. The council was also troubled by the fact that, despite coming to some important agreements, the desired union between the Eastern and Western churches never eventuated.

31. Early synods and councils in North Africa (Hippo Regius [393] and Carthage [397 and 419]), strongly influenced by Augustine, had drawn up a list of the New Testament canon. Although less certain, Pope Damasus I (pope from 366 to 384) may also have drawn up a list at a council in Rome in 382, but this depends on the doubtful association of a document (*Decretum Gelasianum*) that contains the list. It may come from the sixth century. None of these were ecumenical councils, and they all depend on Athanasius.

This decision was ratified at the Council of Trent (April 8, 1546) within the context of the Protestant Reformation. Both before and after Martin Luther, who is popularly regarded as the historical figure who set the Reformation in motion, a number of movements pressed for a reform of the Catholic Church. Part of what was desired was a narrower canon. Luther insisted that authentic Christianity had to be based on the Bible, especially the New Testament. It was to be marked by "faith alone," "Christ alone," and "Word alone." Although James 2:14–26 teaches that true faith must be manifested in good works, Luther regarded its teaching as alien to the true teaching of Jesus and the New Testament, especially Paul. Luther included James in his New Testament, but he regarded it as a "letter of straw." The Protestant tradition also refused to accept anything in the Old Testament that was not written in Hebrew. The Catholic tradition accepted books from the Septuagint, the Greek translation of the Hebrew. As we saw in the previous chapter, this included a number of books not found in the extant Hebrew Bibles (Tobit, Judith, parts of Esther, Ben Sirach, Baruch, parts of Daniel, 1–2 Maccabees).[32] In drawing up the list of books that formed the Old Testament, the fathers of the Council of Trent affirmed books found in the Septuagint and in the subsequent Latin Vulgate. For the New Testament, they went back to the list of the Council of Florence that, in its own turn, looked back to the authority of Athanasius.

What we have traced above is *what happened* across the early centuries of Christianity to produce the collection of books we call the New Testament. It is more important for our purposes to ask *why this happened*. What the above historical sketch of the gradual emergence of a collection of books that we now call the New Testament indicates is that this collection did not emerge from a decision made at any of the early councils, nor did it emerge as the result of direction from the emperor, whatever the characters in Dan Brown's novel might say. The first Church pronouncement on the canon of the New Testament was in 1442, a pronouncement that has its roots in the Easter letter of Athanasius in 367. Only at Florence (1442) and Trent (1546) did ecumenical councils concern themselves with the canon. They affirmed the Church's acceptance of the "grace" of God's gift of these Sacred Scriptures.

The earliest councils took the inspired nature of certain books for granted. They had to argue over a number of passages in the New Testament, finding that the biblical language was not sufficient to express everything that had to

32. Bibles produced by the Protestant tradition often print these books separately, calling them "apocryphal books." Catholic Bibles always contain them, even though they are called "deuterocanonical books" by some Catholics. Although they were not found in the Hebrew Bibles available to the Reformers in the sixteenth century, parts of Ben Sirach, Tobit, and Baruch have been found at Qumran, in Hebrew. These texts are pre-Christian.

be said about the Trinity or Christology. These books were already regarded as part of Scripture, a Word of God, even though no one had imposed on them the label of "canon." They had come to be recognized and accepted as such within the life, prayer, and liturgy of the Christian communities.[33] It is clear that from the second century on they were read because they made sense of the lived experience of believing Christians and were accepted as a gift of God to the Church. Some contemporary scholars are even arguing that some of the original authors of the Gospels, and Paul, understood their writings about the life, teaching, death, and resurrection of Jesus of Nazareth as a continuation of Israel's Sacred Scripture.[34] We have already seen that in the first decades of the second Christian century the author of 2 Peter regarded a collection of the Pauline letters as Scripture (see 2 Pet. 3:15–16). The notion of Christian Scriptures—more precisely, a collection of books regarded as such—was already in place before anyone raised the question of the existence of a Christian canon.

The canon emerged from the life of the Church. Recent scholarship is strongly affirming that "'canonicity' lies in the progressive and mutually forming relationship between certain texts and the Church: a relationship which is complex, historical, but not beyond the bounds of grace."[35] This, after all, was the concern of the letter of Athanasius in 367 and of Pope Innocent I's response to the Gallic bishops in 405. They were acting as "shepherds to their flock," indicating that the stories of Jesus' life, teaching, death, and resurrection, and the various letters that they read from Paul and others, privately and in their liturgies, were indeed Sacred Scripture, a gift of God, *received* by the Church. They trusted and affirmed the faith of their people that these twenty-seven books were "the Word of God."

Conclusion

To this point in our primer we have reflected on the call for all who take Christianity seriously, and live it maturely, to know the Scriptures (chap. 1). We

33. A powerful statement of this can be found in Harry Y. Gamble, "The New Testament Canon: Recent Research and the Status Quaestionis," in *The Canon Debate*, ed. Lee M. McDonald and J. A. Sanders (Peabody, MA: Hendrickson, 2002), 267–94; see esp. 293–94.

34. See D. Moody Smith, "When Did the Gospels Become Scripture?," *Journal of Biblical Literature* 119 (2000): 1–18.

35. Morwenna Ludlow, "'Criteria of Canonicity' and the Early Church," in *Die Einheit der Schrift und die Vielfalt des Kanons* [The Unity of Scripture and the Diversity of the Canon], ed. John Barton and Michael Wolter, Beihefte zur Zeitschrift für die Neutestamentliche Wissenschaft 118 (Berlin/New York: Walter de Gruyter, 2003), 71. See also the important work of Ormond Rush, *The Eyes of Faith: The Sense of the Faithful and the Church's Reception of Revelation* (Washington, DC: Catholic University of America Press, 2009), 116–52.

have seen the need for us to recognize that the books of the New Testament were formed in a Jewish and a Greco-Roman world that was geographically and chronologically very distant from our world (chap. 2). We need to reach back across the centuries in order to read our Scriptures maturely, catching what the original authors were saying to their faithful so that we too might be caught into the same divine rhetoric that has been proclaimed in a life-giving way for two thousand years. Despite the fact that the texts we have in the New Testament show all the signs of belonging to a time and a place very different from our own, Tradition has seen to it that they continue to be proclaimed and lived in the third Christian millennium. We further investigated this process as we asked how the New Testament came into existence (chap. 3). Is there something about the birth of the New Testament that allows it to retain its significance across two thousand years? There are two parts to an answer to this question.

The first is a reflection on the growth of the New Testament traditions themselves. We have found that everything has its beginnings in the death, resurrection, and exaltation of Jesus of Nazareth, now Christ and Lord. Any reading of the New Testament *must* start from the conviction and keen awareness that the stories of Jesus' life; the theological reflection on the significance of what God has done for us in and through Jesus of Nazareth; the admonitions; and the gaze into the future vindication of all who love and suffer that is found in the Apocalypse and in other parts of the New Testament, especially the Gospels (see, e.g., Mark 13), make sense because of Jesus' death and resurrection. The second part of the answer is a reflection on the history of the gradual emergence of the New Testament canon, made up of twenty-seven books that spoke to the faith journey and experience of the Christian faithful. This was neither a political gesture nor a power play. It reflected the experience of the Christian faithful who heard the voice of God in certain documents and did not hear it in others. As John Webster puts it, as "the place where divine speech may be heard, [the canon] is—or it ought to be—a knife at the Church's heart."[36]

This challenging statement takes us back to a comment made by Joseph Ratzinger, later Benedict XVI, in his commentary on *Dei Verbum*, which was mentioned in the preface to this book.[37] In 1968, the then-professor of Catholic systematic theology at the University of Tübingen lamented the fact that the council had not pointed out that Sacred Scripture has an important critical role

---

36. John Webster, "'A Great and Meritorious Act of the Church'? The Dogmatic Location of the Canon," in Barton and Wolter, *Die Einheit der Schrift*, 126.
    37. See pp. x–xii above.

to play in the life of the Christian Church. All too often the great Tradition can be accommodated by human and historically conditioned "traditions." Such an "accommodation" is understandable but must be carefully controlled lest the Christian Church lose its focus on its *culturally unacceptable central mystery: the life-giving death and resurrection of Jesus*. The enigma that a death has produced life is the core of Christianity. Ratzinger pointed out that the Word of God plays the role of a "thorn in the side" of an overly human and overly confident tradition. God's gift of Sacred Scriptures to the Church has the task of keeping the Church honest.[38]

Today's Christians have a hunger for the Word of God. It is the Church's responsibility to respond to that hunger. At the heart of that response is the person of Jesus of Nazareth, his death, resurrection, and exaltation. The rest of this book will focus on those issues. The next step we must take is a brief biography of Jesus of Nazareth. Everything begins with him, his life, his teaching, and—as we have said repeatedly throughout this chapter—his death and resurrection.

38. For further reflection on this, see pp. 199–201 below.

4

Jesus of Nazareth

A Biographical Sketch

Christian prayer and preaching cherish the words and actions of Jesus as presented in the Gospels. Christians sense that they are in touch with who Jesus was as his life unfolded in the Palestine of two thousand years ago. But we do not have a life story of Jesus in any typical sense. Notice, for instance, that there is no single "Gospel story," but rather four: the Gospels of Mark, Matthew, Luke, and John. Many of the words and actions reported in these Gospels can be traced back to the life of Jesus, although they went through various stages of telling and retelling before appearing in their final shape (see *DV* 19). There are also a few episodes recorded by Paul that certainly report events and even words from Jesus himself (e.g., being born of a Jewish woman [Gal. 4:4]; the celebration of a meal that looked forward to his death for its significance [1 Cor. 11:23–26]; being crucified, buried, and seen by many as alive [1 Cor. 15:3–8]). However, reading all four Gospels creates difficulty for anyone wishing to tell Jesus' life story in a way that parallels the biographies of other famous women and men of the past.[1] The fact that Jesus' story was

1. The terminology used in these discussions can be confusing: the historical Jesus, the Jesus of history, the Jesus of faith, the Christ of faith, the glorified Jesus, and so forth. To refer to the Jesus who lived for some thirty years in Palestine, I will speak of "Jesus" and "Jesus of

told by people who believed that he had been raised from death influences the telling of the Gospel stories, unlike any other biography, no matter how significant that person may have proved to be in subsequent history.

The Problem

An immediately obvious challenge of discerning Jesus' life story on the basis of four Gospels is that the same words and actions of Jesus are often set in different contexts in each of the Gospels. In the Gospel of Mark, for example, Jesus asks the disciples who people think he is. They respond that it is generally thought that he is bringing in the messianic era (as John the Baptist, Elijah, or one of the prophets). When he asks them what they think, Peter responds that he is the Messiah. But Jesus warns his disciples not to say anything about this and speaks of his forthcoming passion. Peter objects that Jesus must not undergo such a future, and Jesus calls him Satan, telling him to get behind him, as all disciples are called to follow behind Jesus (Mark 8:27–33; see 1:16–20).

Matthew has much the same series of events, except that Peter is more explicit in his confession of Jesus as the Christ, the Son of the living God. For this act of faith, Jesus blesses Simon Bar-Jona and establishes him as the rock upon whom he would build his Church, entrusting him with the keys of the kingdom and ultimate teaching authority (Matt. 16:13–20). Since the Reformation, this passage has been an important piece of biblical teaching on the Petrine Office, accepted by Catholics as residing in the figure of the bishop of Rome.

Luke has a different point to make at this stage of his story and does not report the encounter between Jesus and Peter in the same way as Mark and Matthew. The question of Jesus' identity emerges as Jesus is praying. Peter confesses that Jesus is the Christ of God, and Jesus immediately announces his passion, without praise or warning for Peter and the disciples. Peter does not object (Luke 9:18–22).

Peter is again a major player in a confession of faith in the Gospel of John (6:66–71). After the multiplication of the loaves and fishes and Jesus' subsequent discourse, many of the disciples decide to leave Jesus. When Jesus

---

Nazareth." The primary concern of the New Testament, written in the light of Jesus' death, resurrection, and exaltation, is the so-called risen Christ, or risen Lord, even when telling his life story. But to drive a wedge between Jesus of Nazareth and the Christ that the earliest Christians believed in is unhelpful for a sound understanding of Jesus. As this chapter will show, one produced the other. For a commonsense approach to this question, see Dale C. Allison Jr., *The Historical Christ and the Theological Jesus* (Grand Rapids: Eerdmans, 2009).

asks whether the Twelve would also like to depart, Peter responds: "Lord, to whom shall we go? You have the words of eternal life; and we have believed, and have come to know, that you are the Holy One of God" (vv. 68–69).

In terms of writing a historical "life of Jesus" that identifies what, where, when, and why Jesus said and did certain things, this example shows that we cannot simply read one or another of the Gospels and claim that they reported words and events exactly as they took place—as though the telling of Jesus' life story is like telling that of Napoleon or Abraham Lincoln. How many are aware that our Christmas stories generally come from the joyous proclamation of Luke 1–2, which includes the annunciation, visitation, birth of our Lord, and presentation and finding of Jesus in the temple? A Christmas pageantry built on Matthew 1–2 would be much darker, with its suspicion of an illegitimate birth, slaying of the innocents, flight into Egypt, return to Israel, and need for another flight to Nazareth. These *different* "stories," however, communicate fundamental truths about the action of God, the person of Jesus, and his future ministry, death, and resurrection. Like everything else in the New Testament, they are written in the light of Jesus' death, resurrection, and exaltation.[2] Indeed, it could be claimed that the "life-story" telling of the beginnings of famous people, even those belonging to our popular culture, is heavily influenced by the achievements of their later careers. The "beginnings" are often described in a fashion that foreshadows eventual achievements (or failures!).

We have to allow for the different perspectives of the Gospels, each with its own point of view, arrangement, and emphasis. Nonetheless, the evidence of all four Gospels points to the fact that at some stage during his ministry the question of Jesus' identity emerged, and the first disciples confessed their faith in him as the fulfilment of Jewish messianic hopes. Each evangelist represented this moment with different words, in different locations, and for different reasons. This example, taken from Mark 8, Matthew 16, Luke 9, and John 6, serves as only one of many possible comparisons. But we can be sure that each of the evangelists was able to look back to solid historical tradition and then tell the recorded memory of that moment *in his own way*, so that each might better address his own audience in the 70s (Mark), the 80s (Matthew and Luke), and at the end of the first Christian century (John).[3] For this reason

2. For further reflection on this, see pp. 132–34 below.

3. Modern scholars have developed a series of criteria that they apply to passages in the Gospels to determine whether they are authentic history. For a good presentation of these criteria, see Meier, *Marginal Jew*, 1:167–95. Today the value of this process is under severe scrutiny. For a sample of newer approaches, see Chris Keith and Anthony Le Donne, eds., *Jesus, Criteria, and the Demise of Authenticity* (London/New York: T&T Clark, 2012). A powerful scholarly presentation of Jesus of Nazareth that rejects these criteria can be found in Dale C. Allison Jr., *Constructing Jesus: Memory, Imagination, and History* (Grand Rapids: Baker Academic, 2010).

alone, what follows will regularly have recourse to all four Gospels in tracing a biography of Jesus.[4]

A Way Back to Jesus?

From what we have already said, it is clear that each of the Gospels contains its own unique portrait of Jesus as the Christ. As we will see in chapter 6, understanding each evangelist's presentation of the person of Jesus is the key to reading the Gospels in a way that appreciates their rich and diverse contribution to the life and faith of the Christian Church. We may not be able to establish a day-by-day account of what Jesus said and did, but the broad contours of his life—what he thought he was doing, why he thought he was doing it, and who he thought he was in relation to God and to those who followed or rejected him—can be traced with confidence.[5]

There is widespread agreement that Jesus of Nazareth thought that his life and teaching were crucial to the establishment of the reign of God in human affairs.[6] His understanding of what that meant is well expressed in his parables. Essential to his sense of mission was an uncanny intimacy with the God of Israel, whom he called "Father." Although Jesus most likely never used the word "son" (outside the expression "Son of Man") to speak of himself, the evidence of the Gospels indicates that he adopted a "son-like" relationship with God. What this meant in the time of Jesus, and for Jesus himself, calls for further reflection. This claim of closeness to God, however, and what he meant in preaching the reign of his God, was daring. It exposed Jesus to rejection and opposition from many in Israel, especially its religious and political leadership, and eventually the Roman authorities.

4. Historical Jesus studies have often disregarded the Gospel of John, which appeared late in the first century and has a well-developed early Christian theology and Christology. However, it contains many authentic memories and traditions about Jesus.

5. Studies that attempt to outline the life of the person Jesus of Nazareth could fill a library. Although different in their approach, the following deserve to be noticed: Meier, *Marginal Jew* (currently in four large volumes, with more yet to come); Ed Parish Sanders, *The Historical Figure of Jesus* (London: Penguin Press, 1993); Theissen and Merz, *Historical Jesus*; Allison, *Constructing Jesus*; and Lohfink, *Jesus of Nazareth*. For a fine survey of a complex discussion, see Mark Allan Powell, *Jesus as a Figure in History: How Modern Historians View the Man from Galilee* (Louisville: Westminster John Knox, 1998). See also Brown, *Introduction to the New Testament*, 817–30 (mainly a discussion of scholarly opinion); Powell, *Introducing the New Testament*, 63–101; and Spivey, Smith, and Black, *Anatomy of the New Testament*, 190–236.

6. The expression "reign of God" attempts to translate the Greek usually rendered as "kingdom of God," found so often in the Gospels. Jesus' use of the expression was more dynamic than a place where God ruled. See Lohfink, *Jesus of Nazareth*, 24–26.

In the Gospels, Jesus regularly points forward to his oncoming death and resurrection in texts that have come to be known as "passion predictions" (see Mark 8:31; 9:31; 10:32–34; Matt. 16:21; 17:22–23; 20:17–19; 26:2; Luke 9:22, 43b–44; 18:31–33; John 3:14; 8:28; 12:32–33).[7] In every one of these "predictions" of Jesus' death and resurrection he speaks of himself as "the Son of Man." It is possible that the words reported in Luke 9:44, "The Son of Man is to be delivered into the hands of men" (see also Mark 9:31), might reach back to words Jesus spoke to his disciples. Jesus was aware that his preaching of the coming of God's reign and the radical manner in which he connected what he was doing with the will of the God of Israel, whom he called "Father," could lead to a tragic end to his life.

Jesus' death by crucifixion is a certain historical fact. Was he aware that such an end was looming? For instance, his use of the expression "the Son of Man" might have explained to himself and others why he persevered in this dangerous ministry. The risks were great, but why would anyone look forward *in hope and faith* despite the likelihood of an ignominious death?

What follows does not pretend to present "a life of Jesus," but it asks fundamental questions of his life journey (indeed, of anyone's life journey).

- *What did Jesus think he was doing?* An answer to this question must be based on his teaching on the reigning presence of God and also on his understanding of his actions, especially his power over the evils of sickness and what was then known as the demonic.

- *Who did Jesus think he was?* In answer to this question, as with every human being, the response can only be very partial. I find it difficult to articulate the mystery of myself. How much more difficult is it for me to talk about the inner workings of Jesus' heart and mind? However, on the basis of the Gospel accounts, his relationship with God can be explored. Finally, we ask whether he was aware of his oncoming death and how he spoke of that death in a way that might make sense for himself and for others.

Such questions lie at the heart of Jesus' identity and mission. We will refer to essential moments in his story, especially his final days in Jerusalem, his final evening and meal with his disciples, and his death and resurrection. Though these events happened, their meaning remains elusive.[8] We need to

---

7. These many predictions, however, depend upon one another. Mark has them, and Matthew and Luke use Mark's sayings in their own way. John's passion predictions (in which Jesus speaks of his being "lifted up" on a cross) are unique. For further evidence of Jesus' awareness of his coming death and its meaning, see Allison, *Constructing Jesus*, 387–433.

8. Given the differences between the Synoptic Gospels (Mark, Matthew, and Luke) and the Gospel of John, even establishing a timeline for the life of Jesus is difficult. For a very helpful

establish essential elements in the life of Jesus of Nazareth that led, through his cross, resurrection, and vindication, to the experience and understanding of a community of people who had followed him. They had seen him as the hoped-for Messiah and came to believe that he was indeed the Christ, but in a way they had not expected. In the light of Jesus' death, resurrection, and exaltation they eventually confessed that he was the exalted Son of God whose life, teaching, death, resurrection, and exaltation offered new hope and life to all humankind.

What Did Jesus Think He Was Doing?

Scholars agree that Jesus of Nazareth saw his mission as intimately linked with the establishment of the reign of God in the world. The Gospel of Mark opens Jesus' ministry with his urgent preaching: "The time is fulfilled, and the kingdom of God is at hand; repent, and believe in the gospel" (Mark 1:15). The notion of God as king is widely used in Jesus' world. In the Old Testament, God is king over creation and especially over humanity, his culminating creation (see Isa. 52:7–9; Pss. 22:28; 45:6; 103:19; 145:11; Dan. 4:3, 34; 1 Chron. 17:14; 29:11). As king he saves, loves, and judges his people, with whom he has established a covenant. The Old Testament notion of God as king also carries with it the idea of an end time, a "day of the Lord" that would spell the end of human history and the final manifestation of God's sovereign rule (see Isa. 2:2–4; 24:1–27:13; Mic. 4:1–4; Zech. 9:1–14:21). These notions were essential background for Jesus' preaching and the idea of a future time when God will definitively establish his sovereign rule.[9]

But Jesus' teaching on the establishment of God's kingdom cannot be totally explained by the Old Testament notion of God as king; there is a further essential element to Jesus' preaching of God's reign. It is best summed up in his debate with his opponents over the source of his authority over the powers of evil. He tells them: "If it is by the finger of God that I cast out demons, then the kingdom of God has come upon you" (Luke 11:20; see Matt. 12:28). The reign of God can already be seen as present and experienced in Jesus'

(and well-documented) attempt, see Meier, *Marginal Jew*, 1:372–433. See also Theissen and Merz, *Historical Jesus*, 151–61.

9. There has been a tendency among some modern scholars to eliminate from the teaching of Jesus all promise/threat of God's decisive and final coming. This suggestion, which makes Jesus into a wandering charismatic or an enlightened, peasant wise man, cannot be found in the Gospels. On Jesus' use of the Old Testament notion of God as king, see Lohfink, *Jesus of Nazareth*, 170–75.

power over evil. Indeed, he tells the Pharisees, who ask when the kingdom of God was coming, "Behold, the kingdom of God is in the midst of you" (Luke 17:21). In and through Jesus the reign of God is present, and one can "enter" the kingdom (see Mark 9:47; 10:15). Jesus' proclamation of God's reign established a tension. His fellow Jews accepted that God, their creator and Lord, was king and that he would establish his reign at the end of all human history. It would be a place and a time where sin and ambiguity would no longer have any place. But Jesus spoke of a startling new possibility. The presence of God as king was already among them in Jesus' person, teaching, and deeds.[10] Jesus' preaching was shot through with a sense of urgency. This urgency was most likely also reflected in his person and his behavior. He moved from place to place preaching the reign of God; gathering disciples, many of whom were marginalized people; healing the sick; and driving out evil spirits. He brought God's rich blessings and shared his belief in an imminent "day of the Lord." Many in Israel looked to him with trust and hope.[11]

The presence and meaning of the reign of God that Jesus embodied and proclaimed was especially communicated in his so-called parables. Although they are told in slightly different ways across the Gospels, they remain our best witnesses to Jesus' own preaching. His parables were closely related to the life, times, and practices of the people who heard them. They were short and pungent and generally struck surprisingly at the heart of religious thought and practice of that time. Jesus' teaching struck a chord in the hearts and minds of his hearers. He spoke of the world they lived in and boldly interpreted their Jewish tradition for them. These parables were remembered and passed on faithfully until they found their way into the Gospels of Matthew, Mark, and Luke.[12] I use the expression "so-called" to speak of parables in general because a

10. The question of the Gospels' reporting of Jesus' miraculous activity is crucial in this respect. It is too large an issue to be discussed in detail here. There can be no doubt that Jesus cured the sick and overcame the powers of evil and that this was seen as the anticipation of God's reigning presence. On this, see the magisterial work of Meier, *Marginal Jew*, 2:509–1038. Meier concludes: "Any historian who seeks to portray the historical Jesus without giving due weight to his fame as a miracle-worker is not delineating this strange and complex Jew, but rather a domesticated Jesus reminiscent of the bland moralist created by Thomas Jefferson" (970). See also the theological reflections of Lohfink, *Jesus of Nazareth*, 121–52. Lohfink rightly concludes: "Every miracle of Jesus reveals a bit of the new heaven and the new earth" (151).

11. The attraction and the urgency of Jesus' person and preaching are creatively presented by Gerd Theissen, *The Shadow of the Galilean: The Quest for the Historical Jesus in Narrative Form*, trans. John Bowden (Minneapolis: Fortress, 2007). See also Lohfink, *Jesus of Nazareth*, 318–28.

12. The Gospel of John does not use parables in the same way as the Synoptic Gospels. There are passages that can be regarded as parables (e.g., John 10:1–6), but John captures the teaching of the parables when he has Jesus use the expression "I am." Jesus is the way, the truth, and the light; he is the true bread from heaven; he is living water; he is the light of the world; he is the good shepherd; he is the resurrection and the life.

helpful distinction can be made between two types of figurative language often referred to as "parables." To speak technically, Jesus preached the kingdom of God using two different literary forms: similitudes and parables.

First, similitudes: Jesus' most explicit teaching about the reigning presence of God is found in his frequent explanations of "the kingdom of God" by *comparing* the kingdom to things familiar to his hearers. Certain realities and experiences from everyday life are *similar to* the kingdom—hence, "similitudes." Some examples, taken from Mark 4 and Matthew 13, sections of Mark's and Matthew's accounts that concentrate on Jesus' teaching about the kingdom, show the rich variety of Jesus' teaching about the reign of God in the here and now of life.

> The kingdom of God *is as if* a man should scatter seed upon the ground, and should sleep and rise night and day, and the seed should sprout and grow, he does not know how. (Mark 4:26–27)

> With what can we compare the kingdom of God? . . . It *is like* a grain of mustard seed, which, when sown upon the ground, is the smallest of all the seeds on earth; yet when it is sown it grows up and becomes the greatest of all shrubs. (Mark 4:30–32)

> The kingdom of heaven *is like* leaven which a woman took and hid in three measures of flour, till it was all leavened. (Matt. 13:33)

> The kingdom of heaven *is like* a net which was thrown into the sea and gathered fish of every kind. (Matt. 13:47)

The list could be much longer. What is most important for our understanding of Jesus' use of similitudes to teach about the reigning presence of God is that there can only be *comparisons*. Throughout the similitudes, as in the examples given above, the kingdom of God *is like* something well known to Jesus' audience. But God's reign escapes everyday categories. Jesus could not even claim that it was his to share. It was "of God," whom he dared to call "Father," as we will see below. The kingdom belongs to his Father (see Luke 12:32; 22:29–30), who alone knows the "hour" of the final establishment of God's reign (see Mark 13:32; Matt. 24:36). The kingdom "comes" (Matt. 6:10; Luke 11:2); it can only be received and prayed for (see Mark 9:36–37; 10:14–15; Matt. 6:10; Luke 11:2). These paradoxes indicate the sovereign freedom of God's intervention. There is no possibility of a neat synthesis. Some sayings indicate a fixed period of time (see Mark 9:1; 13:30; Matt. 10:23), while others reject all attempts to fix a date (Mark 13:32; Acts 1:6–7). Some similitudes speak of "growth" (Mark 4:1–20, 26–32; Matt. 13:24–30); others speak of "entering," as if the kingdom were already in place (see Matt. 7:13; Luke 13:24); others insist on the need for receptivity (Mark 9:36–37; 10:14–15). It *must* be this way. The bafflement of scholars who attempt to decipher whether the kingdom is present or yet to come, or to develop an objective description of the kingdom, shows that no human chronological or geographical system can hope to capture the kingdom as Jesus preached it. The kingdom as it was preached by Jesus is the all-deciding event that breaks into history. From the time of Jesus it is unsleepingly at work in every single situation as the world of God's creation moves toward its consummation. The reign of God cannot be captured and categorized.

Jesus' use of his parabolic "similitudes" shows that realities within history can only very improperly be signs of God's sovereign presence, no matter how meaningful they might be. It is basic to the preaching of Jesus that the world and its situation can only properly be understood in the light of God's sovereignty, but the sovereignty of God can never be seen as simply a projection of anything in this world. Consequently, Jesus' preaching of the reign of God turns upside down the self-sufficient world and its values. God's loving gift to humankind cannot but be experienced as countercultural.

Jesus makes this particularly clear in what can be more strictly classified as parables. Unlike the similitudes, these passages do not *compare* the kingdom with anything. They are stories that leave the listeners gasping as they come to a powerful ending.

> Listen! A sower went out to sow. And as he sowed, some seed fell along the path, and the birds came . . . (Mark 4:3–4)

> There was a man who had two sons; and the younger of them said to his father . . . (Luke 15:11–12)

> There was a rich man who had a steward, and charges were brought to him that this man was wasting his goods. (Luke 16:1)

These opening statements from the storyteller draw the hearer/reader into the story, and by the time the parable comes to closure, a response is required. The similitudes "instruct," while the parables challenge the experience and the worldview of the hearer/reader. "It has been said, and with a great deal of truth, that a similitude *in*-forms, but a parable *re*-forms."[13] The power of

---

13. Jan Lambrecht, *Once More Astonished: The Parables of Jesus* (New York: Crossroad, 1983), 5. As Lohfink closes his study of a collection of Jesus' parables, he comments: "He leads

Jesus' parabolic preaching, in the strict sense, lies in the fact that a parable is incomplete until the listener/reader has responded to it—or has failed to do so. As has often been said, "It takes two to parable."[14]

If the notion of God as king was part of Israel's religious tradition, why was Jesus' teaching so unsettling? Jesus claimed that in his person, his teaching, his establishing of an eschatological group of Twelve (like the twelve tribes of Israel),[15] his calling of disciples, and his healing activity, the kingdom of God was *already present*. The traditional idea of a final establishment of God's sovereignty was being drawn back into history in the life, deeds, and teaching of Jesus. This was a surprising claim for Jesus to make, but even more challenging was his teaching about God. As we have already seen, it is impossible to "control" Jesus' message of the kingdom, as it was not *his* kingdom; he was doing his best, especially through similitudes and parables, to articulate the present-yet-future reign of God as king, but in the end he was introducing the coming reign *of God*. In the parables, in a way different from the similitudes, Jesus spelled out that the kingdom he lived and preached demanded a different understanding of God and a different response to God's reign than was customary in Israel. Here Jesus was treading on dangerous ground.

But an important historical truth about Jesus must be firmly stated at this point. However disturbing Jesus' way of life and preaching may have been to his contemporary fellow Jews, he *did not* reject the laws and practices of Israel. He was an extraordinary Jew but always an observant Jew. The elements in his teaching that *at first sight* seem to contradict Jewish law and practice are in fact startling interpretations of Jewish tradition. His understanding of the law was driven by the urgency of his passion for the reign of God, and he drew people around him who wished to share that passion.[16]

---

his listeners into a world with which they are familiar or at least one they have heard about, a world he describes with accurate realism. But at the same time he makes that world alien and thus blows up the well-known paths of customary pious thinking. Jesus wants to show that the reign of God has its own logic" (*Jesus of Nazareth*, 120).

14. John Dominic Crossan, *The Dark Interval: Towards a Theology of Story* (Niles, IL: Argus Communications, 1975), 87. Crossan's whole paragraph reads: "It is clear that a parable is really a *story event* and not just a story. One can tell oneself stories but not parables. One cannot really do so, just as one cannot really beat oneself at chess or fool oneself completely with a riddle one has just invented. It takes two to parable" (emphasis added).

15. Lohfink, *Jesus of Nazareth*, 127: "If Jesus did anything in the way of creating institutions, it was primarily in the creation of the Twelve. . . . However, it was not for the sake of a church about to be newly founded that would take Israel's place in the history of salvation; it was for the sake of the eschatological Israel that was to be gathered."

16. Jesus' ministry was to Israel but open to the rest of humankind, following established Jewish thought on the gathering of Israel and the nations. See Lohfink, *Jesus of Nazareth*, 39–71, 190–215.

For instance, in his many parables Jesus proclaimed a different understanding of God than the one accepted by the society and religion of his time (see, e.g., the parables of the sower [Mark 4:1–20]; the seed growing by itself [4:26–29]; the wicked tenants [12:1–12]; the weeds among the wheat [Matt. 13:24–30]; the workers in the vineyard [20:1–16]; the wise and foolish virgins [25:1–13]; the places of honor [Luke 14:8–11]; the good Samaritan [10:25–37]; the rich man and Lazarus [16:19–31]; the Pharisee and the publican [18:9–14]).[17] One of Jesus' most striking parables, deliberately not listed above, conveys the unsettling newness of Jesus' presentation of the God of Israel, whose kingdom he claimed to be introducing: the parable of the father who had two sons (Luke 15:11–32).[18]

There is no call for a detailed study of the parable, as it is well known. What must be at the center of attention in any reading of this text is the behavior of the father. This is often missed, as hearers and readers focus their attention on the first son. But there are two sons, and the father is the common factor. Jesus' telling the parable of the "father" reaches into the imagination of the listener and the reader of this parable, asking that she or he recognize "the Father" in the parable and respond accordingly.[19] Most surprising is the attitude of the father, who does not want to dominate or to subject his sons to his own will; he does not want to possess his sons in any morbid way. He sets them free (Luke 15:12, 31–32), and in their freedom they are able to make their mistakes: the younger one in the uselessness of a wasted life (vv. 13–15) and the elder one with his arrogant animosity, rooted in jealousy (vv. 28–30). The point of the parable is that the elder brother might find a home with his father (vv. 31–32), just as his younger brother has, despite the errors of his ways (vv. 22–24). The father never preaches a sermon or demands a confession of sins. The younger son, at the turning point of this story, recognizes the depths to which his wastefulness has led him and decides to return to his father. He prepares a speech that he will give on his arrival: "I will say to him, 'Father, I have sinned against heaven and before you; I am no longer worthy to be

---

17. This list is not exhaustive, but the parables mentioned are familiar and should bring to the mind of a reader the surprising nature of Jesus' teaching. For a full list, classifying them as Markan, Matthean, Lukan, or from Q (i.e., found only in Matthew and Luke), see Lambrecht, *Once More Astonished*, 18–20.

18. This well-known parable of Jesus is generally called the parable of "the prodigal son." But that title cannot be applied to the whole parable. Nowadays it is often referred to as the parable of "the forgiving father." That is better, but it is best to take the name of the parable from the words of Jesus himself: "There was a man who had two sons" (Luke 15:11).

19. For what follows, I have been inspired by commentaries on the Gospel of Luke and in particular by the reflections of Eduard Schweizer in *Luke: A Challenge to Present Theology* (Atlanta: John Knox, 1982), 80–81.

called your son; treat me as one of your hired servants'" (vv. 18–19). When he arrives he finds a father full of compassion, eagerly waiting for him, rushing to meet him, kissing and embracing him (v. 20). He tries to recite his prepared speech, but his father will not allow him to complete it. He will not hear the words of his son: "treat me as one of your hired servants" (see v. 21, where those words do not appear).

It could be said that the father made his first mistake when he divided his living between his two sons (v. 12).[20] He then made another mistake when he received his wayward son back into his home and household (vv. 20–24). He again errs in discretion when, after learning that his second son "refused to go in" and was *outside*, full of rage at not having been treated as well as the sinful son (vv. 25–27), he "came out" (v. 28) to speak with his son. The father thus joins a second son, who is in danger of being lost to the household, outside, no longer in the family hearth where the celebrations are taking place. He tells his angry son that there is every reason for joy, for that which was lost has been found (v. 32). But the danger that the elder son may be lost is not resolved within the parable. Jesus does not tell his listeners whether the second lost son was found, because his main concern is his presentation of the father. He simply reports the words of a loving father to another wayward child: "Son, you are always with me, and all that is mine is yours" (v. 31). As always with Jesus' parables, the sting is in the tail: the father (Father?) is found "outside," with his son in the darkness of his sin and failure, seeking a lost child, promising him all that he has. In much the same way, the parable of the good Samaritan shocked a Jewish audience when Jesus told them that they had to go and be like the Samaritan (Luke 10:37). They are equally shocked when he tells them that they are looking for God in the wrong places! The Father is to be found "outside," seeking his lost child.

But Jesus not only *told* this parable; he *lived* it. In terms of the narrative timespan in Luke's Gospel, shortly after telling this parable Jesus was arrested, tried, and convicted as a criminal.[21] Everyone knows that he is innocent (see Luke 23:4, 14–15, 22, 41, 47). Hanging on the cross, he forgives those who have tried and crucified him (v. 34) and promises paradise to a convicted criminal

20. It has long been claimed that the father behaved inappropriately in dividing his possessions while still alive. This is nowadays questioned. See Callie Callor, "*Adulescentes* and *Meretrices*: The Correlation between Squandered Patrimony and Prostitutes in the Parable of the Prodigal Son," *Catholic Biblical Quarterly* 75 (2013): 260–61n4.

21. "Narrative time" follows the chronology within the story. Jesus tells the parable (Luke 15:11–32) at the midpoint of his lengthy journey to Jerusalem (9:51–19:44). His arrival in Jerusalem leads to conflict, arrest, trial, and crucifixion (19:45–23:49).

(v. 43). He hears the misunderstanding screamed at him by the rulers: "He saved others; let him save himself, if he is the Christ of God, his Chosen One" (v. 35; see 9:29). Jesus' mission is not to save himself but to save others, and thus he is totally powerless because he has decided to love. He has nothing more than his heart full of love and compassion. Like the father in the parable, he forgives the people around him and asks them to come to the banquet hall of his Father (vv. 34, 43). Jesus' life and death instruct that his Father is to be found, first of all, where the father is found at the end of the parable—out in the darkness, doing all he can to save his lost children—even, in Jesus' case, to the point of an innocent death.[22] This parable, like many of Jesus' parables, questioned the way God was understood and revered in the religion and culture of his time.[23] The parables are more dangerous than the similitudes. They invite the hearer of the parable to recognize that Jesus' living of the parable of the compassionate Father renders God present among us. Already in the Gospels it is clear that the parables generated division between an "inner" group who understood the parables, or had them explained, and an "outside" group who did not receive their message (see Mark 4:10–12, 33–34; Matt. 13:10–15, 36–43; Luke 10:23–24). The reigning presence of God is to be found in what Jesus says and does, finally and enigmatically on the cross.

Jesus' all-consuming desire was to communicate the reality and the promise of his Father's reign. Through his person, his teaching, his lifestyle, and ultimately in his death and resurrection, this reign of God was present, touching lives and hearts, looking to a final establishment of God's sovereignty. It necessarily generated difficulties. Regularly throughout the Gospels Jesus' audience asks what kind of teaching this could be (see Mark 1:27; 2:12), by what authority he dared to teach this way (see Mark 2:7; 11:27–33; John 6:30–31). He could lay no claims to have had the long association with a master in Israel necessary for anyone teaching with authority (see John 7:15). What Jesus taught about the kingdom of God was new and was regarded as dangerous by the established authorities, initially in Israel and eventually among the Romans. Yet he taught with a firm authority that was recognized by all who experienced his person and his word. Where did this firm authority come from? This question leads us to the second element in our presentation of

22. Some might object that my use of Luke 15:11–32 in conjunction with Luke 23 goes back not to Jesus of Nazareth but to Luke's interpretation of him. The Lukan theme of the compassion of Jesus, which reveals the compassion of God, did not *begin* with Luke, no matter how beautifully he has incorporated it into his Christology and theology.

23. There are many fine books on the parables that demonstrate this in detail. My favorite remains Lambrecht, *Once More Astonished*. Lambrecht not only shows the surprising message of Jesus' parables in his own time but also rightly points out that they continue to "astonish."

what Jesus thought he was doing and who he thought he was: his relationship with the God of Israel.

Who Did Jesus Think He Was?

Jesus and His Father

The term most consistently used by contemporary Christians to speak of Jesus of Nazareth is "Son of God." But we must be careful not to reach back from this regularly used expression among Christians into the beginnings of the Christian movement in the life story of Jesus of Nazareth. The earliest Church, in the light of Jesus' death, resurrection, and exaltation, quickly began to speak of Jesus as "Son." In Romans 1:3–4, written late in the 50s of the first century, Paul uses an even older confession of faith to tell his readers that Jesus of Nazareth was "constituted Son of God in power" through his resurrection from the dead (AT). In Mark, the earliest of the Gospels, written around 70 CE, the expression "Son" is used throughout as a major literary and theological marker, appearing at the beginning (Mark 1:1, 11), the middle (9:7), and the end (15:39) of the narrative. By the end of the century the author of the Gospel of John writes of Jesus as the "only begotten Son of God" (John 1:18 AT). Throughout the Fourth Gospel Jesus' relationship with the Father as his Son and sent one is crucial for all who believe. Indeed, as John closes his Gospel, he states his purpose: "that you may go on believing that Jesus is the Christ, the Son of God" (20:31 AT).[24]

Even across these earliest years of the growth of the Christian tradition, we can see a steady development in an understanding of Jesus as Son. For Paul he is constituted Son by means of the resurrection; for Mark he is the beloved Son who must be listened to and who goes to his death in unconditional obedience; for John he is a life-giving only-begotten Son of God. The early councils of the Church, especially Nicaea (325 CE) and Chalcedon (451 CE), continue this dynamic tradition. They are dominated by the question of Jesus' sonship: his relationship to the Father and the Spirit (Nicaea) and his being both human and divine (Chalcedon). An understanding of Jesus as Son certainly goes back to Jesus of Nazareth, but we must not associate the *later developments* of a Son Christology, so central to Christian belief, with the Jewish Jesus' own indications of his relationship with the God of

---

24. There are textual debates over the presence of "Son of God" in Mark 1:1 and the verb I have translated "go on believing" in John 20:31 in the original manuscripts that need not delay us here.

Israel. During his life and ministry, Jesus did not regard himself as the only begotten Son of God of John's Gospel, the Second Person of the Trinity of the fourth-century Council of Nicaea, or the divine-human Son of God of the fifth-century Council of Chalcedon. Such doctrines are the *fruit* of the earliest Church's understanding of Jesus' relationship with the God of Israel, whom he called "Father."

As Jesus' understanding of the reigning presence of God came from his Jewish roots, so also his understanding of sonship came to him as his birthright. The Old Testament has no hesitation in speaking of individuals and communities as "son."[25] On at least three occasions an individual is addressed as "son." In 2 Samuel 7, as David worries about the building of a temple to house the Ark of the Covenant, God speaks to him through his prophet Nathan. He tells David that he will not build a temple but that his son (Solomon) will. Not only will Solomon build a temple, but God's prophet proclaims: "I will be his father, and he shall be my son" (7:14). Similarly, in a psalm that may well have had its origins in the enthronement of a Jewish king, the voice of God again calls out: "You are my son, this day I become your father" (Ps. 2:7 AT). A parallel statement is made in Psalm 89, a song that affirms and encourages the Davidic line, perhaps in difficult times.[26]

> He shall cry to me, "Thou art my father, my God, and the Rock of my salvation." And I will make him the first-born, the highest of the kings of the earth. My steadfast love I will keep for him for ever, and my covenant will stand firm for him. I will establish his line for ever and his throne as the days of the heavens. (vv. 26–29 RSV)

There is no suggestion of the "begetting" of a son. The Old Testament thinkers meant that a good king should behave like a son; he *functions* as a son; he lives and rules by following the commandments of God (Torah). As such, the God of Israel anoints, supports, and sustains the king or the dynasty, as a father would. The obedience of the king and the royal dynasty lies behind this notion of a son of God.

The expression is also used to speak of an obedient people, chosen and blessed by God. Moses was told to say to Pharaoh, "Israel is my first-born

---

25. I retain this gender-exclusive term because that is the way it is found in the biblical texts and applied to the male Jesus. Women were, however, part of this oneness with the will of God, especially in its use to speak of faithful Israel.

26. On Ps. 2 as enthronement hymn and Ps. 89 as an affirmation of the Davidic dynasty, see Hans-Joachim Kraus, *Psalms*, trans. Hilton C. Oswald, A Continental Commentary (Minneapolis: Fortress, 1993), 1:123–35 and 2:197–211, respectively.

son" (Exod. 4:22), and the people can cry out, "You, O Lord, are our father" (Isa. 63:16 AT). Hosea can look back to the days of the Exodus from Egypt and say, in the name of God: "When Israel was a child, I loved him, and out of Egypt I called my son" (Hos. 11:1; see the same link with the exodus in Deut. 1:31 and 32:6–7). The notion is widespread (see Deut. 14:1; 18:5; 32:18; Isa. 43:6; 63:8; Jer. 3:4; 31:9; Pss. 34:11; 82:6; 149:2). As with the use of the notion of a king as "son," the idea of the people being the product of a physical fatherhood, a generated sonship, never appears. The expression is used in a number of different ways to claim that Israel must be totally dependent on and subordinated to God if it is to belong to him as God's people. As with the king, the people are asked to behave in accordance with their status, to *function* as children of God, as sons and daughters of their unique God, accepting and living by the commandments (Torah). Jesus, formed in this tradition of obedience to God as the sign of belonging to God as a son belongs to a father, would have been strongly influenced by this vision of reality. In Jesus' relationship with God, he was totally subordinated to the will of God and dependent upon God.[27] In this he *functioned* like a son. Every page of the letters of Paul and the narratives of the Gospels tells of the unconditional obedience of Jesus of Nazareth to the God of Israel.

But the Gospels indicate that there was more to Jesus' relationship with God. One of the most striking features of Jesus' words across all four Gospels is his reference to God as "Father" (Greek: *patēr*). Already in Mark, to which we shall return, it appears three times when Jesus addresses God as his father (Mark 8:38; 13:32; 14:36).[28] On one occasion in the same Gospel, God is indicated as the father of the disciples who will forgive their offenses (11:25). From these beginnings, and based upon the evangelists' own memories, the use of the expression by Jesus explodes. In Matthew, for example, Jesus regularly speaks of God as his father (Matt. 10:20, 33; 11:25–27; 12:50; 15:13; 16:17, 27 [father of the Son of Man]; 18:10; 20:23; 24:36 [father of the Son of Man]; 25:34; 26:29, 39, 42, 53). He also speaks to his disciples about God as their father, especially in his Sermon on the Mount (5:16, 45, 48; 6:1, 4, 6, 8, 14, 15, 18, 26, 32; 7:11; see also 10:29; 23:9). In Matthew Jesus associates himself with the disciples and speaks of "our father" (6:9) and of those who do the will of God as brother, and sister, and mother (12:50). In his final commission the risen Jesus asks his disciples to baptize in the name of the

---

27. Many but not all of the occurrences of "son" and "son of God" directed to Jesus in the Synoptic Gospels refer to this aspect of his life.

28. Jesus directly addresses God as "Father" in 14:36, while he refers to God as the father of "the Son of Man" in 8:38 and as the father of "the Son" in 13:32.

Father, the Son, and the Holy Spirit (28:19). Luke continues Jesus' consistent use of "father" to speak of or to address God, repeating Mark's uses of the expression, continuing many of the sayings that he has in common with Matthew (Q source), and adding more of his own. Memorable is Jesus' prayer from the cross, unique to Luke: "Father, forgive them; for they know not what they do" (Luke 23:34). For the Gospel of John, the relationship between Jesus and the God who sent him is consistently spoken of as the Father sending the Son.[29]

There can only be one source for this strong presentation of the relationship Jesus had with God across all four Gospels. It was so special that he was able to call God "my Father," and he felt free to extend this to his disciples, now sons and daughters of the same father ("your father," "our father"). A late articulation of this is found in the commission the risen Jesus gives to Mary Magdalene in the Gospel of John: "Go to my brethren and say to them, I am ascending to my Father and your Father, to my God and your God" (John 20:17). No doubt, as with the Johannine passage just cited, many of the "father sayings" would have grown as the early Church developed its understanding of Jesus as a son of God, but this notion had to begin somewhere. It was not invented by the Gospel writers.

Matthew 11:25–27 and Luke 23:34, mentioned above, can be singled out as passages where Jesus prays to God, addressing him as "Father." The same could be said for many passages in the Gospel of John. Maybe the best (but by far not the only) example is in Jesus' final prayer in John 17, where he addresses Jesus as "Father" no less than five times (vv. 1, 11, 21, 24, 25). A similar prayer can be found in Mark, but there the evangelist takes us back to an Aramaic word for "father," which he immediately translated for his audience: "*Abba*, father, all things are possible for you; remove this cup from me; but not what I will but what you will" (Mark 14:36 AT). The regular word for "father" in both Hebrew and Aramaic is *ab*. Jesus has added an affectionate diminutive to form the word *abba*. It generates a possessive meaning, "my Father," and would have only been used, in the time of Jesus, within a context of a deep union of intimacy, affection, and respect between a father and his child. It is sometimes compared to the use of "daddy" in English, but this is not a good parallel. While affection and respect are certainly found in the word in English, "daddy" (and similar words in other languages) is a term that tends to disappear from usage as a

---

29. For a comprehensive study, see Marianne M. Thompson, *The God of the Gospel of John* (Grand Rapids: Eerdmans, 2001). For its significance, see Francis J. Moloney, *Love in the Gospel of John: An Exegetical, Theological, and Literary Study* (Grand Rapids: Baker Academic, 2013), 64–68.

child matures. This was not the case for the use of *abba*. The expression in Hebrew and Aramaic was not something used only by a child. It reflected *the quality of a unique relationship* and thus did not fade once a daughter or a son matured.[30]

Within a Jewish world, where reverence for God determined that "the name" should never be pronounced, Jesus' use of the expression *abba*, at least in his prayer life, was extremely bold.[31] Jesus' consistent reference to God as "Father" throughout the Gospels reaches back to the memory of the first Christians that Jesus had spoken to God in prayer with this intimate yet respectful word. The widespread use of the Greek word for "father" (*patēr*) *in the Gospels* had its beginning in the Aramaic (*abba*) *of Jesus.*

Further evidence for this historical claim comes from the boldness of the earliest Church, as it is understood by Paul in the 50s of the first century. Paul is overwhelmed by the remarkable blessings that have come upon those who have been baptized into Christ Jesus. Now that they are sons and daughters in the Son, they too can cry out, *Abba*, Father: "You have received the spirit of sonship. When we cry, 'Abba! Father!' it is the Spirit himself bearing witness with our spirit that we are children of God" (Rom. 8:15–16; see also Gal. 4:6). Addressing churches that were no longer Aramaic-speaking communities (Rome and Galatia), Paul recalled a word addressed by Jesus to his Father. The fact that the Latin- and Greek-speaking recipients of these letters did not use Aramaic did not matter. The expression *abba* had become a precious treasure in the memory of the early Church, indicating the relationship Jesus had with God. Looking back to an authentic memory of the way the Aramaic-speaking Jesus of Nazareth related to God as "Father" (*abba*), Paul rejoices with his fellow Christians that they too can call to God as "our Father" in the same way (*abba*), since they are now sons and daughters of God, the father of Jesus.[32]

Two conclusions can be drawn from the evidence assembled. In the first place, Jesus was part of the long biblical tradition of a sonship generated

---

30. In some English-speaking cultures, the word "daddy" becomes "Dad" as a child matures. This term catches something of the intimate yet respectful relationship indicated by *abba*.

31. It has long been claimed that such an address to God is unique to Jesus and is never found in other Jewish literature prior to Jesus. This is sometimes questioned. We need not resolve that issue here. It is enough to establish that Jesus addressed God as his father in his prayer life, using an intimate and respectful form of address. For the discussion, with due reference to the groundbreaking work of Joachim Jeremias, see James D. G. Dunn, *Jesus and the Spirit: A Study of the Religious and Charismatic Experience of Jesus and the First Christians as Reflected in the New Testament* (London: SCM, 1975), 15–26.

32. See James D. G. Dunn, *The Theology of Paul the Apostle* (Grand Rapids: Eerdmans, 1998), 192–93.

by unconditional obedience to the God of Israel. In keeping with what was expected of the ideal kings and people of the Old Testament, he *behaved* as a son would behave in his obedient and respectful acceptance of all that the God of Israel asked. However, on the basis of his continual use of "father" to speak to God and about God, especially as it was articulated in his use of the Aramaic expression *abba*, there was more. He spoke about the reigning presence *of God* in a way that questioned many traditional assumptions about God, and he spoke with an authority that his contemporaries found hard to challenge (see, e.g., Mark 11:27–12:34). He reduced his opponents to silence: "And after that no one dared to ask him any question" (12:34). He manifested an intimacy with the God of Israel that is apparent in his courageous preaching and in his willingness to accept the consequences. Jesus' use of the expression *abba*, as with the use of the Greek word *patēr*, appears regularly in episodes that report Jesus at prayer (see, e.g., Mark 14:36; Matt. 11:25–27; Luke 23:34; John 11:41–42; 17:1, 11, 21, 24, 25). We must not imagine that Jesus had some otherworldly contact with the God he called "Father." Like all human beings, he encountered his God in and through his prayer life. Most likely, however, his prayer life was more profound and more regular than that of others, as he strove to understand what God wanted of him, brought his petitions to God, and responded accordingly. Rooted in his experience of God as "Father" in his prayer life, the expression spilled over into his preaching about God. He began to speak of God as Father, alluding to the relationship of God to his people as a father (e.g., Luke 15:11–32: the father and his two sons) and referring to God as "my Father" and "your Father" (see John 20:17).

As a son, his unwavering acceptance of what he understood as God's design, the establishment of a reigning presence of God that questioned both the Jewish and the Roman establishment, was bound to generate opposition, conflict, and suffering. Jesus would have been naive in the extreme if he had not been aware that he was following a path that might lead to death. He again turned to the Old Testament to find meaning for himself and for others as such a possibility became more obvious as his ministry unfolded.

Jesus as the Son of Man

In all four Gospels the expression "the Son of Man" is used exclusively by Jesus.[33] Cumulatively it appears more than eighty times, although many of

---

33. John 12:34 is the only place where others use the expression, but it is hardly an exception, as the Jewish crowd asks him how he can speak thus of the Son of Man. They have their own ideas, which Jesus questions. For full detail, see Francis J. Moloney, *The Johannine Son of Man*, 2nd ed. (Eugene, OR: Wipf & Stock, 2007), 181–85.

these texts are parallels shared by Mark, Matthew, and Luke (the triple tradition), or by Matthew and Luke (the Q source). The expression is used *only* by Jesus, and he uses it at all times to speak *of himself.* No other person is called "the Son of Man," and no one else ever addresses Jesus as "the Son of Man." But the expression did not have its biblical origins in Jesus. He used it in a way that shows his dependence upon the use of the expression "one like a son of man" in Daniel 7:13.[34]

To start where Jesus started, we must consider Daniel 7, the central chapter of a book that appeared around 167 BCE in the midst of the persecutions inflicted upon the faithful ones in Israel by the Hellenistic king Antiochus IV of Syria. As we have seen, after the death of Alexander the Great (323 CE), the Hellenistic kings pursued his policy of "hellenizing" all their subjects.[35] Antiochus IV (175–163 BCE) pursued this policy with great vigor (see 1 Macc. 1:1–64; 2 Macc. 4:7–7:42). The tiny nation of Israel had little hope of surviving or of defending its unique understanding of and subsequent loyalty to its one true God. Daniel was written to a suffering people who could find no human solution to the suffering and death that surrounded them in their attempts to remain faithful to the God of Israel. The book of Daniel has a literary form that we call "apocalyptic." In apocalyptic literature the action of God resolves the drama of the seeming destruction of his nation and people by direct intervention. In order to describe the actions of God that defy the possibilities of identifiable human discourse, the author resorts to symbolic language and images to convey the central message: against all evil and suffering, God will have the final word. Addressed to those who strove to remain loyal to the God of Israel despite suffering and death (called "the holy ones"), this message is especially clear in Daniel 7:1–28.

The reader is told of a vision in the night (Dan. 7:1–2) in which Daniel sees four great beasts, with the fourth beast the most horrific of them all. These beasts represent the persecutors of Israel and were immediately identified as such by the first readers of Daniel.

- Babylon is represented as "like a lion and had eagles' wings" (v. 4).
- The Medes follow: "like a bear . . . raised up on one side; it had three ribs in its mouth . . . and it was told, 'Arise, devour much flesh'" (v. 5).

---

34. For two centuries scholars have debated whether Jesus actually used the expression and, if he did, what he meant by it. A survey of the complete discussion can be found in Mogens Müller, *The Expression 'Son of Man' and the Development of Christology: A History of Interpretation* (Sheffield, UK: Equinox, 2008), 140–516. For a detailed presentation of the following interpretation, see Francis J. Moloney, "*Constructing Jesus* and the Son of Man," *Catholic Biblical Quarterly* 75 (2013): 719–38.

35. See pp. 24–26 above.

- A well-known image of Persia appears: "like a leopard, with four wings of a bird on its back; and the beast had four heads; and dominion was given to it" (v. 6).
- Most terrible of all, the present persecution under Antiochus IV is described as "a fourth beast, terrible and dreadful and exceedingly strong; and it had great iron teeth; it devoured and broke in pieces, and stamped the residue with its feet" (v. 7).

Antiochus IV is identified as a small, arrogant horn (v. 8). The scene as Daniel experienced his vision in the night is dark indeed as animal violence gathers, and this was the lived experience in Israel in 168–167 BCE. However, the scene changes as a heavenly court is assembled.

> As I looked,
> thrones were placed
>   and one that was ancient of days took his seat . . .
> The court sat in judgment,
>   and the books were opened. (vv. 9–10)

The three former persecutors lose their power (v. 12), and the fourth "beast was slain, and its body destroyed and given over to be burned with fire" (v. 11).

> And behold, with the clouds of heaven
>   there came one like a son of man,
> and he came to the Ancient of Days
>   and was presented before him.
> And to him was given dominion
>   and glory and kingdom. . . .
> His dominion is an everlasting dominion,
>   which shall not pass away,
> and his kingdom one
>   that shall not be destroyed. (vv. 13–14)

Daniel is puzzled (v. 15), and the rest of Daniel 7 is devoted to the words of an interpreting angel who explains the dream. The phrase "one like a son of man" does not appear; it is replaced by the expression "the saints of the Most High" (vv. 18, 22, 25, 27). The angel tells a well-known story of a persecuted people who place their hope and trust in the final victory of God and the vindication of "the saints."

> And the kingdom and the dominion
>   and the greatness of the kingdoms under the whole heaven
>   shall be given to the people of *the saints of the Most High*;

> their kingdom shall be an everlasting kingdom,
>> and all dominions shall serve and obey them. (v. 27, emphasis
>> added)

In the vision that occupies the first half of Daniel 7 (vv. 1–14), "one like a son of man" is vindicated by God, over against the threats of the animal opponents of God's people and nation. In the second half of the chapter (vv. 15–28), the single "one like a son of man" becomes those in Israel loyal to God's ways: "the saints of the Most High." Daniel 7 (as with the rest of the book) promises that suffering Israel cannot avoid the suffering but that those "saints" who remain loyal and obedient, never betraying Israel's God, will have the last word. God will vindicate them. To "one like a son of man," to "the saints of the Most High," God will give an everlasting kingdom (vv. 14, 27).

Jesus of Nazareth looked back to this dramatic presentation of an apocalyptic victory of God over evil and suffering in Daniel 7.[36] But Jesus took a further bold step. He no longer spoke of the symbolic "one like a son of man" but pointed to himself as "the Son of Man."[37] He takes on in his person the experience of suffering Israel, promised ultimate vindication by God. As we have seen, Jesus' preaching, his immediacy with God, and the bold and courageous lifestyle that this produced eventually led him into misunderstanding, suffering, and persecution. But we must not think that Jesus' ministry was dominated by an ominous expectation of a violent end. No doubt much of his ministry was marked by joy and by a new hope, especially for the less fortunate, as well as by trust, goodness, and warm relationships among an expanding group of women and men who became his friends and companions. Ernest Renan once oversimplified this period into an idyllic "Galilean springtime,"[38] but Jesus certainly did not spend the whole of his ministry looking toward a tragic end. However, strong opposition eventually appeared on the horizon. Relating to God as a son would

---

36. Jewish literature from before and after the time of Jesus shows that the book of Daniel was extremely popular among Jewish writers of that time. For a survey, see Maurice Casey, *Son of Man: The Interpretation and Influence of Daniel 7* (London: SPCK, 1979), 99–141. Jesus of Nazareth, brought up on Israel's Scriptures, was well aware of the message of Daniel 7.

37. This expression on the lips of Jesus in the Gospels has two definite articles in Greek (*ho huios tou anthrōpou*). Such an expression is found nowhere in surviving Greek documents from antiquity. It shifts from the generic "one like a son of man" to the specific and personal "the Son of the Man." See Charles F. D. Moule, *The Origins of Christology* (Cambridge: Cambridge University Press, 1977), 11–22.

38. See Ernest Renan, *Life of Jesus*, trans. Charles E. Wilbour (New York: Modern Library, 1955), 86: "The environs, moreover, are charming; and no place in the world was so well adapted for dreams of perfect happiness." Renan's *Vie de Jésus* was first published in 1869.

relate to a father, Jesus and his life and teaching reflected an immediacy with God that gave authority to what he said and did. A scenario reported in the Gospel of John reflects the difficulty this created for some. The chief priests and the Pharisees lament: "If we let him go on thus, every one will believe in him, and the Romans will come and destroy both our holy place and our nation" (John 11:48).

Jesus' person and message were troubling. The Gospels and other non-canonical documents make it clear that he gathered marginal people; Jesus and his motley entourage of followers would have made both Jewish and Roman authorities uneasy.[39] His calling of disciples from the margins of society, the important role of women in his ministry (see Mark 15:40–41; Luke 8:1–3), his radical interpretation of Jewish law and practices (see Matt. 5:17–48), and his celibate lifestyle (see Matt. 19:12), to mention only some significant "novelties" associated with his ministry, were all part of this. Behind all these manifestations of Jesus' singular life lay his urgent passion (unto death) for the sovereignty of God (the kingdom of God).[40] Unease with nonaligned groups such as those who followed Jesus is well witnessed in Josephus' description of both Herod's and the Romans' handling of opposition to their authority.[41]

The Synoptic Gospels report Jesus as coming to Jerusalem and the temple only once, at the end of his life. He goes there to meet his death. The Gospel of John, more historically reliable in this case, reports that he goes back and forth from Galilee to Jerusalem and regularly enters into conflict with Jewish leadership (see John 2:13–22; 5:16–18; 7:1–10:21; 10:22–39; 11:45–57; 12:9–36a).[42] Jesus' presence in the city of Jerusalem and its temple, coupled

39. See Meier, *Marginal Jew*, 3:40–124.

40. See Lohfink, *Jesus of Nazareth*, 216–44.

41. See, e.g., regarding Herod, Josephus, *Jewish War* 1.325–27; *Jewish Antiquities* 14.450–55 (on the Galilean and Idumean revolt); and regarding the Romans, see *Jewish War* 2.117–18; *Jewish Antiquities* 18 (on Judas the Galilean).

42. On the basis of the timeline of the Gospel of John, coupled with that of the Synoptics, totally determined by the decision of the First Evangelist, Mark, to have Jesus go to Jerusalem only at the end of his life, the following timeline might be suggested: Jesus passed his infancy, youth, and adolescence in Nazareth (Luke 1–2; Matt. 2:19–23). He began his ministry in Galilee (in all Gospels). As the Gospel of John insists, he was present in Jerusalem for the major feasts (called "pilgrim feasts," as Jews outside Jerusalem were expected to go to the temple). Luke 2:41–51 may also be reminiscent of this practice for Jesus and his family. Jesus never set up a permanent presence in Jerusalem. Perhaps because of his unhappy relationship with the religious practices of Jerusalem, his "home" was Galilee, most likely Capernaum, even though his "hometown" was elsewhere (see Mark 6:1–6a; Luke 4:23). Most of his ministry was practiced in Galilee, and he was known as a Galilean (Matt. 26:69; Luke 23:6) and a Nazarene (Matt. 2:23). His final visit to Jerusalem was for the celebration of Passover. There he manifested his customary dissatisfaction with temple practices, and both Jewish and Roman authorities decided

with his taking sides in a first-century Jewish conflict over what represents an authentic understanding of what God requires of his people (see Mark 7:1–23; 12:38–44), would have generated tension between this man from Nazareth and the Jewish religious and political leaders. Jesus' *regular* presence in Jerusalem during his several visits to the city during his ministry was *always* a problem for Jewish leadership. It was not something generated by the final scene in the temple.

Jesus' predictions of his forthcoming passion and death (see, e.g., Mark 8:31; 9:31; 10:32–34) developed in the tradition until they reached the form in which we now have them in the Gospel texts, reporting in detail the events of his arrest, insult, death, and resurrection (see Mark 10:32–34). But we can sense, behind the simplest of them, a Semitic play on words that goes back to Jesus: "For the Son of man is to be delivered into the hands of men" (Luke 9:44b; see Mark 9:31a–b). "The Son of Man" is found in almost all passages in the Gospels when Jesus looks forward to his future suffering and claims that he will be vindicated by God (see also John 3:14; 8:28; 12:32–36). Matthew 26:2 and Luke 9:44 are the only exceptions. But Jesus only indicated in general terms *that* his life would end violently (see Luke 9:44b; Mark 9:31a–b). He did not know *how* it would end or *how* God would enter his story to vindicate his suffering and death as the personification of the Danielic "one like a son of man." But he was convinced that such would be the case (see Mark 8:31c–d). To indicate that conviction, he used a term that he and his listeners understood: "the Son of Man."[43]

His death was not the end of everything; indeed his preaching of God's reigning presence, his oneness with the God of Israel, and his role as "the Son of Man" looked beyond a possible death in the near future. This conviction would have been part of his use of "the Son of Man" to speak of his suffering, death, and ultimate vindication.[44] It is especially present in his last night and final meal with his disciples. Facing death, he can confidently tell them: "Truly, I say to you, I shall not drink again of the fruit of the vine until that day when I drink it new in the kingdom of God" (Mark 14:25; cf. Matt. 26:29;

---

that he needed to be disposed of, as had been the case with other similarly troublesome people, especially those regarded as messianic pretenders.

43. For a different interpretation of "Son of Man/Human One," associating it with majesty, see Lohfink, *Jesus of Nazareth*, 314–17.

44. In all the passion predications, except Matthew 26:2 and Luke 9:44, Jesus tells his hearers that he will rise again or be raised "on the third day." Written many decades after the events of Jesus' death and resurrection, what actually happened is reported. Jesus did not speak of resurrection on the third day, which is already a confession of faith. But based on Daniel 7:13–14 he would have spoken of his vindication by God, his Father. What he actually said is lost to us as what actually happened is reported.

Luke 22:20).[45] His death and vindication was *not for Jesus* but *for others*. At that same meal he points to events of the next day as "my blood of the covenant, which is poured out for many" (Mark 14:24; Matt. 26:28; cf. Luke 22:20; 1 Cor. 11:25; John 6:51; see Jer. 31:31).[46] Although its current articulation is the work of pre-Markan tradition, and its current location as Jesus' closing words in a section devoted to the formation of his disciples is part of Mark's literary and theological creativity, the saying of Jesus in Mark 10:45 is "one of the most important in the Gospels": "For the Son of man also came not to be served but to serve, and to give his life as a ransom for many."[47]

Dale Allison has recently gathered no less than thirty-one texts from across the New Testament that point to Jesus' positive assessment of his forthcoming death. He concludes his analysis of this material by confidently affirming: "They obviously reflect a very widespread belief: Jesus did not run from his death or otherwise resist it. On the contrary, anticipating his cruel end, he submitted to it, trusting that his unhappy fate was somehow for the good."[48] He concludes: "Indeed, next to the fact that Jesus was crucified by order of Pontius Pilate, his acquiescence to his fate is probably the best-attested fact about his last days."[49]

Conclusion

We have attempted to respond to the questions of what Jesus thought he was doing and who he thought he was. Many major issues have been only fleetingly mentioned or taken up in a brief footnote. But the portrait of Jesus articulated in this chapter forms the bedrock for the development of the early Church's interpretation of Jesus of Nazareth, beginning with Paul's letters and then through the narratives of the Gospels, reaching into the later documents of our New Testament. The person of Jesus is fundamentally associated

45. All accounts of Jesus' final meal with his disciples look forward to a time beyond his death. They all use the optimistic word for "until" (Greek: *heōs*). Another word, with the same meaning, is found in the Pauline comment on the final meal (1 Cor. 11:26: "until he comes"). See Lohfink, *Jesus of Nazareth*, 252–56.

46. For a longer summary of the meaning of this final meal with the symbol of the gift of the broken bread and the shared wine, see Lohfink, *Jesus of Nazareth*, 252–56.

47. On this crucial saying of Jesus, see the excursus in Francis J. Moloney, *The Gospel of Mark: A Commentary* (Grand Rapids: Baker Academic, 2012), 213–14. The claim that it is one of the most important sayings in the Gospels comes from Vincent Taylor, *The Gospel according to St. Mark*, 2nd ed. (London: Macmillan, 1966), 444. The Lukan version of this saying (Luke 22:27) appears in Luke's account of the Last Supper.

48. Allison, *Constructing Jesus*, 432.

49. Ibid., 433; see 387–433.

with the God of Israel and the people and institutions of Israel. Jesus of Nazareth preached the reigning presence of God as king. He was able to do so because of his immediacy with God, whom he regarded as his Father. He understood and boldly preached a kingdom different from the one accepted by the religion and culture of his time. But his authoritative word and presence, which appeared to come from closeness to God, marginalized him and his followers in the society of the time. His words, his deeds, and his person generated misunderstanding, rejection, conflict, and suffering and led to his death by crucifixion. But that was not the end of the story. God's intervention in the resurrection vindicated Jesus' way of life and the exciting promise of his word. His preaching of the kingdom, his oneness with his Father, and his preparedness to accept all consequences led to misunderstanding, suffering, death—and a risen life beyond death.[50]

Paul's intense focus on Jesus' death and resurrection as the foundation stone for Jesus' exaltation as the Christ, as Lord and exalted Son of God, is based upon that life story, however little of it he shares with his readers and listeners in his letters.[51] The Gospels' further interpretation of the Son's preexistence (John); of his extraordinary entry into the human story (Matthew and Luke); and of his life, teaching, death, resurrection (Mark, Matthew, Luke, and John), ascension, exaltation, and ongoing presence in the community that looks back to him as its founder (Matthew, Luke, and John) is based on that life story.

What develops across the New Testament and into the faith of the Christian Church has its roots in the life, teaching, death, resurrection, and exaltation of Jesus of Nazareth. One must not drive a wedge between Jesus of Nazareth and what the post-Easter early Church will say about him as it becomes increasingly aware of what God has done in and through Jesus, the Christ, the Son of God, and Lord. The memory of the life of Jesus explodes into the Christologies of the New Testament. The Christian church finds its roots in those first followers of Jesus, who had appointed the Twelve as a symbol of a new Israel. Christian behavior also looks back to Jesus of Nazareth, as all who call themselves Christians are challenged "to walk in the same way in which he walked" (1 John 2:6).

Because of the life, teaching, death, and resurrection of Jesus of Nazareth, his followers in the early Church confidently awaited his return, that—as his followers in whatever situation—they too might share his vindication by God. In the light of Jesus' death and resurrection, his followers *looked back* to his

---

50. For a more detailed study of what actually happened at the resurrection and what it meant (means), see Moloney, *Resurrection of the Messiah*, 137–82.

51. On the "story of Jesus" behind the Pauline letters, see Horrell, *Introduction to the Study of Paul*, 18–23.

story, which marked the decisive in-breaking of God's sovereignty, and his oneness with God, no matter what it cost him, and they knew that such a life did not come to closure with violent death by crucifixion.[52] They thus *looked forward* with confidence as they prayed: "Come, Lord Jesus!" (Rev. 22:20). "*Maranatha*" (1 Cor. 16:22).

52. The approach adopted in this biographical sketch of Jesus of Nazareth, like many such sketches, is the fruit of the epoch-making work of Rudolf Bultmann and the subsequent reaction to his faith-filled but historically minimalist understanding of Jesus on the part of his own students, especially Ernst Käsemann, Günther Bornkamm, Hans Conzelmann, Gerhard Ebeling, and Ernst Fuchs. For a stimulating presentation of this very important moment in the history of New Testament research, see Konrad Hammann, *Rudolf Bultmann: A Biography*, trans. Philip E. Devenish (Salem, OR: Polebridge, 2013), 443–64.

5

Paul

The First Christian Author

Reflection on the contribution of Saint Paul to the developing thought and practice of the Christian community must focus on his influential understanding of what God has done for us in and through Jesus Christ. Although Paul makes very little use of "the story of Jesus," as we have outlined it in the previous chapter, his understanding of Jesus' relationship with God and the crucial event of his death and resurrection lie at the heart of Paul's contribution to emerging Christianity. Without the life, teaching, death, and resurrection of Jesus, there would be no theology of the apostle Paul.

What follows is an introductory sketch of Paul's life and message.[1] It attempts to provide an initial sense of the theological, christological, and

1. As with the biographical sketch of Jesus of Nazareth, so much more could and should be said about the Pauline contribution to Christian thought and life. As well as major commentaries, the following studies have shaped my thought: Ed Parish Sanders, *Paul and Palestinian Judaism: A Comparison of Patterns of Religion* (London: SCM, 1977); J. Christiaan Beker, *Paul the Apostle: The Triumph of God in Life and Thought* (Philadelphia: Fortress, 1980); Jürgen Becker, *Paul: Apostle to the Gentiles*, trans. O. C. Dean Jr. (Louisville: Westminster John Knox, 1993); Dunn, *Theology of Paul*; idem, *The New Perspective on Paul*, rev. ed. (Grand Rapids: Eerdmans, 2008). For briefer helpful studies, see C. Kingsley Barrett, *Paul: An Introduction to His Thought* (London: Geoffrey Chapman, 1994); Morna D. Hooker, *Paul: A Short Introduction* (Oxford: Oneworld, 2003); Jerome Murphy-O'Connor, *Paul: His Story* (Oxford: Oxford University Press,

Christian creativity of a figure regarded as the first and arguably most significant author from the earliest life of the Christian Church. The challenges, successes, and failures of his intense missionary life generated the earliest Christian "literature," through what we call "occasional letters" to various communities.[2] He wrote about Jesus, his death and resurrection, and the demands of Christian life.[3]

Paul's Life and Letters

Saul/Paul of Tarsus was born around 5 CE into a Jewish family living in the Diaspora. It is often suggested that his pre-Christian name was Saul and that his conversion led him to adopt the name Paul. Although Luke insinuates this by using "Saul" across the first half of Acts (up to 13:9) and "Paul" from that point on, most likely the former name is Jewish, and "Paul" is the Latin (Roman) version of the same name. This was a common practice among Jews of that period. He thus grew up with firsthand experience of Judaism lived in the larger Greco-Roman world that we considered in chapter 2. Jewish, Greek, and Roman influences shaped the world he lived in and shaped Paul himself. The fact that he wrote in Greek is evidence of his mixed cultural background. The First Letter to the Thessalonians was probably written in 50 CE, and Paul's last letter was probably the Letter to the Romans, written in about 58 CE. Some suggest that the Letter to the Philippians was written last, shortly before his execution in Rome. His first letter was to a city in northern Greece, Thessalonica, and his last was to (or perhaps from) the capital of the world, Rome.[4] Further letters were directed to other corners of the Greco-Roman world: to major cities in Greece (Philippi and Corinth), to a region in Asia

---

2004); Frank J. Matera, *God's Saving Grace: A Pauline Theology* (Grand Rapids: Eerdmans, 2012); and esp. Horrell, *Introduction to the Study of Paul*. See also Brown, *Introduction to the New Testament*, 409–584; Powell, *Introducing the New Testament*, 215–321, 343–55, 371–85; Spivey, Smith, and Black, *Anatomy of the New Testament*, 271–373.

2. Paul's letters are called "occasional" because, with the exception of the Letter to the Romans, they were all written to communities he had founded and labored in and were written in response to difficulties, misunderstandings, and failures, in order to correct or encourage these fledgling early Christians who were living in the Greco-Roman world. They are not theological tracts, although Romans is sometimes regarded as such.

3. I have used the word "Christian" several times already. Paul never uses this expression. It appears later as a name applied to those who adhered to the new religion that looked to Jesus Christ for its foundation and inspiration (see Acts 11:26; 26:28; 1 Pet. 4:16), but it may have already been in use by the time of Paul. See Dunn, *Theology of Paul*, 185.

4. On the Thessalonian correspondence, see Victor P. Furnish, *1 Thessalonians, 2 Thessalonians*, Abingdon New Testament Commentaries (Nashville: Abingdon, 2004). On 2 Thessalonians, see also pp. 157–58 below.

Minor (Galatia), and to an individual in Asia Minor (Philemon). A number of scholars claim that the Letter to the Colossians, written to Colossae, also in Asia Minor, was written by Paul. If that is the case, it could have been written during Paul's last Roman imprisonment in the 60s.[5]

Debates over the chronology of Paul's life story and catalogs of his journeys abound.[6] What follows focuses on *what he said*. It will refrain from using the accounts of Paul's travels and his speeches in the Acts of the Apostles. That Lukan document is marked by a theological view of the way the history of early Christianity unfolded, and Paul's life and teaching have been shaped to fit that view. This is not to say that there is nothing of value in the Lukan description of Paul and his mission.[7] But the best place to discover what Paul said is within the pages of his own writings.

The interpretative keys provided in what follows indicate Paul's unique contribution to our Sacred Scriptures as the Word of God.[8] Paul, the devout Jew, had been so transformed by the "power of the resurrection" that he rethought the universal Jewish acceptance of God's glorious presence *at the beginning* that would only return *at the end*. With the death and resurrection of Jesus something new and unexpected had broken into the human story. Those who place their faith and trust in Jesus are living in an in-between time, a time between the action of God in and through the death and resurrection of Jesus and the final victory of God at the end of time. Much of Paul's concern was to instruct these followers in how they ought to live during that period and to converse (sometimes bitterly) with those who failed to do so—both Christian individuals and Christian communities.

This chapter's sketch of Paul's life and letters is followed by a snapshot of the Pauline message as it is found in Philippians 3:7–11. I will then describe in three sections Paul's unique contribution to Christian thought and practice. By reflecting on Romans 5:12–21, I will trace Paul's understanding of *what* happened as a result of the death and resurrection of Jesus, followed by a

5. A helpful commentary for each Pauline letter will be suggested when a letter is first mentioned. Further indications can be found in the introductions of Brown, Powell, and Spivey, Smith, and Black, mentioned above in n. 1.

6. For contrasting assessments, see Gerd Lüdemann, *Paul, Apostle to the Gentiles: Studies in Chronology*, trans. F. Stanley Jones (Philadelphia: Fortress, 1984); and Rainer Riesner, *Paul's Early Period: Chronology, Mission Strategy, Theology*, trans. Doug Stott (Grand Rapids: Eerdmans, 1994).

7. See the balanced assessment of Mikael C. Parsons, *Luke: Storyteller, Interpreter, Evangelist* (Peabody, MA: Hendrickson, 2007), 123–37, and the extensive use of Acts to establish the Pauline chronology in Riesner, *Paul's Early Period*.

8. I would like to thank my long-standing friend and colleague Brendan Byrne for support in what follows. Any errors or infelicities, however, are mine.

further reflection on *how* it happened, with the help of Philippians 2:5–11.[9] Only then can we consider Paul's challenge to all who believe in Christ and live in the time between the gracious intervention of God in and through the death and resurrection of Jesus and God's final return in glory at the end of all history.[10]

The Power of the Resurrection

A crucial moment in Paul's biography calls for attention: his conversion. Paul writes that he was a Jew "of the people of Israel, of the tribe of Benjamin, a Hebrew born of Hebrews" (Phil. 3:5; see also Rom. 11:1; 2 Cor. 11:22). He also insists that he belonged to the Jewish sect of the Pharisees (Phil. 3:5), a group that sought a radical holiness.[11] They adhered carefully not only to Torah but also to the teaching of the Prophets, only recently accepted as Scripture by the Jews, and even to the Writings, whose role as Scripture was still being debated in the first century. They also devoted attention to ongoing oral interpretations of the written law that applied Torah to changing society and its practices. Luke informs us that Paul was educated into his Pharisaism in Jerusalem by Gamaliel (Acts 22:3; see also 5:35–39). Paul relates nothing of that background but admits that his passion for the law and its observance led him to a "zeal" that could not tolerate a sectarian Judaism claiming that the crucified Jesus of Nazareth was the Christ.

His repeated references to his former life as a persecutor of the earliest Church (Gal. 1:13, 23; Phil. 3:6; 1 Cor. 15:9) are his way of showing that something dramatic broke into his life. It led to a reversal of his understanding of the way the law was to be understood and lived, and of his understanding of Jesus as Christ, Son of God, and Lord (Rom. 1:3–4).[12] What he had once rejected and persecuted now lay at the heart of his belief in the action of the

9. On Philippians, see Bonnie B. Thurston and Judith Ryan, *Philippians and Philemon*, Sacra Pagina 10 (Collegeville, MN: Liturgical Press, 2005). See also Brendan J. Byrne, "The Letter to the Philippians," in *The New Jerome Biblical Commentary*, ed. Raymond E. Brown, Joseph A. Fitzmyer, and Roland E. Murphy (Englewood Cliffs, NJ: Prentice Hall, 1990), 791–97.

10. For more detailed introductions to Paul's life and letters, see Brown, *Introduction to the New Testament*, 422–55; Powell, *Introducing the New Testament*, 231–53; Spivey, Smith, and Black, *Anatomy of the New Testament*, 271–83.

11. See pp. 31–33 above.

12. In Rom. 1:3–4 Paul explicitly announces: "the gospel concerning his Son, who was descended from David according to the flesh and designated Son of God in power according to the spirit of holiness by his resurrection from the dead, Jesus Christ our Lord." It is widely accepted that this passage is earlier than Paul. Writing to the Romans in 58 CE, Paul received this confession of faith and passed it on as something he knows that the Roman community, not founded

God of Israel: the crucified and risen Jesus of Nazareth was the Christ. Paul was transformed by what we might today call a "religious experience" that turned his life around to such an extent that he spent the rest of it, even to martyrdom, offering the passionate gift of himself to preaching the gospel as he came to understand it (see 2 Cor. 12:1–5, esp. v. 2: "I know a man in Christ who fourteen years ago was caught up to the third heaven"). He told the Corinthians, "For if I preach the gospel, that gives me no ground for boasting. For necessity is laid upon me. Woe to me if I do not preach the gospel" (1 Cor. 9:16). He writes similarly to the Romans: "I am under obligation both to Greeks and to barbarians, both to the wise and to the foolish: so I am eager to preach the gospel to you also who are in Rome" (Rom. 1:14–15). As Jesus was driven by an urgent passion for the reign of God, Paul was driven by his own passionate, and now urgent, belief that God had entered human history in a new way through the death and resurrection of Jesus Christ. Life under the law was a wonderful gift of God, but it was now a thing of the past, an unnecessary custodian, because Christ has come (see Gal. 3:24–25; Rom. 9:1–5).[13]

In the Acts of the Apostles reference is made to Paul's Damascus experience three times (Acts 9:1–30; 22:3–21; 26:9–23). Paul's own direct testimony is less descriptive but more theologically impressive. There is no journey to Damascus, no voice from heaven, no blindness, and no mention of Straight Street and Ananias. What Paul does tell us, however, is that he experienced a "sight" of the risen Jesus and that this revelation was the foundation of his call to be an apostle of Jesus Christ to the gentiles (see 1 Cor. 9:1; 15:8; Gal. 1:12–16). Paul confirms that Damascus was part of his formative experiences (Gal. 1:17; 2 Cor. 11:32), but the geography does not interest him. Scholars debate how "immediate" Paul's transformation was and whether or not he spent several years assimilating his experience and developing his gospel. They also discuss whether Paul experienced a "conversion" or a "call." Many would say that underlying Paul's zeal as a Jew and his zeal as a Christian was a single-minded passion for the one true God that was always with him. His passion for God was not changed by means of a conversion, but he experienced a "call" from that God to recognize and proclaim what God had done for humankind in and through his Son.[14] His passion for the God of Israel never wavered, but his acceptance of Jesus' role in God's action in our world and in human history

---

by him, will immediately recognize and own (see Rom. 16:1–16). See Brendan Byrne, *Romans*, Sacra Pagina 6 (Collegeville, MN: Liturgical Press, 1996), 39–40, 41–45.

13. See Dunn, *Theology of Paul*, 143–50, for a full discussion of this important matter.

14. For a summary of discussions over Paul's conversion and the chronology of his life and mission, see Horrell, *Introduction to the Study of Paul*, 26–43. On his conversion, see especially

transformed him. Jesus Christ's unconditional obedience to and trust in the God of Israel, which led to his death and resurrection, marked a new chapter in God's dealings with humankind.[15]

Paul's Message in Miniature

Writing to the Philippians, a community with which he appeared to have a special bond of affection, Paul bares his soul, telling of his transformation:

> But whatever gain I had, I counted as loss for the sake of Christ. Indeed I count everything as loss because of the surpassing worth of knowing Christ Jesus my Lord. For his sake I have suffered the loss of all things, and count them as refuse, in order that I may gain Christ and be found in him, not having a righteousness of my own, based on law, but that which is through faith in Christ, the righteousness from God that depends on faith; that I may know him and *the power of his resurrection*, and may share his sufferings, becoming like him in his death, that if possible I may attain the resurrection from the dead. (Phil. 3:7–11, emphasis added; see also 1 Cor. 1:18; 2 Cor. 4:7; 12:9; 13:4)

This brief statement, following hard on the heels of Paul's presentation in verses 4 through 6 of his pedigree as a Jew (see also 2 Cor. 11:21–33), presents *in nuce* the Pauline gospel and its source. For Paul, and for the gospel that he preached, the only things that matter are

- to know Christ Jesus as Lord;
- to gain Christ and to be found in him;
- to have right relationship (righteousness) with God through belief in what God has done for us in and through faith in Jesus Christ;[16]
- to reject the idea that such a relationship can be generated by anything human, such as the observance of the Mosaic law;
- to live and die as Jesus of Nazareth lived and died, becoming obedient and faithful like him in suffering and death; and
- to thus eventually share in Jesus' resurrection from the dead.

"Paul's Conversion: A Light to Twentieth Century Disputes," in Dunn, *New Perspective*, 347–65; and Alan F. Segal, *Paul the Convert* (New Haven: Yale University Press, 1990).

15. Sherri Brown, "Faith, Christ, and Paul's Theology of Salvation History," in *Unity and Diversity in the Gospels and Paul: Essays in Honor of Frank J. Matera*, ed. Christopher W. Skinner and Kelly R. Iverson, Early Christianity and Its Literature 7 (Atlanta: SBL, 2012), 256–57, writes of "a fundamental transvaluation of his beliefs."

16. On righteousness as "right relationship," see n. 26 below.

The source for Paul's relentless and passionate conviction that these are the only things that matter is *the power of the resurrection.*

If the only written documents we had from the beginnings of Christianity were the letters of Paul, we would know that in the fullness of time Jesus was born of a woman (Gal. 4:4), that the night before he died he celebrated a meal with his disciples that looked to his suffering, death, and ultimate victory through resurrection for its meaning (1 Cor. 11:23–26), and that he was crucified, buried, raised, and seen by a multitude of witnesses (15:1–8). The last of these witnesses, the one untimely and unworthily born, was Paul himself (15:8–9). Although there are echoes of Jesus' teachings insinuated into the letters, we have no "narrative" of the life of Jesus.[17] For Paul, writing so close to those events, what became the heart of his preaching was Jesus' death and resurrection. As he tells us in his first letter to the Corinthians: "For Jews demand signs and Greeks seek wisdom, but we preach Christ crucified, a stumbling block to Jews and folly to Gentiles, but to those who are called, both Jews and Greeks, Christ the power of God and the wisdom of God. For the foolishness of God is wiser than men, and the weakness of God is stronger than men" (1 Cor. 1:22–25). At the heart of the Pauline gospel is his explanation of how a humiliating crucifixion is transformed into power and wisdom, human weakness into a manifestation of God's strength.

What Happened: Adam and Christ (Rom. 5:12–21)

To explain that Jesus' death, a stumbling block and folly, is the power and wisdom of God, Paul developed a unique understanding of God's threefold intervention within the history of humankind and of all creation

- at the original creation,
- during the span of the human story in the life, death, and resurrection of Jesus,
- and at the end of time.

Paul uses the expression "a new creation" (Greek: *kainē ktisis*) on only two occasions. He does so without any explanation, and the phrase expresses a creative theological and christological point of view. Paul takes it for granted that his readers and listeners know what he means when he tells the gentile

---

17. For a fuller (and optimistic) evaluation of Paul's knowledge of the story of Jesus, see Dunn, *Theology of Paul*, 182–206. See also Becker, *Paul*, 112–24.

Galatians, troubled by whether they should accept or reject Jewish practices that some missionaries are demanding: "For neither circumcision counts for anything, nor uncircumcision, but a new creation" (Gal. 6:15).[18] In a less polemical but profoundly theological context, Paul instructs the Corinthians, "If any one is in Christ, he is a new creation; the old has passed away, behold, the new has come" (2 Cor. 5:17). Paul is not quite as blunt here, as he is dealing more placidly, and almost lyrically, with the newness that has been brought into the human situation by the reconciling love of Christ (see vv. 11–21). He informs the Corinthians that by means of "life in Christ" a believer enters a world of new possibilities, a "new creation." Because of the loving self-gift of Christ, "those who live might live no longer for themselves but for him who for their sake died and was raised" (v. 15).[19]

This theme calls for further exploration. A crucial text for our investigation is Romans 5:12–21.[20] Here we find Paul's conviction that in and through the death and resurrection of Jesus we have a new creation. Like all Jews, Paul accepted that "in the beginning" (Gen. 1:1) everything was exactly as God wanted it. In Genesis, the use of a rich Hebrew word (*tov*), which we translate into the prosaic "good," returns repeatedly to tell the reader and the listener that as a result of God's creating word everything was exactly as it should be. Right order existed (see Gen. 1:4, 10, 12, 18, 21, 25, 31 [as creation is completed God sees that all is "very good"]).[21] In that narrative, Adam was a key player. Paul took the story of Adam and Eve as an account of how things happened. First-century Jews knew nothing of modern criticism of the Old Testament. God's glory and God's will were evident in creation and in the lives of Adam and Eve.[22] However, sin entered the world through the *disobedience* of Adam, and once sin had begun, it gradually spread and took possession of the whole

18. Most early Christians would have heard Paul's letters read to them. Very few in the first century were literate, and oral performance was the widespread way for people to acquaint themselves with what the minority were able to read. See Pieter J. J. Botha, *Orality and Literacy in Early Christianity*, Biblical Performance Criticism 5 (Eugene, OR: Cascade, 2012), 193–250.

19. On Galatians, see Frank Matera, *Galatians*, Sacra Pagina 9 (Collegeville, MN: Liturgical Press, 1992). See also Brendan Byrne, *Galatians and Romans* (Collegeville, MN: Liturgical Press, 2010). On 1 Corinthians, see Pheme Perkins, *First Corinthians*, Paideia Commentaries on the New Testament (Grand Rapids: Baker Academic, 2012), and the still-valuable C. Kingsley Barrett, *The First Epistle to the Corinthians*, 2nd ed., Black's New Testament Commentaries (Grand Rapids: Baker Academic, 1971).

20. Among the commentators, see esp. Byrne, *Romans*, 173–87; Frank J. Matera, *Romans*, Paideia Commentaries on the New Testament (Grand Rapids: Baker Academic, 2010), 124–44. See also Byrne, *Galatians and Romans*, 96–100.

21. See Brendan Byrne, *Inheriting the Earth: The Pauline Basis of a Spirituality for Our Time* (Homebush, Australia: St. Paul Publications, 1990), 15–16.

22. On the question of "what actually happened" to generate sin in the world and the importance of the "truth" communicated by the *biblical story* of Adam and Eve, see Byrne, *Inheriting*

of God's originally perfect creation: "Sin came into the world through one man, and death came through sin, and so death spread to all because all have sinned" (Rom. 5:12 NRSV).

What Paul affirms here is that the disobedience of Adam, as told in the biblical story of creation, had a *universal effect*. Because of the sin of *one person*, death and sin enter the human condition *universally*. Everyone sinned.[23] Long after the universal spread of death and sin, the law was given to Moses. Sin abounded, but not even the law could free us from the slavery of sin. It could protect us . . . but not save us (Rom. 5:13). The tragedy of the disobedience of Adam "at the beginning" was crucial for the Jewish understanding of human history. Paul, along with his Jewish contemporaries, believed that final salvation and the restoration of the world as God had made it, full of his glory, the restoration of a situation of right relationship between God and all creation, would take place only "at the end" of all time. God would restore everything to its original beauty. The "right order" of God's original creation (*tov*) would be restored. God's glory, present at the beginning of time, would be restored by the dramatic action and intervention of God that would bring about the end the world as we know it.[24]

But already in Romans 5:14, in the midst of his description of the tragic universal presence of death and sin, Paul introduces a new and unexpected note of hope. He refers to Adam as "a type of the one who was to come." Adam is "a type" of the one who is to come, Jesus Christ, because his disobedience had universal consequences (vv. 12–13). Paul reverses that story with his strong adversative "but" at the beginning of verse 15 (very strong in Greek: *all' ouch*). God's graciousness has bestowed upon us a "free gift." The similarity with Adam, "a type" of the one who is to come, is that the obedience of the one who was to come, a free gift of God, had universal consequences. Both the disobedience of Adam and the obedience of Jesus Christ have universal consequences. Another similarity between Adam and Christ is that the sin of Adam was an event in human history, just as the obedience, death, and resurrection of Jesus of Nazareth was an event in human history. As sin entered history in and through Adam, so also the free gift of grace entered history in

---

the Earth, 19–25. On the background to Paul's use of "Adam," see Dunn, *Theology of Paul*, 79–90; Matera, *Romans*, 127–29.

23. Scholarship has long debated the use of the difficult Greek expression *eph' hō* in v. 12, explaining how the sin of one had a universal impact. Following Byrne (*Romans*, 177, 183), I regard it as an indication of "an emphatic causal expression" (177). Sin is universally present *because* one man sinned. See also Matera, *Romans*, 126–27.

24. See Robin Scroggs, *The Last Adam: A Study in Pauline Anthropology* (Oxford: Basil Blackwell, 1966).

and through Jesus Christ.[25] Although the effects of the sin of Adam and the effects of the death and resurrection of Jesus are universal, they are radically opposed: Adam's sin brought condemnation; Jesus' obedience brought justification, the possibility of a right relationship with God.[26] The dominance of death is overcome by the free gift of God's grace and graciousness offered to us in and through Christ (vv. 16–17).

Paul's life and teaching were dominated by his passionate belief that history, caught in the chaos and sin generated by Adam and protected but not saved by the law, had been transformed. An unknown Hellenistic Jew wrote late in the second century before Christ: "In his wisdom the legislator [Moses] . . . surrounded us with unbroken palisades and iron walls to prevent our mixing with the other peoples in any matter, being thus kept pure in body and soul, preserved from false belief, and worshiping the only God omnipotent over all creation" (*Letter of Aristeas* 139).[27] This view of history and the role of the law can no longer hold sway. The death and resurrection of Jesus, the free gift of God to a sinful world, opened up a new possibility for humankind. We do not have to wait until the end of time for God's way in the world to be reestablished. God broke into the passage of ordinary human time in and through Jesus Christ. Jesus reversed Adam's sin of disobedience by means of his unconditional obedience to God. "Therefore just as one man's trespass led to condemnation for all, so one man's act of righteousness leads to justification

25. See Matera, *Romans*, 136: "It is because Christ's obedience has countered Adam's transgression that believers can boast in God, through Jesus Christ, through whom they have received reconciliation (5:11)."

26. One of the great battlefields of Pauline studies is the precise meaning of a series of words (a verb, a noun, an adjective) found across the Pauline correspondence. They are all associated in Greek (all have the root *dik-* in them) but are translated in different ways in English: to justify, justification, to make righteous, to be just or righteous, to act justly or righteously. Stated simply, since Luther's reading of Romans (esp. 3:21–26) many have accepted that the death and resurrection of Jesus created a new situation where sin remains but where God's action renders the sinner righteous. We remain sinners, but God declares us righteous. Sometimes called a "forensic" interpretation, it is the key to Luther's celebrated catchphrase *simul iustus et peccator*: at one and the same time justified and a sinner. This interpretation depended heavily on a negative interpretation of the Jewish law as enslaving. The only freedom possible was through the action of God in and through Jesus' death and resurrection. This interpretation (and the negative view of the law) is questioned today, and the interpretation given above in the text is increasingly favored. The death and resurrection of Jesus establishes a right relationship with God, although the Christian must continue to strive to live "in Christ" in the in-between time. See Byrne, *Romans*, 122–35; Matera, *Romans*, 91–104; Dunn, *Theology of Paul*, 385–89. This brief sketch of an increasing rejection of the forensic interpretation is associated with what is now called "the new perspective" in Pauline studies. See the summary of Horrell, *Introduction to the Study of Paul*, 73–80.

27. Text in James H. Charlesworth, *The Old Testament Pseudepigrapha* (New York: Doubleday, 1985), 2:22.

and life for all. For just as by the one man's disobedience the many were made sinners, so by the one man's obedience the many will be made righteous" (Rom. 5:18–19 NRSV).

Paul's claim that we are "made righteous" means that "right relationship" has now been established between God and the human condition.[28] Union with God and a fullness of life are now available. What Jesus had done for us introduced a "new creation." The first creation had been marred by sin and disobedience; the new creation is marked by the free gift of God that produces life through the obedience of one man, Jesus Christ (v. 17). What was wrecked by one man's disobedience has been restored by another man's obedience. God's free and unsolicited gift of his Son is not simply a restoration. Its grace-filled effects abundantly surpass the consequences of Adam's sin. This message is stated over and over: one man's trespass led to condemnation, and one man's act of righteousness leads to life (v. 18); one man's disobedience leads to sin, and one man's obedience leads to righteousness (v. 19); the law made us conscious of sin but did not free us, but where sin increased, grace abounded all the more (v. 20). The life that we have through Jesus Christ is eternal life (v. 21).

But Paul was a realist; the sinful condition established by the sin of Adam has not disappeared. It was as obvious in the world of Paul as it is in our own time that sin still reigns in the hearts of many and, increasingly, in human institutions. Sin and death are still abroad. They run side by side with the grace and freedom established in the new creation, now available in Jesus Christ. We are called to choose which story we would like to join: that of Adam or that of Jesus Christ. The choice before us, both individually and collectively, is: Which story are you going to let be told in your life, in your world? Are you choosing death with Adam or life with Christ? All forms of disobedience, selfishness, exploitation, and even the attitude of "going it alone" apart from God, no matter how well intentioned, place one inevitably on the side of Adam. Surrender to God's gift of righteousness through faith leads to life and to becoming, with Christ, an instrument of life.

For this reason, Paul does not abandon his traditional Jewish understanding of the course of history. The return of God at the end of all time is still firmly in place.[29] The difference now is that we do not have to wait until the end of time to encounter the glory of God in our lives.[30] It is available through faith

---

28. See Byrne, *Romans*, 57–60; Dunn, *Theology of Paul*, 179–81.

29. See the good summary and the helpful diagrams in Horrell, *Introduction to the Study of Paul*, 69–73, and Dunn, *Theology of Paul*, 461–72. This paradigm has been applied to the whole of the Pauline corpus by Beker, *Paul the Apostle*.

30. See Beker, *Paul the Apostle*, 204–12.

in Christ or, as we will see shortly, through our living as Jesus Christ lived, through putting on Christ. For Paul, we still "wait for his Son from heaven, whom he raised from the dead, Jesus who delivers us from the wrath to come" (1 Thess. 1:10). As Brendan Byrne puts it: "You have been part of the Adam story; your human history is marked by its consequences. Do you wish to let the Christ story and its (more powerful) consequences be the final story told in your life and in your world?"[31]

How It Happened: Christ and God (Phil. 2:5–11)

The so-called hymn of Philippians 2:5–11 is an unforgettable synthesis of the passage of the Christ from his preexistent situation of equality with God to a further place where he is Lord of all to the glory of God the Father, via the total emptying of himself in death, even death on a cross. This famous Pauline passage tells us *how* the new creation came about. Philippians 2:5–11 is a passage used by Paul to address listeners and readers who are being challenged, asked to examine the direction of their lives together. Our reflection on Romans 5:12–21 insisted, via the type and antitype of Adam and Christ, that in the affairs of human history—traditionally understood as full of sin and chaos between God's original intervention in the glory of the creation and his final intervention in the glory of his final coming—what Paul elsewhere calls a "new creation" has taken place (see Gal. 6:15; 2 Cor. 5:17). The passage we are about to consider from the Letter to the Philippians may well have been recited or sung to praise Jesus Christ in the Christian community at Philippi. It is widely accepted that Paul did not invent this passage. He took it from the prayer life of the Philippians.[32]

Setting Philippians 2:5–11 within the life of the community helps to explain Paul's request of the Philippians: "Let the same mind be in you that was in Christ Jesus" (v. 5 NRSV). They are to behave as Jesus did. They have a "narrative" of Jesus' obedient descent to death, even death on a cross. It led to his

31. Brendan J. Byrne, *Reckoning with Romans: A Contemporary Reading of Paul's Gospel*, Good News Studies 18 (Wilmington, DE: Michael Glazier, 1986), 224. See his excellent treatment of the Adam-Christ question on pp. 111–20.

32. For an earlier full discussion of this question, see Ralph P. Martin, *Carmen Christi: Philippians ii. 5–11 in Recent Interpretation and in the Setting of Early Christian Worship*, Society for New Testament Studies Monograph Series 4 (Cambridge: Cambridge University Press, 1967), 24–62. Although John Reumann (*Philippians*, Anchor Yale Bible 33B [New Haven: Yale University Press, 2008], 333–77) questions that Phil. 2:5–11 had its origins in a hymn, he also sees this rhetoric at play: "Paul approves the Philippians' composition by citing it, to speak afresh to issues in the house churches there" (374).

exaltation and establishment as Lord. They know of Jesus and praise him on account of his obedient response to God. But to have the same mind as Jesus Christ is another way of stating what the Gospels call "following Christ." The First Letter of John puts it well when the author asks his readers to put their lives where their words are: "He who *says* he abides in him ought to *walk* in the same way in which he walked" (1 John 2:6, emphasis added). The self-emptying of Jesus that lies at the heart of Philippians 2:5–11 should lie at the heart of all who claim to be his followers.

It appears that there was division among the Philippians. Just prior to his insertion of 2:5–11 into his letter, Paul wrote: "Do nothing from selfishness or conceit, but in humility count others better than yourselves. Let each of you look not only to his own interests, but also to the interests of others" (vv. 3–4). Once the Philippians encounter the inserted passage, they become aware that they are hearing familiar words, quoted back to them. Paul reminds them of their praise of Jesus Christ and asks them to praise Jesus not only with *their words* but with their selfless *lives*. The best form of praise is imitation. Their only model can be Jesus, and the hymn that they sing tells his story. Perhaps the story of Jesus' self-abasement was not found among the lives of the Philippians.

Philippians 2:5–11 explains *how* creation began anew in Jesus Christ. This famous passage unfolds in six stages.[33] The first stage describes Jesus' preparedness to accept humiliation by shedding his preexistent divine state (vv. 6–7a).[34] The translation of the hymn in the RSV says that he did not count his equality with God "a thing to be grasped." Scholars have debated for decades why a rough and almost violent Greek word, translated by "grasped" (*harpagmon*), could be used in a hymn dedicated to Jesus. Associated with its verbal form, its primary dictionary meaning is the action of making off "with someone's property by attacking or seizing. *Steal, carry off, drag away.*"[35] More than "grasp" is intended, as there is something violent about the expression. He did not rapaciously and selfishly grasp to himself the honor of being equal to God. The noun is well chosen, despite its offensive overtones, as it spoke eloquently to the selfishness of the readers and hearers of Paul's letter. There is a real possibility that the Philippians were grasping rapaciously for honors (vv. 3–5), and that tendency has not come to an end with the Philippians.

---

33. Following Byrne, "Letter to the Philippians," 794.

34. In the light of current scholarly discussion, see the convincing affirmation of the Pauline notion of Christ's preexistence and its theological importance in Brendan J. Byrne, "Christ's Pre-Existence in Pauline Soteriology," *Theological Studies* 58 (1997): 308–30. See also Reumann, *Philippians*, 366–69.

35. Frederick W. Danker, *A Greek-English Lexicon of the New Testament and Other Early Christian Literature*, 3rd ed. (Chicago: University of Chicago Press, 2000), 134, s.v. *harpazō*. Emphasis added.

What must be noticed is that the verb is negative! This is what Jesus *did not do*: "he *did not* count equality with God a thing to be grasped." Paul speaks directly to all who seek honors and glory in their achievements: Christ Jesus did exactly the opposite. He let go of the most wonderful of honors—his oneness with God. His status was divine and he let it go; the human condition is fragile and prone to sin, but perhaps this was not recognized by some at Philippi who sought human honor and glory. Once they achieved this, they "grasped onto it jealously."

This leads the hymn into the second stage of Christ's humiliation (vv. 7b–8). Jesus does not simply "let go," but he "empties himself" of all dignity, to take on the situation of a servant and slave. Another Greek word that has become central to subsequent Christian thought enters its vocabulary: *kenōsis* (the Greek verb *ekenōsen* is used in the original text).[36] This unconditional self-emptying leaves *nothing* of his being in the form of God, *nothing* of his equality with God. A *kenōsis* is a complete self-emptying. The Christ comes into the history of frail human beings as a frail human being: he became as we are. There can be no holding back on this, as Paul and the Philippians did not hold back in their use and acceptance of the word *kenōsis* to speak of Jesus' taking on the human condition with all its joys, pains, and limitations. Not only is he emptied of all honor (vv. 6–7a), but he takes on the condition of a *doulos*, a Greek word that means either a slave or a servant. Applied to Jesus it means both!

But the second description of Jesus' humiliation points out that to become human was not enough to effect the new creation. He lowered himself in human eyes to the lowest level possible; he accepted the cruelest and most humiliating death—death on a cross. Israel had already been taught by the Torah: "Cursed be every one who hangs on a tree" (Deut. 21:23). But we have lost the sense of what death on a cross meant to people living in the Roman era. The cross has been domesticated, reduced to a bauble that one hangs around one's neck or, as Augustine said, used as a decoration on the emperor's crown. It was the cruelest form of execution that the Romans could devise, generally preceded (as in the case of Jesus) with mockery and the infliction of less mortal insults and suffering. It was reserved only for the lowest of the low, for slaves, hardened criminals, and those who dared to challenge the authority of Rome.[37] When he gives his unconditional "yes" to God on the cross, Jesus Christ's *kenōsis* and subsequent humiliation are complete.

The hymn has a downward swing from Christ being equal to God to Christ as a crucified slave (Phil. 2:6–9). The unconditional obedience of Jesus has

---

36. See ibid., 539, s.v. *kenoō*.
37. On this, see Hengel, *Crucifixion in the Ancient World*.

touched the human story in a "once and for all" fashion, and this has its consequence. Jesus' unconditional "yes" to God is now met by an unconditional "yes" from God. The One who by origin could have claimed "lordship" in the highest degree (v. 6) emptied himself to the very opposite state, to the condition of a human "slave" and, ultimately, the death reserved for slaves. On the basis of this "slave/lord" polarity, God graciously bestowed on him the lordship of the universe, which he had refused to grasp for himself.

In verse 9 the Greek text marks a sharp change of direction. God enters the story of Jesus, a consequence of Jesus' unconditional acceptance of his will. This change of direction is signaled by the use of "therefore" (Greek: *dio kai*), carrying with it the idea of consequence: *because* of what Jesus did out of obedience to God and for all of our sakes, he is highly exalted by God.[38] God's exaltation of Jesus lies at the center of the hymn (v. 9). The theme of the hymn begins its upward swing with this turning point in the unfolding hymn: God has highly exalted him. The Christ returns to the place he "let go" so that we may have life and hope. The result of God's exaltation of his Son does not lead the Christ to a distant place where his journey from equality with God, through the humiliation of the cross, removes him from fragile humankind. Instead it has led to the possibility of a renewed relationship between God and the human condition because of Jesus Christ's unconditional and obedient gift of self—unto death. The text makes clear that believers will bend the knee and confess Jesus Christ as Lord because of what God has done for us in and through him. The crucified "slave" has been raised and exalted by God and is now Lord of the universe.

The first description of the homage that flows from God's action in the resurrection has a subtle but important nuance. "At the name of Jesus every knee should bend" (Phil. 2:10 NRSV). The name "Jesus" was the name of a man who lived among us. It was the name of that human being who had shed all his claims to honor and unconditionally embraced the human condition, even unto death on the cross. The name of this man, now exalted, must be recognized for what he has done. We are all in his debt, and thus every knee should bend. But the exaltation goes further in the sixth and final affirmation of the passage. Not only is the crucified and risen Jesus to be recognized and honored; Jesus Christ must be confessed as "Lord" (Greek: *Kyrios*), an expression used in the Greek Bible for the divinity (v. 11). All creation recognizes what

---

38. The RSV loses this nuance with its weak "therefore." See J. B. Lightfoot, *St. Paul's Epistle to the Philippians* (London: Macmillan, 1913), 113. Jean-François Collange describes the use of *dio kai* as indicating "the gracious sovereign act of God" (*The Epistle of Saint Paul to the Philippians*, trans. A. W. Heathcote [London: Epworth, 1979], 105). Byrne, "Letter to the Philippians," 795, renders the phrase as "wherefore God."

Jesus has done and what God has done in and through him. Every knee bends in recognition of the saving act of God that has taken place through Jesus' obedience unto death in his unconditional "yes" to God and the subsequent unconditional "yes" of God's acceptance of that obedience by means of the exaltation that takes place in resurrection. Through death and resurrection, Jesus Christ is established as Lord of all creation.

Every knee bends and every tongue confesses that the crucified and risen Jesus Christ is Lord (Phil. 2:10–11). Although the words do not appear in the hymn or in this context, the theme of the "new creation" is again shaping the Pauline argument. We no longer have to wait for the end of all time for the establishment of God's "right order." It has been made present among us in the new creation by means of the obedient death, resurrection, exaltation, and universal lordship of Jesus Christ. We confess that Jesus Christ is Lord; we recognize the glory of God . . . but only if we are prepared to accept Paul's initial invitation to walk as Jesus walked: "Have this mind among yourselves, which is yours in Christ Jesus" (v. 5). Believers are called to know Christ Jesus (see Phil. 3:8). The story of Jesus must be repeated in the story of all who claim to follow him. In this way Christian life will be caught up into the rhythm, scope, and ultimate victory of the divine plan.

Living in the In-Between Time: To Know Christ Jesus

Paul was sharply aware of his own fragility (see 2 Cor. 12:7–10; Phil. 3:12–16), and his constant pastoral care for struggling communities led him to accept, with some frustration, that Jesus' death, resurrection, and exaltation had *begun* something that was yet to be *finalized* (see Gal. 3:3; Phil. 3:3–11). James Dunn catches this well when he divides the heart of his study of the theology of Paul into two major sections: "the beginning of salvation" and "the process of salvation."[39] Paul's letters betray that communities had initially accepted his preaching of the gospel but were being severely tempted by other "gospels" (especially in Galatia, Corinth, and Philippi).[40] Jesus' death and resurrection

---

39. Dunn, *Theology of Paul*, 317–459 and 461–532, respectively.

40. Debates about the problems faced by Paul in these (and other) communities are never-ending. The Letter to the Romans was written to a community that he did not know. But it is clear that the gentile Galatian converts were being urged to accept fundamental Jewish practices (especially circumcision) as the sign of their conversion to Christ. The Corinthians are beset with a number of problems that arose from their charismatic enthusiasm (divisions, misuse of the body, sexual irregularities, divorce and remarriage, eating food offered to idols, poor eucharistic practice, use and abuse of the gifts of the spirit, the resurrection of Jesus and the Christian [esp. in 1 Corinthians], tensions between Paul and the community, and the attempts

had transformed once and for all the way God related to the world, but the human condition was too often trapped by the propensity to sin that resides in "the flesh" (see esp. Rom. 7:7–25), despite the promise of the blessings that flowed from life "in the spirit" (see esp. Rom. 8:1–39).[41] Written at different times to different people facing a variety of differing situations, Paul's letters nevertheless have a consistent approach in his exhortations to early Christians living in the time between God's gracious gift of grace through the death and resurrection of his Son and the victory of God in the final return of the Christ.

Paul introduces material into his letters that the people receiving and hearing them knew very well. These significant passages serve as a lesson in Paul's way of calling his fellow believers to return to "life in Christ." Paul had heard that there were serious problems with the community celebration of the Lord's Table in Corinth. Apparently the wealthy were using these festive meals to show their authority and wealth, gathering at sumptuous tables and making the eucharistic meal into a feast that left many of them inebriated. However, at that same meal, they disregarded the poorer members of the community. Paul's language suggests that they did not wait for the arrival of those who were not masters of their own time—for example, slaves and lowly servants. Thus little food was left when the latter did arrive. They were allowed only a marginal participation at the table. As he described the situation: "I hear that there are divisions among you. . . . For in eating, each one goes ahead with his own meal, and one is hungry and another is drunk. What! Do you not have houses to eat and drink in? Or do you despise the church of God and humiliate those who have nothing?" (1 Cor. 11:18, 21–22). His mind on this matter is quite clear: "When you meet together, it is not the Lord's supper that you eat" (v. 20).

To instruct the Corinthians on the true significance of the eucharistic meal, he reminds them of something they knew very well: the actions and words of Jesus on the night before he died (1 Cor. 11:23–25). These are *the words and deeds that they recall as they celebrate the Lord's Supper.* But their lives do

---

of some to denigrate his person and his gospel [esp. in 2 Corinthians]). As we have seen, there were disturbing internal divisions at Philippi (see Phil. 2:3–5) and also the danger of a return to Jewish practices (3:2–11). Although Paul affirms the Thessalonian community, there are concerns about how they are to live as they await the imminent return of Christ in glory and about the destiny of those believers who have died before that event (see 1 Thess. 4:13–5:11). Even Philemon is challenged to continue what he has begun: to accept back his former slave Onesimus, now a Christian, as his "beloved brother" in Christ (Philem. 8–20). On 2 Corinthians, see Jan Lambrecht, *Second Corinthians*, Sacra Pagina 8 (Collegeville, MN: Liturgical Press, 1999). See also the still-valuable C. Kingsley Barrett, *The Second Epistle to the Corinthians*, Black's New Testament Commentaries (Grand Rapids: Baker Academic, 1973). On Philemon, see Thurston and Ryan, *Philippians and Philemon*.

41. On the use of "flesh" in Paul, see Dunn, *Theology of Paul*, 62–72. On Paul's use of "the spirit," see pp. 413–41.

not match what Jesus did for them, despite the fact that Jesus told them: "Do this in remembrance of me" (vv. 24, 25). Jesus' loving self-gift for them on the cross, where his body was broken and his blood was shed, has been forgotten in real life. Nevertheless, in their neglect of one another, they continue to use gestures and words of Jesus that summon them to break their bodies and spill their blood in memory of him.[42] If they pray that way, they ought to live that way. For Paul, Eucharist was not a ritual to be celebrated by the privileged but the grammar of life for all who had accepted God's salvation through Jesus Christ's self-giving obedience, revealed in his death and resurrection. Indeed, the lives of a eucharistic people should proclaim the Lord's death until he comes again (v. 26).

The same rhetorical practice is found in the passage we examined above, Philippians 2:5–11. In the midst of their divisions and arrogant affirmation of their own dignity, Paul reminded the Philippians of *words* they prayed regularly: their praise of Jesus' self-emptying and his subsequent exaltation by God. If they are to participate in the new creation, they are to let go of their selfishness, so reflective of the arrogance left in human history by the sin of Adam, and are to become imitators of Jesus Christ. In this way their lives will proclaim what God has done for us in and through Jesus until he comes again (see 1 Cor. 11:26).

A number of rich and oft-repeated Pauline expressions that indicate an association between the believer and Jesus Christ are spread across the letters. Several of them run together in Paul's words to the Galatians: "I have been crucified with Christ; it is no longer I who live, but Christ who lives in me; and the life I now live in the flesh I live by faith in the Son of God, who loved me and gave himself for me" (Gal. 2:20). Equally evocative is the value Paul places on "knowing Christ Jesus" (Phil. 3:8). These claims presuppose not an "otherworldly" existence for the believer but rather a lifestyle determined by the obedient life and death of Jesus Christ that generated God's saving and liberating action in his resurrection and exaltation. There is an interpretative tradition that explains these associations (living in Christ, knowing Christ) with a mystical appropriation of Jesus Christ.[43] But this is hardly satisfactory. Other relational expressions abound across Paul's letters, including "in" Christ (Rom. 6:11; 8:1–2, 39; 9:1; 12:5; 14:14; 15:17; 16:3, 7, 9–10; 1 Cor. 1:2, 4–5, 30–31; 3:1; 4:10, 15, 17; 7:22, 39; 9:1–2; 11:11; 15:19, 22, 31; Gal. 3:26–28; 5:6; Phil. 2:19, 24, 29; 3:3, 14; 4:1–2, 4, 7, 10, 19–21), to "put on" Christ (Rom. 13:14;

42. See Francis J. Moloney, *A Body Broken for a Broken People: Eucharist in the New Testament*, rev. ed. (Peabody, MA: Hendrickson, 1997), 165–74.

43. For a recent and carefully articulated restatement of this position, see Dunn, *Theology of Paul*, 390–412.

Gal. 3:27), "with" Christ (Rom. 6:8; 2 Cor. 4:14; 13:4; Phil. 1:23; 1 Thess. 4:14; 5:10), and "through/by" Christ (Rom. 1:8; 2:16; 5:1, 11, 17, 21; 7:25; 15:30; 16:27; 1 Cor. 15:57; 2 Cor. 1:5; 3:4; 5:18; Gal. 1:1; Phil. 1:11; 1 Thess. 4:2; 5:9).[44]

Each one of these affirmations must receive an interpretation determined by its own context, but at least one of the many ways in which the Christian is associated with Jesus Christ is in imitating his lifestyle. Life "in Christ" is marked by a radical change in the freedom, joy, and love that mark *this life* for the Christian (see Rom. 6:11; 8:1–2, 31–39; 14:14; 15:17), in the way one speaks (see Rom. 9:1), in the community's sense of being one body of believing people, all the time maintaining their individuality "in Christ" (see Rom. 12:5; 16:3, 7, 9–10). Jerome Murphy-O'Connor has shown that these passages point to the possibility of a new way of living in which the loneliness and alienation generated by sin have been overcome by living "in Christ," "with Christ," "through Christ." The way the believer lives is evidence that she or he has "put on Christ."[45] The measure of this, possible in the "here and now" (the in-between time), is a lifestyle modeled on the life, death, and resurrection of Jesus Christ: "The life I now live in the flesh I live by faith in the Son of God, who loved me and gave himself for me" (Gal. 2:20).

I have used the RSV translation of a Greek expression in Galatians 2:20 as "faith in the Son of God." Not all follow this translation, as the Greek verb "to believe" (*pisteuein*) also means "to trust," and the noun "faith" (*pistis*) also means "faithfulness/trustworthiness." The Greek *pistis Christou*, found in some major Pauline texts (esp. Rom. 3:22, 26; Gal. 2:16, 20), is traditionally rendered in English as "faith in Christ." Paul instructs believers to place their faith and trust in the crucified and risen Christ if they wish to have life (see also Phil. 3:9). Some contemporary Pauline scholars interpret the Greek expression as a reference to "the trustworthiness of Christ" or "the faithfulness of Christ." This translation argues that Paul wishes to say that the faithfulness of the believer is to be modeled on the faithfulness of Jesus Christ.[46] If this is the case, then Paul is claiming that Jesus' faith-filled *obedience* transformed the human condition and is inspired by the Jesus we sketched in the previous chapter. Jesus of Nazareth was so overwhelmed by the urgency of God's

---

44. The texts listed are only a sample. For a comprehensive analysis of all the Pauline expressions indicating union with Christ, see Constantine R. Campbell, *Paul and Union with Christ: An Exegetical and Theological Study* (Grand Rapids: Zondervan, 2012).

45. Jerome Murphy-O'Connor, *Becoming Human Together: The Pastoral Anthropology of St. Paul*, Good News Studies 2 (Wilmington, DE: Michael Glazier, 1982), 141–98.

46. In Greek the genitive case (as found in *pistis Christou*) can be either "objective" or "subjective." The former means that Christ is the object of faith (i.e., "faith in Christ"), while the latter means that Paul is speaking of the faith that the subject himself, Jesus, has in responding to God (i.e., "the faithfulness of Christ"). See Horrell, *Introduction to the Study of Paul*, 78–80.

reigning presence that he never wavered in his obedience to the God of Israel, whom he called "Father," no matter what it cost him. So must it be for the believer. The debate is very alive among Pauline scholars, but the centrality and widespread presence of Paul's call for "faith in Christ" suggests that the Greek *pistis Christou* always summons the believer to faith in Christ (objective genitive) rather than a presentation of the faithfulness of Jesus Christ (subjective genitive). Christian life flows from faith in the crucified and risen Christ, and not only in an imitation of his faithful and obedient lifestyle. [47]

The initiative for God's saving action in Jesus Christ lies entirely with God, who showed his love for us while we were yet sinners (Rom. 5:8). Christ died for us, and we were thus reconciled with God by means of the death of his Son. In Romans 8:31–39, Paul is lyrical in his description of the immensity of the saving love that God has made available through Jesus Christ our Lord. Equally lyrical is his description in 1 Corinthians 12:31c–13:13 of the never-ending quality of Christian love, the greatest of all gifts. This must be understood within the context of Paul's presentation of God's action in rendering the sinner (see Rom. 1:18–3:20) righteous through the death and resurrection of Jesus (see Rom. 1:16–17; 3:21–26), drawing back into human history the revelation of God's glory through Jesus' death and resurrection.

But the traditional expectation of a final end of all time was still in place. Paul uses older traditions (e.g., 1 Thess. 4:13–18) and his own formulae (see 1 Cor. 15:51–57; Phil. 3:20–21) to refer to an event that is to come in the uncertain future.[48] Paul must devote attention to the instruction of his Christians on how they are to live in the in-between time. There is a strong sense of living between God's gift of the new creation in and through the death and resurrection of Jesus and the final coming of God and Jesus Christ at the end of time. Believers wait in hope and love through the in-between time (see Rom. 8:24–25). The whole creation waits with eager longing, as do those who already enjoy the firstfruits of the Spirit. They groan inwardly, "as we wait for adoption as sons, the redemption of our bodies" (Rom. 8:23). Already caught up in the anticipated presence of the glory of the end time, given by God through the obedient death and resurrection of his Son, yet aware that the end time is yet to come, the Christian lives the law of love.

The law does not save; that can be effected only by the death and resurrection of Jesus. Paul even speaks of "the curse of the law" (Gal. 3:13). Yet Paul preserves the values enshrined in the commandments of the law, reducing

---

47. For a defense of *pistis Christou* as "faith in Christ," see Dunn, *Theology of Paul*, 379–85. For a good survey of the unresolved discussion, also leaning toward the objective reading, see Campbell, *Paul and Union with Christ*, 252–53.

48. See Dunn, *Theology of Paul*, 294–315.

them all to love (see Rom. 13:8–10). He nevertheless regards life under the law as an enslavement (see esp. Gal. 3:1–5:1), all the while claiming that he upholds the law (Rom. 3:31). How he does this is debated. Does he understand the law as Scripture that must be upheld (see Rom. 4:1–25), or is the law being fulfilled through the Spirit in love (Rom. 8:1–4)?[49] "To be justified by God's saving grace, those under 'the law' needed to be transferred to the realm of the Spirit."[50] The law guides the believer in a response to God's love and grace. This is made particularly clear in Romans 13:8, where Paul teaches that "the one who loves another has fulfilled the law" (NRSV), spelled out with explicit references to the law in verses 9–11: "The commandments, 'You shall not commit adultery, You shall not kill, You shall not steal, You shall not covet,' and any other commandment, are summed up in this sentence, 'You shall love your neighbor as yourself.' Love does no wrong to a neighbor; therefore, love is the fulfilling of the law." In Galatians 5:13–14, the call to freedom resulting from God's saving action sets the believer free: "Through love be servants of one another. For the whole law is fulfilled in one word, 'You shall love your neighbor as yourself.'" The practice of love within the community is indicated in Galatians 6:2: "Bear one another's burdens, and so fulfil the law of Christ."[51]

Conclusion

Jesus Christ is the model of how the law of love must be lived in response to the loving initiative of God. It is unwise to claim that Paul tells very little of the story of Jesus because he has no interest in the life and ministry of Jesus. On the contrary, the way Jesus lived and loved, in unconditional obedience

49. Brendan Byrne, "The Problem of *Nomos* and the Relationship with Judaism in Romans," *Catholic Biblical Quarterly* 62 (2000): 294–309, esp. 296–303, is a lucid presentation of this debate, insisting that Paul, from "within" Judaism, looks back to the association of the Spirit with the promise to Abraham (Gal. 3:15–18). In the light of Jer. 31:33 and Ezek. 36:26–27, Paul teaches that the law must be upheld as Scripture, fulfilled through the Spirit in love, yet he is critical of the pursuit of righteousness through the law that led Israel to "stumble" over the rock of the cross (Rom. 9:32–33; 10:2–3). Only the cross can free the sinner from enslavement (see Byrne, "Problem of *Nomos*," 303–9).

50. Matera, *God's Saving Grace*, 102; see 84–124 for a fine treatment of the Christian experience of the saving grace of Christ.

51. For a careful examination of how believers should live in the in-between time, see Dunn, *Theology of Paul*, 626–69 (on internal and external motivating principles) and 670–712 (on ethics in practice). What has been shared above devotes little attention to Paul's pastoral concerns for the day-to-day life of his believers, how they are to relate to authority, to one another, especially to the fragile. He regularly deals with this as his letters conclude, as can be seen in Rom. 12:1–15:13. See Matera, *Romans*, 281–326.

to God, is the model for all Christians. Christian life, for Paul, is an *imitatio Christi* (imitation of Christ).[52] The believer has been "overtaken" by Christ (Phil. 3:12 AT), in whom God's own love has been bestowed (Rom. 5:8). Living in the in-between time, believers must "put on Christ" (see Gal. 3:27–28; Col. 3:10) and live no longer for themselves but for Christ who lives in them: "And the life I now live in the flesh I live by faith in the Son of God, who loved me and gave himself for me" (Gal. 2:20; see also 2 Cor. 5:14–15). For Paul, repeating the obedient love of Jesus Christ is the way of a believer in the in-between time. The believer has been claimed by love. "As a new man in Christ, the believer *is* love; that is the total meaning of his life and the reason why his obedience is the yielding of his whole life to God."[53]

Through the death and resurrection of an obedient Son, Jesus Christ, God's love and glory have entered the human story, dominated as it is by chaos and sin (see Rom. 1:18–3:20). Since the time of Moses, Israel has been protected but not saved by the law (see esp. Rom. 7:7–25; see also Rom. 5:14). The creative action of God, present at the beginning of all time and expected again at the end of all time, has now become available within the span of human history (see Gal. 6:15; 2 Cor. 5:17). To be "a new creation," one must be "in Christ." The death and resurrection of the obedient Jesus Christ have reversed the universal sin and death that flowed from the actions of the disobedient Adam. "If any one is in Christ, he is a new creation; the old has passed away, behold, the new has come" (2 Cor. 5:17). We already have privileged access to God's glory in a way that was expected only at the end of time.[54] Using theological language, we can say that for Paul, believers are an "eschatological people of God." The Christian Church, despite its perennial ambiguity, because of God's gracious presence made possible in and through the death and resurrection of Jesus, already has the possibility to anticipate and partially participate in God's final glory.

---

52. See Dunn, *Theology of Paul,* 193–95.

53. Victor Paul Furnish, *Theology and Ethics in Paul,* 2nd ed., New Testament Library (Louisville: Westminster John Knox, 2009), 200. Emphasis and gender-exclusive language in original.

54. One major Pauline concern that has not been dealt with in this all-too-brief summary is Paul's concern for Israel. Israel's rejection of Jesus makes Paul wonder about God's faithfulness to his chosen people. Paul wrestles with this problem in Rom. 9–11. See the fine treatments of Byrne, *Romans,* 281–361, and Matera, *Romans,* 211–80.

6

The Four Gospels

Stories of Jesus

For the first Christians, the memory of Jesus' life, teaching, death, and resurrection was still powerfully alive. As we have seen, even though there are good indications that he was aware of Jesus' story, Paul did not tell it. But with the passing of time and the gradual spread of the Christian communities beyond Israel into the larger Greco-Roman world, a question began to emerge: Who was this man Jesus of Nazareth, now confessed as the Christ, the Son of God, and even Lord? Paul had focused intensely upon the saving effects of his death and resurrection, his role as the Christ, the Son of God, and his exaltation as Lord through his death and resurrection. However, if his life story *ended* with crucifixion, burial, resurrection, and exaltation, questions necessarily emerged about the life he had lived and why his story had come to such a dramatic end.

Stories Emerge

The best way to answer these questions, some believed, was to tell his story. Even though Paul did not tell any "stories of Jesus," that does not mean that these stories were not being told; it only means that they were not written down. But even in Paul we hear the story of what Jesus had said and done "on the night before he died." Jesus, crucified and risen, continued to be with his followers, as they "remembered" him in a way that made him present (see 1 Cor. 11:25–26).

Early Gospel Stories

From the evidence of the Gospels, it appears that another "story" was told from the very beginnings of Christianity. The fact that Jesus was crucified as a criminal was a challenge to all who followed him as the Christ and the Son of God. The narratives of Jesus' final night with his disciples, his prayer in Gethsemane, his arrest, his trial before Jewish and Roman authorities, his crucifixion and death, the discovery of an empty tomb three days after the crucifixion, and a number of encounters between the disciples and the risen Jesus are very old. All the Gospels tell this particular "story" in the same sequence. This does not happen anywhere else in the Gospels. The sequence of events of Jesus' passion and resurrection stories never changes because they were told this way *from the beginning*.

The parables of Jesus rang in the ears, minds, and hearts of the original listeners. They were told over and over again as the generations passed. Yet no single "story of Jesus" existed in written form until the Gospel of Mark appeared in about 70 CE. But the Gospels, which adopted the literary form of an ancient biography, did not invent what they said about Jesus' life, teaching, and deeds.[1] What we call "oral tradition," the passing on of stories from the life and teaching of Jesus by word of mouth, would have played a major role in faith sharing among the first believers. The early Christians would have encouraged one another in times of difficulty by recalling Jesus' words and deeds, instructing their children, speaking about Jesus to their friends, and using these stories when they shared with those whom they wanted to draw into their community of faith. Indeed, the main purpose of all the Gospels (but not the only purpose) is the encouragement, education, and support of those who already believed but who were facing difficulties or asking questions. Those few who could read and write provided a "book" about the life, teaching, death, and resurrection of Jesus, but most early Christians, like their contemporaries, could not read or write. These Gospel

---

1. Scholars have long debated whether the Gospels were related to the Greco-Roman biographies that were being written at about the same time. Most are now convinced that they are, as the result of the work of Richard A. Burridge, *What Are the Gospels? A Comparison with Graeco-Roman Biography*, 2nd ed. (Grand Rapids: Eerdmans, 2004).

stories would have been heard as they were read, and even seen performed, by the vast majority.[2]

Many "gospels" existed that are not found in the New Testament, including some that you may have heard of: the *Gospel of Thomas*, the *Gospel of Philip*, the *Gospel of Peter*, the *Protoevangelium of James*, the *Gospel of Judas*, the *Gospel of Mary*, and the *Gospel of Mary Magdalene*.[3] As we have already seen, by the middle of the second century four Gospels were accepted and read in the Church as part of the Christian Scriptures: the Gospels of Mark (written about 70 CE), Matthew (written about 85 CE), Luke (written about 85 CE), and John (written about 100 CE). The names, associated with their traditional authors (Matthew, Mark, Luke, and John), appeared late in the second century. They were not attached to the original writing of the Gospels but were added to the manuscripts of each respective Gospel *to ensure that the uniqueness of each one was preserved*.[4] Although we cannot be sure of the identity of the original authors or of their names, it is less distracting to retain these traditional names. They have served well for almost two thousand years and will continue to do so, no matter who originally wrote each Gospel.[5]

The Synoptic Gospels

Matthew, Mark, and Luke are called the "Synoptic Gospels."[6] When you place these three Gospels side by side, you can see that they compare quite

2. On orality and performance, see Kelly R. Iverson, "Orality and the Gospels: A Survey of Recent Research," *Currents in Biblical Research* 8 (2009): 71–106; Botha, *Orality and Literacy*.

3. These works are available and accessible in English in the first volume of Wilhelm Schneemelcher, *New Testament Apocrypha*, rev. ed., trans. R. McL. Wilson, 2 vols. (Louisville: Westminster John Knox, 1991).

4. Martin Hengel, "The Titles of the Gospels and the Gospel of Mark," in *Studies in the Gospel of Mark* (Philadelphia: Fortress, 1985), 64–84 (esp. 72–77), has shown the importance of the addition of authorial names to the Gospels so that readers and hearers would be aware of *which* Gospel was being used. Hengel would date that process earlier than most, claiming that it was in place by the end of the first century CE.

5. Interestingly, modern and contemporary Christians concern themselves about the exact identity of each author. However, not one of the authors has allowed his or her name to appear in the Gospel. Only in the Gospel of John are we told that the author was "the disciple whom Jesus loved," often called "the Beloved Disciple" (John 21:20, 24). But we are not provided with the identity of the Beloved Disciple.

6. See also Brown, *Introduction to the New Testament*, 99–125; Francis J. Moloney, *The Living Voice of the Gospel: The Gospels Today* (Peabody, MA: Hendrickson, 2006), 13–42; Powell, *Introducing the New Testament*, 81–101; Spivey, Smith, and Black, *Anatomy of the New Testament*, 49–61. Charles H. Dodd, in a wonderful series of lectures for the BBC in 1949, described the point of view in each Gospel in a way that continues to capture the Christian imagination. See Charles H. Dodd, *About the Gospels* (Cambridge: Cambridge University Press, 1952).

closely. This can be seen with one look of the eye. This is what is meant by the Greek word *synopsis* behind "synoptic": "with the eye." Only forty of Mark's 675 verses are not found in Matthew. Luke is different, as he is a more creative writer. However, when Matthew and Luke agree in their ordering of events from the life of Jesus, they always follow Mark. The Synoptic Gospels all begin with Jesus' ministry in Galilee and have him eventually journey to Jerusalem. After a brief but intense ministry in Jerusalem, he is eventually arrested, tried, and killed. It is in Jerusalem that he dies and is raised. However, the reader must be wary. There are many places where Matthew, Mark, and Luke tell the same story, in the same order as one another, and almost with the same words, but each of the Synoptic Gospels has a unique point of view.

If Mark's Gospel was written first, Matthew and Luke most likely had Mark in front of them. But they did not follow Mark slavishly. Indeed, there are many places where Matthew and Luke share material from Jesus (especially his teaching) that is not found in Mark or John. They appear to have had another common "source," independent of Mark. As noted above in chapter 3, this material has come to be known as "Q," the first letter of the German word for "source" (*Quelle*). In addition to this special material from a common source, both Matthew and Luke had their own memories of Jesus, their own stories of Jesus told in their communities. Thus there are stories and teachings of Jesus found only in Matthew and Luke, and there are stories and teachings of Jesus found *only* in Matthew and *only* in Luke.

What must never be forgotten, of course, is that for all the material that was included in the written books, the communities and the authors looked back to their memories of Jesus of Nazareth. Now they understood more.

> The first Christians firmly believed that they had a story to tell which was worth telling just because it was not only about what happened under Pontius Pilate, but also about what God had done for mankind. . . . Any other way of telling it would have seemed to them false to the facts as they had experienced them. If we give them another meaning, we do so on our own responsibility, and not on the evidence. There is a challenge in the Gospels, and sooner or later we are bound to face it.[7]

In the light of the resurrection and the life of the Spirit, they were able to confidently claim that he was the Christ and the Son of God (see, e.g., Mark 1:1; Matt. 16:13–16; Luke 1:26–38; John 20:30–31). Jesus never used these

7. Dodd, *About the Gospels*, 20.

terms to speak of himself. But now they were beginning to understand the full significance of what God did for humankind in and through Jesus.

The Gospel of John

The Gospel of John is very different from the Synoptic Gospels. In the Fourth Gospel, Jesus is regularly in Jerusalem, especially for the celebrations of the great feasts (Pentecost [John 2], Sabbath [chap. 5], Tabernacles [7:1–10:21], and Dedication [10:22–42]). Written at the end of the first Christian century, after more time for reflection, for life in the Spirit, and for prayer, the understanding of Jesus as the Christ and the Son of God had developed even further. Though some of the stories from the Synoptic Gospels reappear (e.g., the multiplication of the loaves and fishes, the confession of Peter, the passion story), the Jesus of the Gospel of John is different. He is presented as the preexistent Word (Greek: *Logos*) who became flesh, dwelt among us, and made God known (John 1:1–18). He knows all things and leads the believer—both the disciples in the story and the readers of the story—into an ever-greater commitment of faith, so that everyone might believe more deeply that Jesus is the Christ, the Son of God, and might have life because of this belief (see 20:30–31). Guided by the Paraclete, who was given by Jesus as his ongoing presence among his followers (14:15–17, 25–26; 15:26–27; 16:7–11, 12–15), John writes to Christians who did not know Jesus but who are specially blessed: "Blessed are those who have not seen and yet believe" (20:29).

It could be claimed that all four Gospels were written for those who have not seen, yet believe. In a famous study of the Fourth Gospel, J. Louis Martyn argued that this Gospel reflects a "two level drama."[8] By this he meant that the people *reading* and *hearing* the Gospel were living a particular Christian experience. That was their "level." In order to speak to that experience the author of the Gospel looked back creatively to the life, teaching, death, and resurrection of Jesus. This was another "level." The story of Jesus was told in a way that looked back to the "level" of the life and experience of Jesus and his first disciples, to address the "level" of those reading and hearing this story. What Louis Martyn said of John's Gospel could be said of all the Gospels. We continue to tell the story of Jesus found in the Gospels because, after two millennia of Christian history, they still address and challenge

---

8. J. Louis Martyn, *History and Theology in the Fourth Gospel*, rev. ed. (Nashville: Abingdon, 1979), 129–51.

us in our "level" of faith and experience, *reading the New Testament in the Church*.

The Gospel of Mark

The Shape of Mark's Gospel

A careful reading of this Gospel,[9] even for the beginner, reveals that Mark has designed his "storytelling" in two halves: Mark 1:1–8:30 and 8:31–16:8.[10] An outline of the literary structure of the Gospel of Mark takes the following shape:

1:1–13	Prologue: informing the reader/listener who Jesus is and what he will do
1:14–8:30	The mystery of Jesus as the Christ (see 8:29)
8:31–15:47	The mystery of Jesus, Son of Man and Son of God (see 14:62; 15:29–32, 39)
16:1–8	Epilogue: resurrection and discipleship

After being told in 1:1–13 who Jesus is and what he will do, through various episodes in the first half of the Gospel that involve an interaction between Jesus and characters *who have not read the prologue*, a single question emerges: "Who is Jesus?" It is asked by different people throughout (see 1:27, 37; 2:7, 16, 18; 3:6, 11–12, 20–22; 4:41; 5:16–17). The questioning ceases after Jesus

9. For reliable single-volume commentaries on the Gospel of Mark, see Brendan Byrne, *A Costly Freedom: A Theological Reading of Mark's Gospel* (Collegeville, MN: Liturgical Press, 2008); R. Alan Culpepper, *Mark*, Smyth & Helwys Bible Commentary (Macon, GA: Smyth & Helwys, 2007); Sharon Dowd, *Reading Mark: A Literary and Theological Commentary on the Second Gospel*, Reading the New Testament (Macon, GA: Smyth & Helwys, 2000); Morna D. Hooker, *The Gospel according to St. Mark*, Black's New Testament Commentaries (Grand Rapids: Baker Academic, 1991); John R. Donahue and Daniel J. Harrington, *The Gospel of Mark*, Sacra Pagina 2 (Collegeville, MN: Liturgical Press, 2003); and Moloney, *Gospel of Mark*. For readers of this book, the most helpful might be Byrne, Dowd, Hooker, or Moloney. See also Brown, *Introduction to the New Testament*, 126–70; Moloney, *Living Voice*, 44–70; Powell, *Introducing the New Testament*, 125–45; Spivey, Smith, and Black, *Anatomy of the New Testament*, 62–88.

10. In the literary structure that follows, Mark 1:1–13 is described as a prologue to the whole Gospel. Before Jesus begins his ministry in 1:14–15, the author has informed the reader (speaking himself, using words of God from the Prophets, and using the witness of John the Baptist and the events surrounding Jesus' baptism) that Jesus is the Christ, the Son of God (vv. 1, 11), the Lord (v. 3), the Stronger One (v. 7), one who will baptize with the Holy Spirit (v. 8). Full of the Spirit, he is driven into the desert to reverse the tragedy of the Adam and Eve story (vv. 12–13). Those who have read or heard this prologue know much more about Jesus than the characters populating the story. For more detail, see Moloney, *Gospel of Mark*, 27–41.

asks his disciples at Caesarea Philippi, "Who do people say that I am?" (8:27 NRSV). Peter responds: "You are the Messiah" (8:29 NRSV). This sounds fine to us—but not to Jesus. Jesus warns his disciples severely not to talk about him in this way (8:30).

The second half of the Gospel opens with an immediate explanation of who Jesus is: the Son of Man who must go up to Jerusalem to suffer and to die and to be raised on the third day (8:31). Jesus is the Messiah, but he will be a suffering Son of Man. The second half of the Gospel explains this further. On three occasions he is presented to his disciples as the suffering and raised Son of Man (8:31; 9:31; 10:32–34). As a result of his suffering he will take his place at the right hand of God and come at the end of time as the universal judge (8:38; 13:24–27; 14:61–62). During his passion, as they mock him, his opponents ask that he come down from his cross that they might believe (15:29–32). They have not understood the nature of Jesus' messiahship. It is as the crucified and risen Son of Man that he is both Messiah and Son of God (see 1:1; 14:61–62). To come down from the cross would be a denial of Jesus as Son of God and Messiah (see 15:21–32). It is the saving effect of God's action in Jesus' suffering, death, and resurrection that makes sense of his story.

As Jesus dies his agonizing death on the cross, a gentile, the Roman centurion, confesses: "Truly, this man was the Son of God" (15:39). Three times across the Gospel, acting almost as signposts in the story, Jesus has been proclaimed "Son of God": at the beginning by the voice from heaven (1:11); in the middle, again by a voice from heaven (9:7); and finally on the cross in his moment of death (15:39). This way of obedience unto death so that God might enter his story and raise him from death (see 16:6) must be the measure of the life of all who claim to be his followers. Each of the passion predictions in the second half of the Gospel (8:31; 9:31; 10:32–34) is directed to his disciples, to instruct them in what they must do if they are to "follow" him (see 1:16–20). But they are never able to accept this challenge. They succeed reasonably well in the first half of the Gospel (see 6:6b–13), but in the second half their obtuseness becomes clear. They will not, or cannot, understand what it means to follow the crucified Messiah and Son of God.

The presentation of Jesus in the Gospel of Mark is strongly focused on a suffering Jesus who dies asking God why he has forsaken him (15:34). This portrait challenges all who follow the Son of God. He responds to his Father through his unconditional self-gift, whatever it may cost him (see 14:36). His followers are asked to do the same (see 8:34–38). Mark faced a problem stated by Paul some twenty years before the Gospel appeared: "For Jews demand signs and Greeks seek wisdom, but we preach Christ crucified, a stumbling block to Jews and folly to Gentiles, but to those who are called, both Jews and

Greeks, Christ the power of God and the wisdom of God. For the foolishness
of God is wiser than men, and the weakness of God is stronger than men"
(1 Cor. 1:22–25). This is dramatically shown in Mark's brief resurrection
story (Mark 16:1–8), where the action of God raises Jesus from death and
promises the reconstitution of a failed discipleship (see vv. 6–7), despite the
failure of the women (v. 8).[11]

Mark 8:22–9:7: The Centerpiece of Mark's Gospel

The centerpiece of the Gospel of Mark is 8:22–9:7, in which the story of
Jesus tells the central message of this Gospel.[12] On Jesus' arrival at Bethsaida,
a blind man is led to him. Jesus leads the blind man out of the village, makes
spittle and puts it on his eyes, and asks him whether he can see. The man receives imperfect sight: men look like walking trees, he says (8:24). He has only
partially recovered his vision. In a second moment, Jesus lays his hands upon
the man, and total sight is restored. He sees clearly (8:25). The blind man has
gone from blindness (v. 22) to partial sight (v. 24) to a fullness of sight (v. 25).
This journey of sight, from no faith to the fullness of faith, is matched among
the disciples in the episode that follows: the confession of Peter at Caesarea
Philippi (vv. 27–29).

The disciples journey with Jesus to Caesarea Philippi, and on the way, Jesus
asks them: "Who do men say that I am?" (Mark 8:27). They respond that most
people think he is one of the expected messianic precursor figures: John the
Baptist, Elijah, or one of the prophets. To understand Jesus as yet another precursor is *blindness*. He turns to his followers and asks: "But who do you say that
I am?" and Peter confesses: "You are the Christ" (v. 29). This passage has rightly
been regarded as a central moment in the Gospel of Mark. For the first time in
the story, a character in the action confesses that Jesus is the Christ (see 1:1).
In the name of the disciples, Peter proclaims Jesus as the Christ. Surprisingly,
the confession is followed by a command from Jesus, insisting that the disciples
say nothing about this to anyone (8:30). Peter may only manifest *partial sight*.

Jesus immediately begins to teach them that the Son of Man must go to
Jerusalem, suffer, and be rejected and slain by the elders, the chief priests, and

11. In our discussion above of this Gospel's literary structure, Mark 1:1–13 was described as
a prologue addressed to the reader. It is matched by 16:1–8, an epilogue, addressed to disciples
of all ages. See Moloney, *Gospel of Mark*, 339–54. The original Gospel of Mark ended at 16:8.
Later scribes added a number of further endings, some of which are found in our Bibles. See
ibid., 355–62.

12. For a more detailed study of this passage, see Moloney, *Gospel of Mark*, 171–82, and
the references there.

the scribes (Mark 8:31). Jesus' own words reveal his true identity; to accept this Messiah is *fullness of sight*. The disciples' false messianic hope is already made clear in Peter's response to Jesus' self-identification as a suffering, dying, and rising Son of Man. He refuses to accept that Jesus should face such a destiny, but Jesus tells him to take his correct place where all disciples should be: behind him, following him down *his* way.

The discourse that follows (8:34–9:1) enlarges upon what has happened in Jesus' command to Peter to take up his correct place as a disciple following Jesus. It is addressed to all his disciples and to the crowd (v. 34). If they wish to be followers of Jesus they must take up their cross and follow him. They must be prepared to tread the same path he trod and in this way eventually come to the glory of the resurrection, also with Jesus (see v. 38; 9:1). Is it possible that the Christ must suffer and die? What is more incredible is that he asks all who wish to be his disciples to follow him down this same path, if they also hope to join him in his glory. Who is this man who has called them into this way of suffering and death? Some of them will see, as in his resurrection they will "see that the kingdom of God has come with power" (9:1).

But for the moment an answer is found in the Markan account of the transfiguration that follows (9:2–7). Jesus, in the company of two figures who had ascended to heaven, is a heavenly figure. The voice from heaven explains his heavenly appearance: "This is my beloved Son; listen to him" (v. 7). What Mark has proclaimed through the narrative made up of the series of events found side by side in Mark 8:22–9:7 can only make sense in the light of the transfiguration. It is absurd to ask followers to commit themselves to death in the light of a promise that such commitment is life-giving (8:35). It can only make sense because of the authoritative words of God, the voice that comes from heaven. The readers must pay attention to the story they are hearing: "This is my beloved Son; listen to him" (9:7). Mark instructs his audience that Jesus, the one who has called them to follow him into a life of self-gift, suffering, and death (8:34–9:1), is the Son of God. This alone is sufficient reason for all readers to "listen to him" (9:7).

The Gospel of Matthew

Matthew's Gospel contains three-quarters of the Gospel of Mark, and much of the story line of the life of Jesus in Mark is found again in Matthew.[13] As

13. There are 675 verses in the Gospel of Mark. Only forty of them are missing from Matthew's Gospel. For reliable single-volume commentaries on the Gospel of Matthew, see

in Mark, and in much the same way as Mark, Jesus is the Christ, the Son of God, and the Son of Man (see esp. Matt. 16:13–16). However, Matthew, written for a Jewish-Christian community some fifteen to twenty years later than Mark, develops further important teachings about Jesus and in so doing both *rewrites* sections of Mark's Gospel and *adds* further teaching and episodes that are not found in Mark. Matthew argues that Jesus does not abolish the old law; rather, Jesus perfects the law, both in what he does and in who he is.

Matthew has made two major additions to Mark. In the first place, Matthew reports the birth and infancy of Jesus (chaps. 1–2). For Matthew, the story of Jesus' beginnings builds a bridge between God's former covenant with his chosen people, Israel, and the life of Jesus. Jesus is the fulfillment of the promises of old. Almost every scene in the Matthean infancy narrative indicates that the events of Jesus' birth and infancy are "to fulfil what the Lord had spoken by the prophet" (1:22–23; see also 2:5–6, 15, 17–18, 23). The same theme also flows into the ministry of Jesus (see 3:3; 4:6–7, 14–16). Matthew taught that Jesus was the perfection of the promises made to Israel.

The Gospel of Matthew begins in the Old Testament, through the genealogy of Jesus (1:1–17), where God's providential handling of the history of a chosen people is already obvious. The promises to Israel are fulfilled in the events of the birth and the public life of Jesus. He lives the law perfectly, and he exhorts his followers to do the same. This exhortation is found in the second major feature of Matthew: five lengthy discourses during which Jesus instructs how a "new people of God" founded on a new and perfect Moses (see 5:1–2) should live. The five discourses match the five books of the Law: 5:1–7:29 (the Sermon on the Mount), 10:1–11:1 (a discourse on the future mission of the community), 13:1–53 (teaching the new people of God by parable), 18:1–35 (a discourse on the future life and order of the new people of God), and 24:1–25:46 (a discourse on the end of time and the final judgment).

Brendan Byrne, *Lifting the Burden: Reading Matthew's Gospel in the Church Today* (Collegeville, MN: Liturgical Press, 2004); David E. Garland, *Reading Matthew: A Literary and Theological Commentary* (Macon, GA: Smyth & Helwys, 2001); Craig S. Keener, *A Commentary on the Gospel of Matthew* (Grand Rapids: Eerdmans, 1998); John Nolland, *The Gospel of Matthew*, New International Greek Testament Commentary (Grand Rapids: Eerdmans, 2005); Donald Senior, *Matthew*, Abingdon New Testament Commentaries (Nashville: Abingdon, 1998); John P. Meier, *Matthew*, New Testament Message 3 (Wilmington, DE: Michael Glazier, 1980). For readers of this book, the most helpful might be those of Byrne, Meier, or Senior. See also Brown, *Introduction to the New Testament*, 171–224; Moloney, *Living Voice*, 93–126; Powell, *Introducing the New Testament*, 103–23; Spivey, Smith, and Black, *Anatomy of the New Testament*, 89–119.

The Shape of Matthew's Gospel

The argument of Matthew's Gospel is consequently more complex than the simple, twofold division of Mark. But Mark's basic story line is evident. Matthew retells it in the following fashion:

1:1–4:16	Prologue: informing the reader/listener who Jesus is and what he will do as Messiah, Son of Abraham, and Son of David
4:17–11:1	The Messiah's ministry of preaching, teaching, and healing in Israel
11:2–16:12	The crisis in the Messiah's ministry
16:13–20:34	The Messiah's journey to Jerusalem
21:1–28:15	The Messiah's death and resurrection
28:16–20	The Messiah's commissioning of his disciples

During his ministry, Jesus insisted that he has come to change not an iota or a dot from the Law and the Prophets (Matt. 5:17–18). He and his disciples were sent only to "the lost sheep of the house of Israel" (see 10:5–6; 15:24) in order to live the Law and the Prophets perfectly. But at the end of the Gospel a different message is heard. In Jesus' appearance after his death and resurrection his followers are instructed to reach beyond the perfect living of God's design for Israel and to go boldly into a gentile mission—to the ends of the earth (28:16–20).

Jesus is more than simply the perfection of all that was promised in and through Moses. The members of Matthew's church are sent out by a new Lord, Jesus, to whom all authority in heaven and on earth has been given. Caught up in the gentile mission, they are to teach what Jesus taught, and he will be with them until the end of all time (see 28:16–20). Jesus fulfills the hopes of Israel as the Son of David, and he reaches out to all nations as the Son of Abraham (see 1:1). From his vantage point, Matthew's Jesus looks back to the past and into the future, and the person who tells the story describes himself as a scribe "who brings out of his treasure what is new and what is old" (13:52).

In addition to insisting upon Jesus' perfection of the law and the promises made to Israel, especially in and through the events of his death and resurrection (see especially 27:51–54; 28:1–4), Matthew shows particular concern for the community of believers whom only he calls "the church" (Greek: *ekklēsia*; see 16:18; 18:17). The death and resurrection of Jesus may have been a turning point in the history of God's relationship with his chosen people, but Jesus makes it clear that the end time is yet to come (see 24:1–44). He will be "with" this community as the Emmanuel until the end of time (1:23; 28:20). More than any other Gospel writer, Matthew insists upon the figure of Peter (see 4:18; 14:28–31; 16:22–23; 17:1–6, 24–27; 18:21–22; 26:34–35, 40, 75) and the importance of Petrine leadership (see especially 16:13–18) and instructs the members of this community on their behavior, their relationships, and their mission (see 10:1–11:1; 18:1–35). In a long passage during which Jesus speaks harshly of the Pharisees (23:1–36), he is also speaking to his disciples, who run the danger of falling back into the secure ways of their past, creating a ghetto Christianity.

Matthew 28:16–20: The Universal Mission of the Disciples

After the Easter events (see Matt. 28:1–15), the disciples return to Galilee, to the mountain indicated by Jesus (v. 16).[14] Events on a mountain recall Sinai (see Exod. 19; Matt. 5:1; 17:1). The reaction of the disciples to the sight of Jesus is ambiguous. Some worship him, yet Matthew still reports: "but some doubted" (Matt. 28:17). They believe, yet they falter in their belief.

The risen Jesus claims that all authority on heaven and earth has been given to him (v. 18). Jesus has taken over the authority and dignity that traditional Israel allowed only to YHWH.[15] On a mountain with his hesitant disciples, Jesus claims to have been given all the authority that, according to traditional Judaism, belonged to YHWH alone. This is a bold claim. It would not have been well received by the Jews of the 80s of the first century. After the destruction of the temple-city Jerusalem and of Israel as a political entity in 70 CE, Judaism had to struggle through a period of religious reconstruction. The Jews no longer had a capital city with its temple; they no longer had a land. Judaism gradually established its identity after the disastrous effects of the Jewish War of 70 CE. A universal (although still varied) approach to YHWH, the unique and traditional God of Israel, was developed from the earlier Pharisaic form of prewar Judaism. Over against the synagogue's attempts to reestablish YHWH and his law at the center of postwar Judaism, this Gospel presents Jesus as having been given the authority and privilege allowed only to YHWH.

14. For a more detailed study of this passage, see Moloney, *Resurrection of the Messiah*, 49–58, and the references there.

15. The use of this expression (YHWH) is a respectful written abbreviation for the name of Israel's God. It comes from the Hebrew word used in the Old Testament, and it is never pronounced by a Jewish reader. Similar respect for the name of God should be practiced by all readers of the Bible.

Flowing from the uniqueness and universality of his authority, the Matthean Jesus then breaks through three further elements basic to post–70 CE Jewish belief and practice, promising to be with them always, to the "end of the age" (see also 1:23).

1. He commands his disciples to "Go therefore and make disciples of all nations" (Matt. 28:19a). This is in direct opposition to the belief in Israel's exclusive place among the nations of the world as God's chosen people. Although there had been openness to the idea of a universal salvation in the Prophets (see, e.g., Isa. 2:1–4), it had always meant a movement from the gentile world toward Zion. Here this is reversed: the new people of God, founded by Jesus of Nazareth, are to "go out" to make disciples of all nations.
2. The disciples are further instructed to "baptize" in the name of the Father and of the Son and of the Holy Spirit (Matt. 28:19b), thus introducing a new initiation rite for the new people of God, setting out on its mission. It is to replace the centrally important Jewish rite of circumcision. The Christian missionary is told to replace the Jewish rite of initiation with baptism.
3. As if what had been commanded so far was not enough, the final command demolishes the very basis of traditional Jewish faith, built upon the teaching and the learning of the Torah. Jesus uses words commonly found in passages on the importance of the Torah—"to teach," "to observe," "commandments" (see, e.g., Deut. 5–6, esp. 6:1, where all these terms appear)—to indicate a new teaching: "teaching them to observe all that I have commanded you" (Matt. 28:20a). The command to teach and observe looks no longer to the Torah but to the commandments of Jesus. As the Gospel had made clear (see 5:17–18), the law of Moses has been perfected by the life, teaching, death, and resurrection of Jesus.
4. Jesus' final words are not words of departure but words assuring that he will always be with his disciples (Matt. 28:20b). The abiding presence of Jesus will never leave his community of disciples. God has established and will sustain a holy people in and through the death and resurrection of Jesus.

Earlier in the Gospel Jesus taught that heaven and earth would have to pass away before the Law and the Prophets could be perfected (5:17–18). This has happened in Jesus' death (see 27:45, 51–53) and resurrection (28:2–3). The end of Matthew's Gospel shows that Jesus' mission and the mission of the disciples can no longer be limited to "the lost sheep of Israel." Jesus' death and resurrection mark a turning point in God's relationship with humankind. But we still face a long history between that turning point in God's relationship with humankind and the end of all time. In this in-between time we are sent out on a journey into a universal mission, confident in the abiding presence of Jesus, but always remembering where we came from, bringing out of our treasures "what is new and what is old" (13:52).

The Gospel of Luke

Although Luke's Gospel is one of the Synoptic Gospels (along with Mark and Matthew), Luke is a very creative storyteller.[16] Only Luke portrays the image of Mary, the Mother of Jesus, in the fashion that many Christians have come to love and accept. Many narratives and parables are found *only in Luke*: the restoration of the only son to a widow at Nain (Luke 7:11–17); the shock generated by Jesus' attention to and forgiveness of a sinful woman who enters the house of a Pharisee to perform an erotic ritual (7:36–50); the scandal of the women who journey with this itinerant preacher (8:1–3); the Good Samaritan (10:25–37); Martha and Mary (10:38–42); the parable of the great banquet (14:15–24); the parable of the lost sheep (15:3–7); the parable of the lost coin (15:8–10); the parable of the father with two lost sons (15:11–32); the parable of the cunning steward (16:1–9); the rich man and Lazarus (16:19–31); the one cured leper, a Samaritan, who returns to thank Jesus (17:11–19); the parable of the Pharisee and the tax collector (18:9–14); Jesus and Zacchaeus (19:1–10); and Jesus' weeping over Jerusalem (19:41–44).

Jesus' final words of despair in Mark and Matthew ("My God, my God, why have you forsaken me?" [Mark 15:34; Matt. 27:46 NRSV]) in Luke become: "Father, forgive them; for they know not what they do" (23:34); "Truly, I say to you, today you will be with me in Paradise" (v. 43); "Father, into your hands I commend my spirit" (23:46 NRSV). The Roman centurion does not say, "Truly this man was the Son of God" (Mark 15:39; see also Matt. 27:54), but he praises God, exclaiming, "Certainly this man was innocent" (Luke 23:47). The resurrection is highlighted by the story of the journey to Emmaus (24:13–35) and Jesus' commission as Risen Lord: "Thus it is written,

16. For reliable single-volume commentaries on the Gospel of Luke, see Brendan Byrne, *The Hospitality of God: A Reading of Luke's Gospel* (Collegeville, MN: Liturgical Press, 2000); Luke T. Johnson, *The Gospel of Luke*, Sacra Pagina 3 (Collegeville, MN: Liturgical Press, 1991); Robert C. Tannehill, *Luke*, Abingdon New Testament Commentaries (Nashville: Abingdon, 1996); John T. Carroll, *Luke: A Commentary*, New Testament Library (Louisville: Westminster John Knox, 2012). For readers of this book, the most useful might be those of Byrne, Tannehill, or Carroll. See also Brown, *Introduction to the New Testament*, 225–78; Moloney, *Living Voice*, 165–201; Powell, *Introducing the New Testament*, 147–67; Spivey, Smith, and Black, *Anatomy of the New Testament*, 121–53.

that the Christ should suffer and on the third day rise from the dead, and that repentance and forgiveness should be preached in his name to all the nations, beginning from Jerusalem. You are witnesses of these things. And behold, I send the promise of my Father upon you; but stay in the city, until you are clothed with power from on high" (24:46–49).

The Shape of Luke's Story

Despite Luke's creativity, the story still recalls the simple design of Mark's Gospel.

1:1–4	Dedication to Theophilus
1:5–4:13	Prologue: informing the reader/listener who Jesus is and what he will do as Messiah and Son of God.
4:14–9:50	Jesus' ministry in Galilee
9:51–19:44	The journey of Jesus and his disciples to Jerusalem[17]
19:45–21:38	Jesus in Jerusalem
22:1–24:53	Jesus' passion, death, resurrection, and ascension

Although a physical journey is reported in 9:51–19:44, the theme of "journey" appears important to Luke's overall message. In Luke's ongoing story (the Acts of the Apostles) the apostles do as they were commanded: "You shall receive power when the Holy Spirit has come upon you; and you shall be my witnesses in Jerusalem and in all Judea and Samaria and to the end of the earth" (Acts 1:8). The story that follows tells of the gift of the Holy Spirit (2:1–4), the community in Jerusalem (2:5–8:1), the mission into Judea and Samaria (8:2–13:12), and, by means of Paul's journeys, a journey to the ends of the earth. As the second volume of Luke's work comes to a close, indeed, in its very last line, Paul is in Rome "preaching the kingdom of God and teaching about the Lord Jesus Christ quite openly and unhindered" (28:31). Luke tells the story of the birth, life and teaching, death, resurrection, and ascension of Jesus, followed by the journey of the earliest Church to the ends of the earth. It could be said that contemporary readers of the Gospel of Luke and the Acts of the Apostles are part of an as-yet-unfinished story that will be told until the end of time.

Luke continues the tradition initiated by Mark and continued by Matthew. Jesus is the Christ, the Son of God, and the suffering and risen Son of Man who will come as judge. However, this overview of the elements in Luke's

---

17. This section is very different from its counterpart in the other Gospels, as Luke inserts a large amount of Jesus' teaching while on a long journey to Jerusalem.

Gospel that are *unique to Luke* shows that Luke wants to teach something further about Jesus. In the first place he is the Lord of all history. Exercising this lordship enables Jesus to demonstrate particular attention to the marginalized in society: women, sinners, lepers, Samaritans, the poor, and other such groups. Luke's Gospel is sometimes regarded as the Gospel of compassion. As we have already seen in our reading of Jesus' parable of the father with two sons (Luke 15:11–32), this title is well earned.[18]

But there is more to Luke. In Jesus' instruction of the disciples, especially during the journey to Jerusalem, both before (9:51–14:35) and after (16:1–19:44) the parables of compassion (15:1–32), he relentlessly spells out the cost of discipleship. He demands ceaseless prayer (11:1–13); unconditional commitment; repentance; the elimination of all hypocrisy (11:37–52; 12:1–3; 18:9–14); courage in the face of adversity (12:4–12); the shunning of wealth, possessions, and worldly achievement (12:13–21, 22–34; 16:1–31; 18:18–30); discernment and an ability to see the presence of the kingdom (12:49–56; 17:20–37); forgiveness of those who offend (12:57–59; 17:1–4); humility and recognition of one's own faults (14:7–14); simplicity and openness to God's kingdom (18:15–17; 19:1–10). Only Luke reports Jesus' harsh words: "Strive to enter by the narrow door; for many, I tell you, will seek to enter and will not be able" (13:24–25); "If any one comes to me and does not hate his own father and mother and wife and children and brothers and sisters, yes, and even his own life, he cannot be my disciple" (14:26); and "Whoever of you does not renounce all that he has cannot be my disciple" (14:33).[19]

This rigorous teaching is driven by Luke's concern that "the journey" of those hearing this Gospel may be in danger of coming to an end. They think they have done enough; they are prepared to rest on their laurels. This is unacceptable. As followers of the crucified and risen Christ they are summoned to continue their faith-filled journey as his witnesses to him, to the ends of the earth (see Luke 24:44–49; Acts 1:6–11).

Luke 24:13–35: The Walk to Emmaus . . . and the Return to Jerusalem

Luke's journey seems to stop once Jesus arrives in Jerusalem. In fact, a feature of Luke's resurrection account is his insistence that everything took place

---

18. See pp. 74–76 above.

19. David P. Moessner, *Lord of the Banquet: The Literary and Theological Significance of the Lukan Travel Narrative* (Harrisburg, PA: Trinity Press International, 1989), helpfully argues that Jesus' presence and teaching across the travel narrative is that of a "prophet," urgently calling disciples to authentic discipleship. He traces the same theme in the travel narratives of Acts on pp. 296–307.

on the one day (see Luke 24:1, 13, 29, 36, 51). The whole of Luke's Gospel has been directed toward this "day." As Jesus began his journey toward Jerusalem in 9:51, the narrator commented, "When the days drew near for him to be received up, he set his face to go to Jerusalem." That "journey" comes to its close in Jerusalem through "the things that have happened there" (24:18). On this resurrection "day" we sense that we are at the end of a long journey. The Lukan use of this theme is at the center of his account of the journey of two disciples to Emmaus (24:13–35), where it serves as background to a number of other central Lukan themes: the compassion of Jesus, the fulfillment of the Scriptures, the fulfillment of God's plan, the forgiveness of sin, the breaking of the eucharistic bread.[20]

The opening remarks of the journey to Emmaus are an indication of the wrong choice made by two disciples. "That very day"—in the midst of the paschal events—two disciples were going to Emmaus, "about seven miles from Jerusalem" (Luke 24:13). They are walking *away from Jerusalem*, the central point of God's story; away from God's journey, making himself known in his Son, from Nazareth (Luke 1–2) to the ends of the earth (Acts 1:8; 28:16–31). They walk away from the place and the day of the paschal events. This aspect of the journey to Emmaus is central to Luke's resurrection story.

This impression is further reinforced once the reader/listener notices the details of the account itself. The paschal events are in the forefront of their minds and are the subject of their conversation as they walk away (Luke 24:14) and as the risen Jesus "drew near and went with them" (v. 15). He has regularly reached out to sinners with pardon and offered salvation from his cross (23:34, 39–43). Now, as the risen one, he "walks with" two disciples who are abandoning God's saving story. God is also behind this encounter. Luke says not that they were unable to recognize Jesus but that "their eyes were kept from recognizing him" (24:16). There is a mysterious "other" directing the presence of Jesus with his disciples, indicated by the use of the divine passive voice of the verb. God is not mentioned as the subject of the action, but despite the absence of the name, God is responsible. However much they may be abandoning God's story, God is not abandoning them. Jesus opens the conversation by asking them what they were discussing with each other as they walked. They continue to walk away from Jerusalem as they discuss the events that took place there. But at Jesus' question they stop (v. 17).

A hint of something new has entered the story, but it does not last, as one of them, named Cleopas, responds to Jesus' question. He wonders how Jesus could

---

20. For a more detailed study of this passage, see Moloney, *Resurrection of the Messiah*, 81–86, and the references there.

even ask such a question. Surely every visitor to Jerusalem would know "the things that have happened there in these days" (Luke 24:18). This is incredible irony, since Cleopas is speaking to Jesus, indeed a visitor to Jerusalem who had journeyed from Galilee to the city in order to bring to a climax part of God's saving design. This journey has been under way since 9:51, when Jesus set his face for Jerusalem, "when the days drew near for him to be received up." Cleopas asks the very "visitor"—to whom these events happened—why he does not know about them. Jesus, who has been at the center of the events, is also the measure of their significance. But the two disciples know only of the "events," not their ultimate significance. Indeed, "their eyes were kept from recognizing him" (24:16).

A catechetical-liturgical process begins in verse 19, where, in response to Jesus' further query about the events, the disciples show the extent of their knowledge of "what has happened" in Jerusalem. Crucial to their response to Jesus is their explanation of their expectations of Jesus: "We had hoped that he was the one to redeem Israel" (v. 21). They have not understood the significance of the life, teaching, death, and resurrection of Jesus. They are yet to discover that the resurrection of Jesus is "the resurrection of the Messiah," although not the Messiah of their expectations but "the Messiah of God" (see 9:20 NRSV). His way of responding to the Father has not fulfilled their hopes for the one who would redeem Israel. But they do know *the facts* of his life, teaching, death, and resurrection.

- They know of his life, teaching, and miraculous ministry: Jesus of Nazareth, "a prophet mighty in deed and word" (24:19).
- They know of his death: "Our chief priests and rulers delivered him up to be condemned to death, and crucified him" (v. 20).
- They know of the events at the tomb: "it is now the third day" (v. 21), and women have been at the tomb early in the morning but "did not find his body" (v. 23).
- They have even heard the Easter proclamation: there has been a vision of angels, "who said that he was alive" (v. 23).
- Perhaps the witness of the women was not enough, as "some of those who were with us" have been to the tomb and likewise found it empty. "But him they did not see" (v. 24).

The two disciples on the way to Emmaus know everything . . . but him they did not see (vv. 15–17). Thus they do not understand the significance of these events, and they continue their walk away from Jerusalem.

Jesus chides them for their foolishness. He opens the Scriptures for them, explaining that it was necessary that the Christ should suffer many things to enter his glory (Luke 24:25–26). He "interpreted to them in all the scriptures the things concerning himself" (v. 27). Jesus journeys with these disciples who have abandoned God's journey, and on the way a "liturgy of the Word" takes place. He calls to their memory the necessity for the Christ to suffer in order to enter into his glory (v. 26). Not only did Jesus teach these truths (see 9:22, 44; 18:31–33), but it was the true meaning of "all the scriptures," beginning with Moses and the prophets, whose promises Jesus fulfills (24:27). The narrative has now reached a turning point. Initiative must come from the erring disciples themselves. Has the word of Jesus made any impact upon them? The Greek of verse 28 reads: "He pretended to be going further."[21] Jesus has unfolded God's plan through the explanation of the Scriptures. The disciples must now take some initiative in response to Jesus' biblical catechesis. They do so generously: "Stay with us, for it is toward evening and the day is now far spent" (v. 29). As the evening of the Easter "day" draws in, the littleness of faith that led them to leave Jerusalem and the eleven is being overcome by the presence of the risen Lord (v. 15) and the instruction of his word, asking them to remember (vv. 25–27). A process of repentance and forgiveness is under way, generated by the action of Jesus, who walks with his fragile disciples.

At the meal the disciples recognize him in the breaking of the bread (vv. 30–31). Jesus has set out to follow and to journey with these failing disciples as they walked away from God's designs for his Messiah (see v. 26). Yet he has accompanied them, made himself known to them, and opened the Word of God to them. Finally, he is recognized in the breaking of the bread. The memory of the many meals that Jesus has shared with them, and especially the meal he shared on the night before he died (22:14–38), opens their eyes and anticipates the many meals that will be celebrated in the future. The failed disciples are touched by Jesus' word and presence, and their immediate reaction is to turn back on their journey: "And they rose that same hour and returned to Jerusalem" (v. 33). The journey away "from Jerusalem" (v. 13) has been reversed as they turn back "to Jerusalem" (v. 33). Once they arrive back to the place they should never have abandoned and the eleven apostles upon whom the community is founded, before they can even utter a word about their experience, they find that Easter faith is already alive. They are told: "The Lord has risen indeed, and has appeared to Simon!" (v. 34). Easter faith has already been born in Jerusalem.

As the Gospel opens, the reader/listener comes to know of a man called "Simon" (Luke 4:38). Within the context of a miraculous catch of fish he is

---

21. This is the dictionary meaning of the Greek verb *prospoieō*: "make/act as though, pretend."

called to be a disciple of Jesus, and Jesus introduces a new name for him: "Peter" (see 5:8). The reader/hearer is reminded of this transformation in the Lukan list of the twelve apostles: "Simon, whom he named Peter" (6:14). From that point on, throughout the whole of the Gospel, he is called "Peter" (see 8:45, 51; 9:20, 28, 32–33; 12:41; 18:28). At the Last Supper, where the mingling of the themes of Jesus' sharing his table with the broken and the commissioning of his future apostles is found, he is still "Peter" (22:8, 34, 54, 55, 58, 60–61). Only in foretelling his future denials does Jesus emphatically revert to the name he had before he became a disciple: "Simon, Simon, behold, Satan demanded to have you, that he might sift you like wheat" (22:31). The return to "Peter" at the end of Jesus' words is, in itself, a sign that all is not lost (v. 34). Yet, it is to the failed Simon that the risen Lord has appeared, to restore him to his apostolic role. The name "Simon," without any link with the apostolic name "Peter," appears only before this man's call to be a follower of Jesus (4:38) and at the end of the Emmaus story, when two failing disciples are restored to God's saving story that is taking place in Jerusalem. There another sinner, Simon, has also been blessed by the presence of the risen Lord (24:34). The failed disciples have returned to another disciple who had failed his Lord. This return home, however, has happened because the risen Lord reached out to them in their brokenness and made himself known to them in the breaking of the bread.

Two disciples with inadequate faith had decided to walk "away from Jerusalem" (Luke 24:13), and the Easter proclamation announced the presence of the risen Lord to the fragile Simon: "The Lord has risen indeed, and has appeared to Simon!" (v. 34). This unforgettable story, the subject of imaginative art, poetry, and dramatic representation across the centuries, retains the powerful message that lies at the heart of Luke's Gospel: despite all human sin and frailty, the kingdom of God has been definitively established through the death and resurrection of Jesus.

The Birth Stories in Matthew 1–2 and Luke 1–2

Before leaving the Synoptic Gospels, it will be useful to reflect upon the stories of Jesus' birth and infancy as told in the Gospel of Matthew (1:1–2:23) and the Gospel of Luke (1:1–2:52).[22] The celebration of Christmas, and the symbols we use during that celebration, nearly all come from the Gospel of

---

22. The fundamental study of the infancy stories remains Raymond E. Brown, *The Birth of the Messiah: A Commentary on the Infancy Narratives in Matthew and Luke* (New York: Doubleday, 1977).

Luke. Similarly, the Joyful Decades of the Rosary in the Catholic tradition all come from the Gospel of Luke: "The Annunciation" (Luke 1:26–38), "The Visitation" (1:39–56), "The Birth of Jesus" (2:1–24), "The Presentation of the Child Jesus in the Temple" (2:25–40), "The Finding of the Child Jesus in the Temple" (2:41–52). These are joy- and faith-filled stories of wonderful women (Elizabeth and Mary), John the Baptist, shepherds, angels, Simeon, Anna, and the child Jesus among the wise men in the temple. The dominant character is Mary, the Mother of Jesus, who hears the Word of God and does it.

The only episode from the Gospel of Matthew that creeps into the Christmas celebrations is the Magi and their association with the shadowy account of the slaying of the innocents (Matt. 2:16–18). The joyful proclamation of the Lukan story is absent as Matthew tells Jesus' genealogy (1:1–17), the suspicion of an illegitimate child to be born of Mary (1:18–25), the visit of the Magi while Herod plots (2:1–12), the flight into Egypt (2:13–15), and the return to Judea of Joseph and his family followed by their flight to Nazareth in Galilee (2:19–23). The dominant character is Joseph, the supposed father of Jesus, who (like Mary in Luke) hears the Word of God and does it.

As with so much in the Gospels, Matthew and Luke have told the story in different ways. No doubt there were popular stories that Luke knew, and that is what appears in his account, while Matthew also used familiar stories. They did not "invent" these narratives but created them from traditions that came to them. Matthew and Luke shaped their stories differently for at least two reasons: to serve as an introduction of the person of Jesus to their different readers/listeners (Matthew to a largely Jewish-Christian community and Luke largely to gentiles) and to serve as a prologue to the whole story. In other words, the reader/hearer can only understand the Lukan and Matthean portraits of Jesus in the light of the birth and infancy stories. Once one understands who Jesus is and where he comes from (Matt. 1–2 and Luke 1–2), one is in a position to read or hear the story of his ministry, his teaching, his death, and his resurrection. As Matthew's story of Jesus is different from that of Luke's, so are the birth and infancy stories of these two Gospels.[23]

But are we able to find anything behind these different stories that may go back to the events that surrounded Jesus' birth? Both stories tell of Mary and Joseph, Jesus' mother and his supposed father. Both locate Jesus' birth

---

23. The birth narratives thus play a similar theological and literary role to Mark 1:1–13, which also serves as a prologue. The Prologue to the Gospel of John (1:1–18) is well known. The theological heart of each Gospel narrative is found in these prologues. They all tell the reader/listener of Jesus' origins and his mission. The characters *in the narrative* have not read that narrative's prologue, so the reader/listener is in a privileged position, able to assess the various responses to Jesus that are recorded in the story—and measure their own response accordingly!

around the time of the end of the reign of Herod the Great (4 CE). Both stories (although in different ways) tell that Jesus' conception is the result of the action of God and not of a union between Mary and Joseph. Both stories locate the place where Jesus grew up as Nazareth, even though he is born in the city of David, and Joseph is of the line of David. Thus, for both accounts, Jesus is understood as from the Davidic line. For Matthew everything happens in Bethlehem, while for Luke, Jesus is born on a "journey" from Nazareth to Bethlehem, where there is no room in an earthly resting place (see Luke 2:7).[24] Behind the two different stories there is something they share. Ultimately, there is also something that cannot be explained: Jesus is from God, and his mission is to "save his people from their sins" (Matt. 1:21), to be the salvation of God, a "light of revelation to the Gentiles, and for glory to your people Israel" (Luke 2:32 AT).

There are two moments in the New Testament's story of Jesus that defy human measurement and understanding: how he came into the world (virgin birth) and how he went out of it (resurrection and ascension). This is the case because they are outside our human experience.[25] Jesus embraces the human condition without reservation. But the Gospels leave his origins and his destiny in the mystery of his being one with God. It is here that the New Testament summons its readers to abandon all attempts to "control and measure" the person of Jesus and to recognize that we are being blessed by God's action among us and for us. "She will bear a son, and you are to name him Jesus, for he will save his people from their sins" (Matt. 1:21 NRSV). "My eyes have seen your salvation that you have prepared in the presence of all peoples" (Luke 2:30–31 AT).

The Gospel of John

The Gospel of John is a much-loved Christian document.[26] Many of its passages "ring a bell" with any Christian. No scholarly training is needed for us

24. This subtlety already tells Luke's readers and listeners that the theme of journey is not limited to 9:51–19:44 but reaches across the whole of Luke-Acts. The Greek word generally translated as "inn" in Luke 2:7 (*katalyma*) does not refer to some form of hostelry. It indicates a pitched tent by the side of the road where care was provided for weary travelers.

25. It is beyond the scope of this book to study the different presentations of the resurrection of Jesus in the four Gospels. See Moloney, *Resurrection of the Messiah*.

26. For reliable single-volume commentaries on the Gospel of John, see the older but extremely rich Edwyn C. Hoskyns, *The Fourth Gospel*, ed. Francis N. Davey (London: Faber & Faber, 1947); as well as R. Alan Culpepper, *The Gospel and Letters of John*, Interpreting Biblical Texts (Nashville: Abingdon, 1998); Francis J. Moloney, *The Gospel of John*, Sacra Pagina 4 (Collegeville, MN: Liturgical Press, 1998); Mark W. Stibbe, *John*, Readings: A New Bible Commentary (Sheffield, UK: JSOT Press, 1993); Andrew T. Lincoln, *The Gospel according to Saint*

to be moved by the proclamation, "The Word became flesh and lived among us, and we have seen his glory, the glory as of the Father's only son, the fullness of a gift which is truth" (John 1:14 AT). We share the belief expressed by the Samaritan villagers: "We know that this is truly the Savior of the world" (4:42 NRSV); by Martha: "Lord, I believe that you are the Messiah, the Son of God, the one coming into the world" (11:27 NRSV); and by Thomas: "My Lord and my God!" (20:28). We respond with joy to Jesus' promises: "You will know the truth, and the truth will make you free" (8:32), and "I am the way, and the truth, and the life" (14:6). But this Gospel was not written as a collection of inspiring and comforting words. On the contrary, it came into existence to create *crisis*, not *comfort*.

The Shape of John's Story

The Gospel of John, at first sight, is relatively simple to divide into the Prologue, two major sections, and a conclusion, followed by an additional chapter that functions as an epilogue.[27]

1:1–18	Prologue: informing the reader/listener who Jesus is, where he is from, and what he will do
1:19–12:30	Jesus' public ministry in Galilee and Jerusalem, often called the "Book of Signs" because all his miraculous activity, called "signs" by John, occurs here
13:1–20:29	Jesus' final encounter and farewell with his disciples and his passion and resurrection, often called the "Book of Glory" because John presents Jesus' death and resurrection as events that reveal the glory of God and generate the glorification of Jesus
20:30–31	Conclusion: addressing the reader/listener on the purpose of the Gospel
21:1–21	Epilogue: a later addition to the Gospel yet nonetheless a part of it, facing problems of community and leadership not dealt with in 1:1–20:31

John, Black's New Testament Commentaries (Grand Rapids: Baker Academic, 2005); Brendan Byrne, *Life Abounding: A Reading of John's Gospel* (Collegeville, MN: Liturgical Press, 2014). For readers of this book, the most helpful might be Culpepper, Moloney, or Byrne. See also Brown, *Introduction to the New Testament*, 333–82; Moloney, *Living Voice*, 237–75; Powell, *Introducing the New Testament*, 169–89; Spivey, Smith, and Black, *Anatomy of the New Testament*, 155–88. See also the extremely helpful introduction to this Gospel, its structure, and its theology by Ruth Edwards, *Discovering John: Content, Interpretation, Reception*, 2nd ed. (London: SPCK, 2014).

27. For a more detailed presentation of this structure and the Johannine theology behind it, see Moloney, *Love in the Gospel of John*, 11–35.

The Prologue (John 1:1–18) is one of the most remarkable passages in the New Testament, and it stands alone, introducing the story of the life and teaching of Jesus. Before entering the day-to-day telling of the life and ministry of Jesus, the reader knows that the Logos existed before all time in intimate union with God. As such, the Logos made God known but came among his own and was refused. But those who accepted him could become his children. The Logos became flesh, and his name was Jesus Christ. We have seen him, and in him we have had God made known to us.

With this information in their minds and hearts, readers and listeners begin to experience a narrative about Jesus' public ministry. It opens with John the Baptist's activity (John 1:19–34), but once Jesus enters the scene, he calls his disciples and becomes the main focus of attention. He journeys with his disciples, from one miracle at Cana (2:1–12) to another (4:46–54), summoning various people to true faith. He then journeys to and from Jerusalem for the feasts of Israel: Sabbath (5:1–47), Passover (6:1–71), Tabernacles (7:1–10:21), and Dedication (10:22–42). Across these feasts he presents himself as the sent one of the Father who embodies the central celebration of the feasts: lord of all (Sabbath); bread from heaven (Passover); living water, the light of the world, and the Messiah (Tabernacles); and the living presence of God in Jerusalem (Dedication).

The raising of Lazarus (John 11:1–54) is not really about sickness but about life, and through this miracle Jesus begins his journey to the cross, the revelation of the glory of God and the means by which Jesus will be glorified (see v. 4). The decision is made that he must die not only for the nation but to gather into one the children of God who are scattered abroad (vv. 49–53). Jesus enters Jerusalem, the Greeks seek him, and the hour of his glorification—his lifting up, his drawing everyone to himself on his cross—has come (12:1–36)!

John's account of Jesus' last night with the disciples is very different from the accounts in Mark, Matthew, and Luke. He washes their feet and shares bread with them, despite their failure, because he loves them to the very end (John 13:1–38; 17:1–26). He tells them he must leave them, but he will not abandon them. They will be given the Spirit Paraclete (14:1–31; 16:4b–33), and they must live according to Jesus' commandments of faith and love in the midst of hatred and persecution (15:1–16:3).

John's story of Jesus' passion repeats the story told in the Synoptic Gospels: the Garden of Gethsemane (18:1–11), Jewish hearing (18:12–27), Roman trial (18:28–19:16), death and crucifixion (19:17–37), burial (19:38–42). But it is told differently. Jesus is in control at all times. He is crowned and proclaimed as a king by Pilate (see 19:1–3), and he is crucified as a king (see 19:17–22), despite being rejected by those who will not accept this revelation of God's love for us. Similarly, while the events of the resurrection are the same—empty tomb, Mary Magdalene, appearances and a commission to his disciples—the story is different. Mary Magdalene, the Beloved Disciple, the disciples, and Thomas all come to true faith in Jesus.

However, this story is written for us also. Jesus blesses those who believe without seeing (John 20:29), and John tells us he wrote this Gospel so that we might come to believe and have life (vv. 30–31). A further chapter (John 21), added after the author had penned 20:30–31, has always been part of this story of Jesus. More was to be said to the disciples, and to all subsequent disciples who might read this Gospel, about the universal mission of the Church (21:1–14), the authority of Peter the shepherd (vv. 15–19), and the witness of the Beloved Disciple (vv. 20–24), which must be affirmed before the book can be closed (v. 25).

John 13:1–38: Loving to the Very End

Jesus knows the hour has come for his return to the Father (13:1).[28] He has brought to perfection the work his Father gave him to do (see 4:34), loving his own "to the end." The expression "to the very end" has two meanings. It means a point in time, to the end of his life on the cross. It also tells of the quality of his immeasurable love. Jesus' departure from this world to the Father, in a consummate act of love for "his own," will be *via* the cross.

In the Gospel's report of the final moments of Jesus' public ministry with his disciples and among the crowds of people who either accept him, reject him, or remain indifferent, Jesus has already set the agenda for what is now about to be explained by his deeds and words. As the Greeks arrived, the hour of the glorification of the Son of Man was announced (John 12:23) and explained as a "lifting up" (vv. 32–33). The disciples are swept up into Jesus' love by means of two gestures. In the first, Jesus adopts the position of the most menial servant or slave. He takes off his clothes and washes the feet of the disciples (13:1–20). This remarkable gesture of his love for them "to the very end" is met only with rumblings of Judas' future betrayal (vv. 2, 10–11), with Peter's inability to understand what Jesus is doing for them (vv. 6–9), and with the general ignorance of the other disciples (v. 12). Despite their failure, ignorance, denial, and betrayal, they have a part in Jesus (see v. 8), and he challenges them to be his disciples by accepting the new example he has shown them: as he has done for them, so they must do for one another (v. 15).

---

28. For a more detailed study of this passage, see Moloney, *Love in the Gospel of John*, 104–17, and the references there.

Why is he doing this for them, showing how much he loves them in the midst of their betrayal, ignorance, and failure? He tells them in verse 19: "I tell you this now, before it occurs, so that when it does occur, you may believe that *I am he*" (NRSV, emphasis added). What he is doing and saying by loving them to the end and asking them to love in the same way is leading them into belief in him as the revelation of the love of God. The Greek behind the words "I am he" (*egō eimi*) is taken from the Greek Bible to indicate the presence of the living God.

In the second half of the chapter, another loving gesture is seen in the gift of the morsel (John 13:21–28). This symbolic gesture of Jesus' love for his own takes place in the shadow of Judas' betrayal, of Peter's denials (vv. 36–38), and of the ignorance of all the disciples (vv. 28–29). As Judas leaves the room to go into the darkness of the night, the same theme returns. The Son of Man is now glorified, and God is glorified in him (vv. 30–32). As the symbol of the foot washing was an example of his never-ending love, meant to be imitated by the disciples, he makes a parallel request after the gift of the eucharistic morsel. He tells them: "I give you a new commandment, that you love one another. Just as I have loved you, you also should love one another. By this everyone will know that you are my disciples, if you have love for one another" (vv. 34–35 NRSV).

The stage is set for Jesus' lifting up on the cross, so that all can gaze upon the pierced one and see in him the revelation of God's love (see 19:37). Later in the final discourse that Jesus has with his disciples he explains why his death tells us how much he loves us: "No one has greater love than this, to lay down one's life for one's friends. You are my friends if you do what I command you" (15:13–14 NRSV). The love that is to be revealed in Jesus' self-gift will be continued in the lives of "his own," whom he leaves in the world (13:12–17, 33–35). Jesus tells these things to fragile disciples, whom he has chosen and will send out, so that when this moment of glorification takes place they might believe that Jesus is the revelation of God: "so that . . . you may believe that I am he" (v. 19 NRSV). Jesus makes God known in the perfect love he shows for his fragile disciples, even washing their feet and giving the morsel to Judas. In and through his loving, Jesus is glorified, and God is glorified in him (vv. 31–32). The disciples are to be recognized as the sent ones of Jesus—who loved so much and was himself sent by a God who loves the world so much (see 3:16)—by the unity created by the love they have for one another (13:15, 34–35).

Conclusion

Many stories of Jesus' life, ministry, death, and resurrection existed in the early centuries of the Christian Church. The Gospels of Mark, Matthew,

Luke, and John were received by believing Christians by the end of the second century because they were relevant, because they made sense when they were read, listened to, seen performed, and interpreted in the Church. The brief introduction to each of these Gospels and the sketched interpretation of a few sample passages from each of them provides only an echo of the ongoing relevance of these inspired accounts of the life, teaching, death, and resurrection of Jesus of Nazareth, who is the Christ and the Son of God. Each one of them is different, despite the fact that all four evangelists looked back to the memory of Jesus of Nazareth for the source of what they wanted to tell. But the Gospels were *never intended* to be simply biographies in any modern sense. To read them in that way, as most of us do, is to lose an important gift of God to the Church.

The evangelists told the story of Jesus to address the joys, hopes, sufferings, doubts, hesitancy, pains, and perplexities of their Christian communities. Ultimately they all wished to proclaim the saving action of God in and through the person of Jesus of Nazareth. Each one presented this action differently in a uniquely inspired "telling" of the story of Jesus, but it is precisely that difference that makes our fourfold Gospel tradition so rich. It is wonderful that the Gospel of Mark is not the Gospel of John—and we are all the richer because of this *difference*. What the evangelists communicated to early Christians made great sense to them *then*.

These same stories have been read in private and in public; have provided the centerpiece for the liturgies of all Christian traditions from both East and West; and have been recited, performed, and sung for almost two thousand years. From a high Byzantine liturgy, to a Pontifical Mass at Saint Peter's Basilica in Rome, to an unornamented proclamation of the Word in the evangelical tradition in the southern states of the United States, to a Christmas pageant played by our children and grandchildren: the Gospel stories continue to speak to us. The Gospel books have been encased in jeweled covers and reproduced in wonderful manuscripts that contain some of the great art of Christian history. The four Gospels form the core of the life and tradition of the Christian community because, in their different and mutually enriching fashion, they take us back to Jesus and bring Jesus into our communities. Even in the increasingly secularized third millennium we continue to read and interpret Mark, Matthew, Luke, and John as Sacred Scripture *in and for the Church*.

7

The Acts of the Apostles

Telling God's Story to the End
of the Earth

The Acts of the Apostles continues the narrative tradition that highlights the literary form of the Gospels and is the second volume of the single work known as Luke-Acts. It follows the story of the experience of the founding apostles, from their first days after the resurrection and at the ascension of Jesus (Acts 1:1–14), over several decades, until it closes with the apostle Paul under house arrest in Rome, still "preaching the kingdom of God and teaching about the Lord Jesus Christ quite openly" (28:31).[1] There is, of course, much else that is found in this exciting narrative, including earthquakes (16:26), shipwrecks (27:41–44), avenging angels (12:23), harrowing escapes (9:23–25; 21:30–36), riots (19:23–41), murder plots (9:23; 23:12–15), political intrigue (16:35–39; 22:22–29; 24:26–27), courtroom drama (23:1–10), and much more,[2] which clearly reflects the desire on the part of the evangelist we call Luke to continue his storytelling. In a story dedicated to Theophilus (Luke 1:1–4), Luke had told of Jesus' birth,

1. There are hints in Acts that Luke was aware of Paul's death (see Acts 20:22–25, 38), but he has chosen to omit a tragic ending. It did not suit his purpose, as there is no place for pessimism in a story of a God-directed triumphant march from Jerusalem to Rome.
2. Powell, *Introducing the New Testament*, 191.

life, teaching, death, resurrection, and ascension. His second volume is also directed to Theophilus (Acts 1:1–2) and tells the story of the apostles.[3]

The Gospels were narrative proclamations of what God had done for humankind in and through his Son, Jesus Christ. Even though many literary patterns and theological themes from the Gospel of Luke continue into the Acts of the Apostles, a different theological interest drives the narrative. Luke wishes to share with his readers and listeners his passionate conviction that the God and Father of Jesus continues to be present in the steady outreach of the witnessing to what God had done in and through Jesus. It begins in Jerusalem (1:8) and reaches the end of the earth (28:30–31). Both the Gospel of Luke and the Acts of the Apostles were written to confirm and strengthen the belief of Luke's fellow Christians (see Luke 1:4).[4] This agenda has already been set as the Gospel closes. Jesus has instructed the founding apostles: "Thus it is written, that the Christ should suffer and on the third day rise from the dead, and that repentance and forgiveness of sins should be preached in his name to all nations, beginning from Jerusalem. . . . And behold, I send the promise of my Father upon you; but stay in the city, until you are clothed with power from on high" (Luke 24:46–47, 49). The theme is taken up again at the beginning of Acts in the risen Jesus' final words to his apostles as he departs from them in his ascension: "You shall receive power when the Holy Spirit has come upon you; and you shall be my witnesses in Jerusalem and in all Judea and Samaria and to the end of the earth" (Acts 1:8). If the Gospel of Luke was a history of Jesus, then the Acts of the Apostles is a history of the God-directed witness to Jesus by the founding apostles, especially Peter and Paul. The messenger, Jesus, of Luke's Gospel has become in the Acts of the Apostles the subject of a message of what *must* happen for God's design to be fulfilled.[5]

3. For helpful commentaries on Acts, see Beverly R. Gaventa, *Acts*, Abingdon New Testament Commentaries (Nashville: Abingdon, 2003); Luke T. Johnson, *The Acts of the Apostles*, Sacra Pagina 5 (Collegeville, MN: Liturgical Press, 2006); and Mikael C. Parsons, *Acts*, Paideia Commentaries on the New Testament (Grand Rapids: Baker Academic, 2008). See also Brown, *Introduction to the New Testament*, 279–332; Powell, *Introducing the New Testament*, 191–213; Spivey, Smith, and Black, *Anatomy of the New Testament*, 241–70.

4. Luke states this purpose explicitly in Luke 1:4, using a Greek word (*asphaleia*) to explain to Theophilus that he is writing that he "may have full confidence concerning the words in which you have been instructed" (AT). The word *asphaleia* is not about intellectual "truth" but "a mental state of certainty and security." See Johnson, *Gospel of Luke*, 28.

5. One of Luke's favorite words in both the Gospel and Acts is the Greek expression *dei*. It means "must" or "it is necessary." It was necessary that Jesus die and rise from the dead (Luke 9:22; 13:33; 17:25; 24:7, 26; Acts 17:3), that Judas be replaced (Acts 1:22), that Paul visit Rome (Acts 19:21; 23:11; 25:10; 27:24), for the gospel to be proclaimed to the Jews first (13:46), for the Christians to suffer tribulation and suffer for Christ's name (9:16; 14:22). On the theme of God's dominant role in Acts, see Powell, *Introducing the New Testament*, 200–204.

The command of Jesus in Acts 1:8 drives the structure of the narrative of Acts. The story begins with the disciples in Jerusalem, wondering when the end time will come. Jesus departs as an angel tells them not to gaze into the heavens or worry about when and how the end time will come. They have a mission that will take them to the end of the earth. Only when that is completed will Jesus return (1:1–11). Subsequent to the promised gift of the Holy Spirit (2:1–4), the disciples, especially Peter, reach beyond the city into other parts of Palestine (all Judea and Samaria) and then, through the ministry of Paul, across Syria, Asia Minor, and Greece, into a gentile mission. The journeys of Paul take the mission into an unfailingly successful journey to Rome, at that time "the end of the earth." On the basis of this overall narrative scheme, established by the command of Jesus in 1:8 and the instruction of the angel to the "men of Galilee," much lies ahead of the apostles. A God-directed story unfolds in four major narrative, literary, and theological stages.[6]

1:1–2:47	The beginnings of the apostolic community
3:1–12:25	The gospel in Jerusalem, all Judea, Samaria, and Galilee (see 1:8)
13:1–21:14	The triumphant progress of Christianity
21:15–28:31	To the end of the earth: Rome (see 1:8)

Acts 1:1–2:47: The Beginnings of the Apostolic Community

Jesus departs in his ascension, and the original disciples are ordered to cease looking into the heavens and begin their mission (1:1–11). The apostolic witness of the twelve apostles is established; Matthias replaces the failed Judas Iscariot. The number twelve must be maintained, as it was the number of foundational tribes of Israel and the number of "apostles" originally established by Jesus (1:12–26; see Luke 6:12–16).[7] The Spirit, "the promise

6. The following division depends on my use of Jesus' words in Acts 1:8 as determining the shape of the narrative. See Johnson, *Acts of the Apostles*, 26. Other divisions are possible. See, e.g., Brown, *Introduction to the New Testament*, 280; Parsons, *Acts*, 19. Luke obviously used sources for his account and certainly regarded himself as a "historian," but in the sense of his contemporary "historians." Their main objective was not simply to record facts from the past but to tell them in a way that "persuaded" readers to accept the author's values and point of view. As we will see, in Luke's case, it was a profoundly theological point of view (i.e., it tells about the action of God). See Brown, *Introduction to the New Testament*, 316–22; Parsons, *Acts*, 3–22.

7. See Johnson, *Acts of the Apostles*, 38–40. Only Luke and Paul refer to the Twelve as "apostles." Paul regarded himself as an apostle, even though he was not one of the Twelve (see esp. 1 Cor. 15:3–11; 2 Cor. 10–12). The Greek word for "apostle" means "one sent out." Luke

of the Father" (see Luke 24:49; Acts 1:4), the "power from on high" (Luke 24:49), is given to the infant Church, and the apostles break out of their fears (so enthusiastically that they are thought to be inebriated [see Acts 2:13]) to proclaim what God has done in and through Jesus (2:14–36), leading to sorrow, repentance, and conversion (about three thousand on that first Pentecost day [v. 41]).

Signs associated with the foundation of the original people of God at Sinai (see Exod. 19:16–20: thunder, lightning, and fire) return at this first Christian Pentecost (Acts 2:1–4).[8] The confusion of tongues that began at the Tower of Babel is overcome (see Gen. 11:1–9) as people of many tongues and nations understand the disciples' words (Acts 2:5–12). "The parallelism [between the Genesis stories and Acts 2:1–4] fits the pattern of Luke's story: Jesus is the prophet who sums up all the promises and hopes of the people before him; in his apostolic successors, that promise and hope (now sealed by the Spirit) will be carried to all the nations of the earth."[9] This pattern of preaching that Jesus' mission, death, and resurrection were part of God's plan, already foretold in the Old Testament, and the subsequent response of conversion and baptism, already established in Peter's Pentecost speech and its aftermath (2:14–42), is found across the many long speeches in Acts.[10] A community attentive to the teaching of the disciples, breaking bread and praying together, with one heart and mind, emerges as the founding model of the future missionary community (vv. 42–47).[11]

---

and Paul are especially concerned with the outreach of the Christian message and the Christian community "to the end of the earth." The Lukan "twelve apostles" has become part of traditional Christian language, even though Mark and Matthew know nothing of that terminology. For Paul, it was possible to be an apostle without being one of the Twelve. The title "The Acts of the Apostles" was added to this document in the second century, even though "apostles" are only rarely mentioned (1:2; 4:36–37; 5:12; 8:1) and the central figures are Peter and Paul rather than the Twelve.

8. The Jewish celebration of Pentecost (to this day) is the commemoration of the gift of the law, the establishment of a covenant between God and a people at Sinai.

9. Johnson, *Acts of the Apostles*, 47.

10. This is the case no matter who gives the speech. Comparisons between the speeches in Acts (delivered by Peter, all the Jerusalem believers, Stephen, or Paul) show they are very similar. This does not mean that Luke "invented" everything, but he has certainly shaped all the speeches so that they correspond to his theological idea of Jesus as the fulfillment of God's will, already manifested in the Old Testament, and the need for everyone to have a change of heart and receive forgiveness and baptism. See Spivey, Smith, and Black, *Anatomy of the New Testament*, 248–50, for a good summary.

11. Luke will regularly insert summary statements about the unity and peace that existed in the Jerusalem community (see 1:14; 2:43–47; 4:32–37). This is Luke's way of indicating the ideal Christian community. His rhetoric suggests to readers: it was like this in the beginning and thus should always be like this. On the content of the summaries, see Brown, *Introduction to the New Testament*, 285–89.

Acts 3:1–12:25: The Gospel in Jerusalem, All Judea, Samaria, and Galilee

The outward spread of the witness of the apostles is related in 3:1–12:25. Following the indications of 1:8, it begins in Jerusalem, highlighted by the power manifested in the apostles' preaching and healing in the city (3:1–26, Peter and John at the temple and another speech from Peter; 4:1–37, Peter and John before the council and the response of the community in another speech; 5:1–42, Ananias and Sapphira betray the community, signs and wonders are performed, and the apostles are persecuted, closing with Gamaliel's warning that these men may be doing a work of God). Luke wants his readers and hearers to recognize that Christianity emerged from the very heart of Israel: Jerusalem and its temple. For Luke, God's design has not changed direction with the life, teaching, death, and resurrection of Jesus that climaxed in Jerusalem, and neither did it change in the beginnings of the community witnessing to Jesus, which had its origins in Jerusalem. "Christianity emerged from Israel's very heart and is, therefore, the true expression of that ancient faith."[12]

A further turning point of the story is found in the problem of the "Hellenists." It leads to the appointment of seven men to serve them (6:1–7). The existence of Greek-speaking Hellenists and "the Hebrews" within the community is a first indication that the Gospel is reaching beyond its origins in the small group of frightened disciples of Jesus (see 1:1–14).[13] One of those servants, Stephen, is specially gifted in continuing the power and signs that mark God's presence.[14] He may be one of the "servants," but his ministry of power indicates that he continues the mission of the foundational apostles. Falsely accused, he is arrested, and he delivers the longest speech in Acts (6:1–7:53). The speech does not deal with the charges against him, but by means of a long reflection on Israel's history it points to the past disobedience of the chosen people, questions the relevance of the temple (see 7:47–50), and strongly denounces those who have betrayed and murdered Jesus (vv. 51–53). It closes: "You who received the law as delivered by angels and did not keep it" (v. 53). Regardless

---

12. Spivey, Smith, and Black, *Anatomy of the New Testament*, 252.

13. It is also one of several indications in the text, like the story of Ananias and Sapphira, that there were divisions in the community, but Luke makes nothing of this in his story of the unfolding of God's design for the Christian community. See Brown, *Introduction to the New Testament*, 293–94; Parsons, *Acts*, 81–85.

14. The Greek word for "servant" is *diakonos*, and Catholic tradition has long looked back upon Acts 6 as the beginnings of a sacramental Order called the Diaconate. Stephen is often presented in Christian art in the vestments of an ordained deacon. Although there were certainly appointed people who had a ministry of "service" in the early Church (see as early as Rom. 16:1; Phil. 1:1; Eph. 6:21; 1 Tim. 3:8), the sacramental Order appeared much later.

of the accusations of 6:11–14, on the basis of his speech alone he is condemned to death.[15] In death he prays as Jesus prayed: "Lord Jesus, receive my spirit" (7:59; see Luke 23:46), and "Lord, do not hold this sin against them" (Acts 7:60; see Luke 23:34). Those who die for Christ repeat the death of Christ.[16] As the episode closes, the reader is introduced to the hero of the second half of Acts: "And Saul was consenting to his death" (Acts 8:1a; see 7:58).[17]

The fruits of martyrdom are reported in 8:1–40. The Christians scatter as Saul persecutes them (8:1b–4). Philip makes converts of many in Samaria (vv. 5–25) and of an Ethiopian eunuch on the road south from Jerusalem to Gaza (vv. 26–40). He is then transported to Caesarea in Galilee (v. 40). Others preach the word, but only the actions of Philip are reported in any detail. The command of the ascending Jesus is being fulfilled as the gospel is preached outside Judea, in Samaria (vv. 5, 9, 25; see 1:8), accompanied by baptism, the presence of Peter and John, and the pouring out of the Spirit when the apostles' hands are laid upon the newly baptized (vv. 14–18).

The gospel has now reached out from Jerusalem into the whole of Judea, Samaria, and Galilee. The next stage in God's plan to take the gospel to the end of the earth is prepared in the well-known account of Paul's conversion (9:1–22). The encounter with the risen Jesus on the Damascus road, his encounter with Ananias in Damascus, and his preaching there, which "confounded the Jews who lived in Damascus" (9:22), are recorded on two further occasions in Acts (see 22:3–21; 26:12–18).[18] Hunted by some Jewish people in Damascus, Paul escapes and returns to Jerusalem, the cradle of Christianity. From there he is sent home to Tarsus (9:23–30). Luke shows his skills as a storyteller by introducing the Christian Paul in 9:1–30. The hero of the second half of Acts (13:1–28:31) enters the narrative here, but he disappears in 9:30, only to return in 12:25–13:3, fully commissioned as an apostolic missionary. In the meantime (9:32–12:23), Peter dominates the action.

Peter is crucial to this section of Acts, as he continues to work wonders in the name of Jesus Christ (9:32–35, the healing of Aeneas; vv. 36–42, the raising of

---

15. Parsons, *Acts*, 85–108, shows how this speech should be read through the lens of ancient rhetoric, to show that "Stephen is not pitting Christianity over against Judaism; rather he is aligning himself and his group with what he considers to be the 'best' in Jewish history" (108).

16. See Johnson, *Acts of the Apostles*, 142–44. Here and throughout his commentary Johnson rightly points out that the apostles are not only "witnesses" but continue Jesus' "prophetic" presence.

17. As Brown, *Introduction to the New Testament*, 296, comments: "Just as Jesus' death was not the end because the apostles would receive the Spirit to carry on the work, the death of Stephen is not the end, for observing is a young man named Saul (7:58). He consents to the death (8:1a), but in God's providence he will continue the work of Stephen."

18. On the threefold telling of Paul's conversion, see Johnson, *Acts of the Apostles*, 170.

Tabitha/Dorcas) and is the key figure in the explicit acceptance of the mission to the gentiles through the baptism of the Roman centurion, Cornelius, whom he accepts without first demanding that he become a member of the Jewish community (10:1–11:18). It is a complex and somewhat repetitious account. Cornelius has a vision at Caesarea, at this stage the frontier of the gospel's outreach (see 8:40), instructing him to summon Peter from Joppa (10:1–8). Simultaneously Peter has a vision, insisting that what has once been regarded as "unclean" can no longer be so (vv. 9–16). Cornelius' servants bring Peter to Caesarea, where the two men have a moving encounter (vv. 17–29). Cornelius tells Peter of his vision (vv. 30–33). Peter's response is a missionary speech (vv. 34–43) dominated by the theme of his opening words: "Truly I perceive that God shows no partiality, but in every nation any one who fears him and does what is right is acceptable to him" (vv. 34–35). *Before* anything else happens, as Peter ends his words, the Holy Spirit falls upon all who heard them. As a *consequence* of the gift of the Holy Spirit, Peter baptizes Cornelius and his company (vv. 44–48). "The gift of the Holy Spirit has been poured out even on the Gentiles" (v. 45). This moment in the story of Acts is sometimes called the Pentecost of the gentiles.

Peter returns to Jerusalem, where he is criticized by the circumcision party. He should not have gone to an uncircumcised man and eaten with him (11:2–3). In response, Peter retells all the events (vv. 1–18).[19] As always in Acts, Peter's report meets no opposition. It is received in silence as they glorify God, saying, "Then to the Gentiles also God has granted repentance unto life" (v. 18).[20] Even though Peter's speech in 11:1–18 repeats what has happened in Caesarea, this occasion is used to spell out further the theological importance of this moment: "If then God gave the same gift to them as he gave to us when we believed in the Lord Jesus Christ, who was I that I could withstand God?" (v. 17). God is the unseen but ever-central character in the Acts of the Apostles. Peter will return to this moment in his defense of the gentile mission at the so-called Jerusalem Council (see 15:7–9).

A series of episodes is reported in 11:19–12:25 that continues the spread of the gospel within the context of opposition that is always vanquished. Stephen's

---

19. Peter's retelling of the story in 11:1–18 is not entirely consistent with the earlier report of the events. However, the alterations only serve to make even clearer Luke's message about the inevitability of God's design to bring the gospel to the gentiles. See Johnson, *Acts of the Apostles*, 180–202.

20. This is one of many occasions in Acts where Luke writes an account to show that God's plan will broach no failure or opposition. We are aware from other early Christian literature, especially Paul's Letter to the Galatians, that the passage into the gentile world—especially the question of circumcision—was conflicted and that even Peter and Barnabas were ambiguous about it (see Gal. 2:11–14).

martyrdom generates a mission to Phoenicia and Cyprus. Some converts go to Antioch preaching the Lord to the Greeks. The field is ripe for harvesting, so Barnabas of Cyprus goes to Tarsus, seeking out Saul. It is at Antioch that "the disciples were for the first time called Christians" (11:26). The disciples determine to bring goodness, through the ministry of Barnabas and Saul, to all who are suffering (vv. 27–30), but this goodness is met by hatred as Herod executes James and puts Peter in prison (12:1–5). God will not be thwarted, and Peter is miraculously released from prison (vv. 6–19), and Herod, who has no interest in the sufferings of the people of Tyre and Sidon (in contrast to the attitude of the Christians to the poor in Judea in 11:27–30), is struck down by "an angel of the Lord" and dies ignominiously (12:20–23). As opposition fails, the community grows, and the power of the word increases as Barnabas, Saul, and John Mark come together (vv. 24–25). The scene is set for the third major section of the narrative.

Acts 13:1–21:14: The Triumphant Progress of Christianity

This section of Acts is dominated by the three journeys of Paul, interrupted only by the Jerusalem Council. The journey theme, so central to Luke's Gospel, is resumed with considerable effect. In the Gospel, Jesus was on the move from Nazareth in Galilee, through Jerusalem, to return to his Father. In the Acts of the Apostles, it is the good news *about* Jesus that is on the move from Cyprus and Asia Minor (first missionary journey, 13:1–14:28), into Greece (second missionary journey, 15:36–18:22), and then consolidated in Ephesus and Greece (third missionary journey, 18:23–21:14). But Jerusalem is not forgotten. The only interruption to this triumphant march from Jerusalem to Ephesus, Athens, and Corinth is the Council of Jerusalem. After the success of the first formal mission to the gentiles (13:1–14:28), the Church gathers to assess whether this mission is part of God's plan (15:1–35). Jerusalem, the fulcrum of God's saving history, remains an essential point of reference for a movement that has its roots in God's promises to Israel.[21]

Paul and Barnabas are commissioned by the church at Antioch (13:1–3), which had been founded by Christians fleeing persecution in Jerusalem (see 11:19–20). Historically these two ancient churches had their tensions and their different perspectives, but this is all smoothed out in the narrative of Acts. Barnabas and Paul, initially with the company of John Mark, successfully preach the gospel, always using the Jewish synagogue as their point of

---

21. See Johnson, *Acts of the Apostles*, 225–27.

departure. They sail from Seleucia to Cyprus, cross the island from Salamis to Paphos, and eventually arrive in Asia Minor in Perga. Asked to preach in the synagogue, Paul speaks as an Israelite to Israelites. Regularly throughout this section of Acts, Paul tries to show that Jesus Christ is the fulfilment of Jewish hopes (13:16–41). The message is heard by some and rejected by others (vv. 44–45). Rejection leads Paul to go to the gentiles (vv. 46–50) and eventually to journey to Lystra, initially addressing both Jews and gentiles but eventually turning only to the gentiles (14:1–20). This missionary strategy is repeated regularly across Acts. The wonders they perform lead to a false understanding of the two apostles as "gods." We can sense the early Christian message to the pagans: "We also are men, of like nature with you, and bring you good news that you should turn from these vain things to a living God who made the heaven and the earth and the sea and all that is in them" (v. 15; see 1 Thess. 1:9–10). Neither Jew nor gentile is happy with this message, and the missionaries are forced to flee, which results in their preaching successfully in Derbe (vv. 20–21). As is regularly the case in Acts, all ends well. The apostles go back on their tracks to Antioch, finding that they "had made many disciples" (v. 21). They appoint elders for every community to lead them in prayer and fasting (v. 23). After their journey to Antioch (vv. 24–28), they announce their success, declaring "all that God had done with them, and how he had opened a door of faith to the Gentiles" (v. 27).

The missionary journeys are put on hold as a group of Christians from Judea insists that circumcision is essential for admission to their ranks (15:1–5). The so-called Council of Jerusalem follows, during which, through the crucial intervention of the foundational figures of Peter (vv. 6–11) and James (vv. 15–21), a decision is made in favor of Paul and Barnabas: circumcision is not required (vv. 22–29).[22] After a dispute over the role of John Mark, who had abandoned the first missionary journey (see 13:13), Paul and Barnabas separate. Paul resumes his mission to Asia Minor, taking Silas with him (15:36–16:5). But this journey takes him further west, to Troas, the seaport on the western coast of Asia Minor. Summoned in a dream to go to Macedonia, Paul arrives in Philippi, where he is immediately successful in his conversion of Lydia (16:6–15).[23] But his saving and curing presence to a possessed slave

22. Paul also records this meeting in Gal. 2:1–10.
23. In the second half of Acts the author uses "we" in a number of reports. These reports begin at Troas and are regularly but not always associated with sea voyages (see 16:10–17; 20:5–15; 21:1–18; 27:1–28:16). For many, this shows the presence of the author of Acts and is thus an indication of a firsthand witness to the events reported and is evidence of the historical reliability of Acts. Not all agree. For a balanced study of the "we" passages, see Brown, *Introduction to the New Testament*, 322–27.

girl leads to his being accused by the girl's angry owners and then imprisoned. As is now a familiar pattern, Paul is miraculously freed; the doors are opened and he baptizes his repentant jailer (vv. 16–34). Subsequent discussion over the treatment of Paul and his companions leads to Paul's first indication to his oppressors that he is a Roman citizen. He receives the apologies of the authorities, visits Lydia, and leaves to continue their mission (vv. 35–40). Passage and preaching in Thessalonica and Beroea lead to the usual mixed response (17:1–15). From here Paul journeys to Athens, where he not only uses his initial approach to the Jews but also confronts the pagan culture and religion of the city. Set in the heart of Greek culture and religion, this passage is highlighted by Paul's speech on the Areopagus, a central point for public speech in Athens. Paul's speech does not use the Hebrew Scriptures but cites Greek authorities (the poet Aratus) to point them to the unknown God, a man who has been raised from the dead (vv. 16–34).[24] As always, the response is mixed: "Some mocked; but others said, 'We will hear you again about this'" (v. 32).

A parallel narrative pattern and theological message shape Paul's ongoing journey through Corinth, where his rejection by the Jews leads to a definitive choice: "From now on I will go to the Gentiles" (18:6). But even here he meets conflict and is eventually led to the Roman authorities by his Jewish enemies. Gallio, the Roman proconsul of Achaia, dismisses the charges (18:1–17), and Paul returns to Antioch via Cenchreae (the port of Corinth) and Ephesus. From there he sets sail, promising to return if God so wills (vv. 18–21).[25]

God's will leads Paul to return to Asia Minor and Greece on his third journey. After initiating the final missionary journey in Galatia and Phrygia (18:23), Paul commits himself to a long and trouble-filled experience in Ephesus (18:24–19:41). The figure of Apollos appears briefly (18:24–28; see also 1 Cor. 1:12; 3:4–6), and Paul is persuaded to go to Ephesus, where he preaches boldly in the face of many obstacles, chief among them the riot initiated by the silversmiths who see that Paul's preaching against false gods will bring their trade to an end. Paul leaves Ephesus with the problem unresolved and journeys through some of his earlier mission fields (20:1–6). Returning to Asia Minor, he preaches at such great length at Troas that a young man sitting in a window

---

24. In Athens the death of Jesus is not mentioned, only Jesus' being raised from the dead.

25. The reference to Gallio as the proconsul of Achaia is one of the fixed points for determining a chronology for Paul. There is archeological evidence (an inscription found in Delphi) that Gallio was the proconsul sometime during 51–52 CE. See Jerome Murphy-O'Connor, *St. Paul's Corinth: Texts and Archaeology*, Good News Studies 6 (Wilmington, DE: Michael Glazier, 1983), 141–52. See Spivey, Smith, and Black, *Anatomy of the New Testament*, 277, for a fine photograph of the inscription.

falls asleep and crashes to his death, but Paul restores him. Nothing can stop the spread of God's word (vv. 7–12).

In a fashion that matches many "farewell speeches" found in both biblical and classical literature, Paul sails from Troas to Jerusalem, stopping at Miletus so that he can address the leaders of the church from Ephesus, who are assembled there (20:13–38). It is a moving speech, full of emotion and affection, and a commissioning that they persevere in their faith mission.[26] Paul looks back to what has been achieved and courageously ahead to all that God may have in store for him: "I am going to Jerusalem, bound in the Spirit, not knowing what shall befall me there; except that the Holy Spirit testifies to me in every city that imprisonment and afflictions await me" (vv. 22–23). From there he travels directly to Jerusalem (21:1–14). This is the first time that Paul's journeys have not returned to his home church of Antioch. The God-directed cycle of Jerusalem to Rome must be accomplished (see 1:8). As he bids farewell to a dedicated group in Caesarea before the final leg of his journey to Jerusalem, he tells them, in a way that renders more explicit what he said at Miletus: "For I am ready not only to be imprisoned but even to die at Jerusalem for the name of the Lord Jesus" (v. 13). The narrative stage is set for the final journey: the word of the Lord will journey from Jerusalem to Rome.

Acts 21:15–28:31: To Rome, the End of the Earth

The final pages of the story of the apostles are devoted to Paul's visit to Jerusalem, his arrest, his various trials, and his arrival in Rome. The book closes with Paul preaching the gospel freely in Rome (28:31). As throughout Acts, Lukan literary and theological themes determine the shape and message of the narrative. On arrival in Jerusalem, Paul visits James, the leader of the Jerusalem community, and shares with him the success of the gentile mission. He is able to announce that what was decided at the Jerusalem Council (see 15:1–29) has been put into effect among those received into Christianity without circumcision (21:15–26). Immediately following this episode, however, Jews from Asia, aware of Paul's work among the uncircumcised, create a disturbance in the temple, accusing Paul of "teaching men everywhere against the people and the law and this place; moreover he also brought Greeks into the temple, and he has defiled this holy place" (v. 28). Paul is arrested by Roman authorities (vv. 27–36). From this point on, the narrative consists of a series of encounters

---

26. For a summary of the use and message of these farewell testaments, see Francis J. Moloney, *Glory Not Dishonor: Reading John 13–21* (Minneapolis: Fortress, 1998), 4–7; Johnson, *Acts of the Apostles*, 359–68.

between Paul and Roman authorities in which Paul must answer the accusations of his Jewish enemies.[27]

He defends himself in Jerusalem by calling himself "a citizen of no mean city" (v. 39), reporting the account of his conversion and his mission to the gentiles (see 21:37–22:21). None of this is of interest to the Romans. Discovering that he is a Roman citizen, they send him back to the Jewish Council (22:22–29). His Jewish credentials impress some but not others, and that night "the Lord stood by him and said, 'Take courage, for as you have testified about me at Jerusalem, so you must bear witness also at Rome'" (23:11; see 22:30–23:11). As Paul's opponents concoct a plot to murder him, "the son of Paul's sister" (v. 16) hears of it and informs Paul, who is being held in the Roman barracks. Paul is swept away by the authorities to the governor Felix in Caesarea, the seat of Roman authority in Palestine (23:12–35).

A series of trials take place at Caesarea before Felix, who leaves the case unresolved, with the result that Paul remains in prison for two years (24:1–27). Felix's successor, Porcius Festus, resumes the hearings, and Paul's appeal to be heard by Caesar is granted (25:1–12). Festus, however, brings Paul before King Agrippa and his wife, Bernice (25:13–26:32), during which Paul again tells of his conversion (26:12–18). Paul fulfills the destiny promised by Jesus to his disciples: "And you will be brought before kings and governors in my name" (Luke 21:12). In a dramatic conclusion to this trial, he appeals to Agrippa to believe (Acts 26:27–29). At each trial Paul's defense is the same: he has done nothing to discredit the traditions of Israel, as he has been singled out by an act of the God of Israel to proclaim the saving effects of the death and resurrection of Jesus. "To this day I have had the help that comes from God, and so I stand here testifying both to small and great, saying nothing but what the prophets and Moses said would come to pass: that the Christ must suffer, and that, by being the first to rise from the dead, he would proclaim light both to the people and to the Gentiles" (vv. 22–23; see Luke 2:31–32). The message of Luke 24:1–49, more so than that of the Pauline Letters (although they are not at odds), can be heard in this defense. At each stage throughout these trials, Paul is declared innocent (23:29; 25:25; 26:31–32). It is as an innocent witness to the truth (like Jesus in the Lukan passion narrative [see esp. Luke 23:47]) that Paul sails for Rome (27:1–2).

The perilous sea journey, described as Luke's "literary *tour de force*,"[28] is reported in 27:1–28:10. After an initial easy journey at the right time of the year

27. On the Lukan theological and rhetorical agenda throughout these encounters, see Johnson, *Acts of the Apostles*, 399–400.

28. See Johnson, *Acts of the Apostles*, 450. It is precisely this exciting story's literary elegance that makes the interpreter wonder why so much time and effort has been put into it.

(27:1–8), a decision is made—against Paul's advice—to continue the journey in the winter (vv. 9–12). From that point on, every possible peril is faced: storm at sea (vv. 13–20), starvation (vv. 21–25), and possible shipwreck (vv. 26–32). Paul advises correctly in every situation and even miraculously provides food for everyone as they are starving (vv. 33–38). They come to land in Malta, where they experience dangers (28:3–6, the episode with the viper), again overcome by Paul, and they are made welcome by the local people (27:39–28:10). They set sail from Malta and finally "came into Rome" (28:16; see vv. 11–16). As throughout Acts, the Christian community, Peter, and Paul continually face danger and opposition, but difficulties are overcome by the power of their miraculous activity and the persuasion of their proclamation of the gospel.

In Rome, Paul tells his story of trial and is asked to further explain himself to the local authorities. As always (reflecting the way the gospel has been received everywhere), some believe and some reject what Paul has to tell them (28:17–25a). Acts closes with Paul's final use of Israel's Scriptures to legitimate his message and his turning away from Israel to the gentiles: "Let it be known to you then that this salvation of God has been sent to the Gentiles; they will listen" (v. 28; see vv. 25b–28). Paul's mission to the Jews has come to a close, and from Rome the gospel will be preached to the gentiles. Luke tells of the relentless and unstoppable proclamation of the message of what God had done in and through Jesus. His second volume closes with the information that Paul remains in Rome for two years, courageously and openly "preaching the kingdom of God and teaching about the Lord Jesus Christ" (vv. 30–31). It is "an assurance that 'the ends of the earth' is not the arrival at a boundary, but realization of the limitless promises of the dominion of God."[29]

Conclusion

I have provided this overview of the theological narrative of the Acts of the Apostles for two reasons. In the first place, the story is not well known to Christians. We hear pieces of Acts read on various occasions, often unhelpfully for an understanding of its faith-filled motivation. For example, Paul's conversion, the subject of spectacular artistic renditions over the centuries and the origin of an English turn of phrase, "a Damascus experience," is not understood as the action of God, in and through the risen Jesus, to turn the preaching of the gospel toward the gentiles. The appointment of deacons is

---

29. Richard I. Pervo, *Luke's Story of Paul* (Minneapolis: Augsburg Fortress, 1990), quoted in Parsons, *Acts*, 367. See also Johnson, *Acts of the Apostles*, 473–76.

regularly misread as the beginnings of a rite of ministerial ordination. The summary statements on the unity of the Jerusalem church are read in an idealistic way, as though this was exactly how things were back then rather than a rhetorical challenge issued by Luke to his readers: this is the way things should be *now*. The aggressive overall story of the fulfillment of God's plan, the word concerning what he has done in and through his Son, from Jerusalem to the end of the earth, is neither known nor understood.

Christians are far better informed about the martyrdom of Paul, which is only found in later Christian tradition and never in the Acts of the Apostles. They thus miss the message that the commands of Jesus in Luke 24:46–49 and Acts 1:8 have been fulfilled, thanks to the never-failing presence of a saving God who protects, empowers, and directs his apostles, and especially Paul, to take the gospel from Jerusalem to the end of the earth. Opposition emerges not only from the Jews, who will not accept an uncircumcised Christian, and from the Romans, who cannot—and do not want to—understand what Paul represents, but also from believers who want a closer adherence to the law of Moses. He is even opposed by the elements, as storm, starvation, and shipwreck threaten this journey from Jerusalem to Rome. But all such opposition fails as, accompanied by signs and wonders that manifest God's power, the preaching of the kingdom reaches to the end of the earth.

Second, there is much in the Acts of the Apostles that is fundamental to the faith life of believing Christians.[30] God is in control of history and guides his "apostles" of all ages through their difficulties, sinfulness, and rejection. Starting with God's promises to Israel, and on through the story of Jesus Christ, eventually preached as the Messiah, Lord, and Savior at the end of the earth, God has been faithful to Israel, and his promises to them have been fulfilled. Although unexpected by the earliest Christians, these promises have come to incorporate the gentiles, who are included as part of a long journey that began in the fulfillment of the promises of the Old Testament in a child from Nazareth, but born in Bethlehem, the City of David (Luke 1–2). That journey of fulfillment reached its crucial turning point in Jerusalem, where Jesus took control of the temple, preached, was opposed, and was ultimately tried, crucified, raised, and taken up to heaven (Luke 19:44–24:53). However, as he leaves he instructs his disciples that "repentance and forgiveness of sins should be preached in his name to all nations, beginning from Jerusalem" (Luke 24:47), and he commissions them: "You shall be my witnesses in Jerusalem and in all Judea and Samaria and to the end of the earth" (Acts 1:8).

---

30. For a good summary, which I have used in what follows, see Powell, *Introducing the New Testament*, 200–211.

The Church's mission to reach out to the end of the earth will be accompanied by the presence of Jesus in his Spirit, in his word, in the lives of his followers, and in the use of his name, as salvation is proclaimed and experienced and as believers have access to the power of God in the Christian community. They are thus "liberated from whatever prevents them from experiencing life as God intends."[31] We may look back on the narrative of the Acts of the Apostles, discover there a word of God that makes these claims, and wonder: is this really the case? There has been so much ambiguity in the ongoing story of the community of Jesus down through the centuries, and this ambiguity remains with us in the contemporary Christian Church. How can this story of God's unfailing success, despite all forms of opposition, be relevant in today's Church? But Luke was aware of these ambiguities even in his own time and in his own experience of church. Yet he chose not to focus on tales of such messiness! Luke wanted to proclaim, by means of this narrative, that miracles *can happen*. God's outreach to the end of the earth *can be successful*. Indeed, our own experience of church is an indication that the gospel has reached the end of the earth.[32] The challenge of the Acts of the Apostles is that those who read and hear it, living their Christian life at the end of the earth, might accept Luke's view of *how things should be* in God's Church, where Jesus is present and where the saving power of God can be found. In this way we *can be the witnesses* who fill the pages of a third volume of what God has done for us in and through Jesus Christ.

---

31. Ibid., 208.

32. Writing in Australia, I am particularly conscious of the presence of the good news about Jesus, and the presence of God's realm, in the midst of our ambiguity, in Christian communities at the end of the world.

8

Later Writings
of the New Testament

Letters from Apostles and a Homily

Checking the index of our New Testament shows that there are a number of documents that we have not yet discussed. They all have their importance within the life and liturgy of the Church, but history has located the Pauline Literature and the Four Gospels at its center. For that reason we have devoted the bulk of this book to Jesus, Paul, Mark, Matthew, Luke, and John. But before we close our reflections, we must ask how the remaining documents emerged within early Christianity and sketch their significance as they are read in the Church.

Many of the remaining documents are associated with the name of an apostle or a leading figure in the earliest Church. Paul's name is regularly associated with 2 Thessalonians, Colossians, Ephesians, Titus, 1 and 2 Timothy, and Hebrews. Most scholars today would regard these letters as "post-Pauline" or, in the case of Hebrews, non-Pauline. While they have their roots in the Pauline experience and continue his tradition into a later era, Paul, who was most likely executed in 64–65 CE, was no longer alive when these documents were produced. Because of their thematic similarity with the Fourth

Gospel (especially the theme of love), 1, 2, and 3 John have been associated with the name "John." John's name is also associated with the book known to us as the Apocalypse, or Revelation, where the author identifies himself by that name (see Rev. 1:1, 4, 9; 22:8).[1] "Peter" is named as the author of two letters (1 and 2 Peter), and "James" and "Jude" claim authorship for two further letters. The Letter to the Hebrews names no author, but it has long been associated with Paul.

Second Thessalonians, Colossians, Ephesians, Titus, and 1 and 2 Timothy claim that they were written by Paul. On the basis of that claim, they are proclaimed in the liturgical life of the Christian churches as letters of Paul. Nevertheless, a number of theological themes, problems faced, and language found *in the documents* do not appear to be Pauline. But they were regarded by those who wrote them, and even by those who received them, as "Pauline." We Christians of the third millennium have a sense of "literary ownership," and even "intellectual property," that was unknown and made no sense in antiquity. It was quite common to use the name of a significant figure from the past as the author of a document, especially when that figure remained the inspiration and model for the original writer.

The name of the historical author does not appear, as he or she wishes to continue the tradition of a figure from the past. These letters that look back to Paul for their authority are an example of this widespread practice in antiquity, known as "pseudonymity."[2] We must be careful not to apply our twenty-first-century criteria to this widely used practice. The exhortations and teachings of 2 Thessalonians, Colossians, Ephesians, Titus, and 1 and 2 Timothy continue the Pauline tradition and are the inspired Word of God, accepted as such by the end of the fourth century.[3] The authors of these documents, at a later time in the development of the Church's life and practice, consciously placed themselves within the trajectory of Paul's thought and teaching. They wished to continue the lively presence of the authoritative word of the apostle Paul in

1. The Greek word *apokalypsis* means "revelation." Both "The Apocalypse" and "Revelation" have been traditionally used as a title for this document.

2. For a clear description of the practice of pseudonymity in antiquity and in the New Testament, see Brown, *Introduction to the New Testament*, 585–89. "Pseudonymous" must not be confused with "anonymous." Pseudonymity means that the actual writer supplies the name of another as the author ("false name"). An anonymous document has no indication of the name of an author (e.g., the four Gospels). Pseudonymity is very common in the Old Testament (e.g., Moses as the author of Deuteronomy, David as the author of all the Psalms, Solomon as the author of Wisdom, Daniel as the author of a book set in the sixth century BCE but in fact addressing Israel's political and religious situation in the second century BCE). See also Green and McDonald, *World of the New Testament*, 367–78; Powell, *Introducing the New Testament*, 222–29; Spivey, Smith, and Black, *Anatomy of the New Testament*, 375–78.

3. See pp. 57–61 above.

these different circumstances. The simple fact that these writings eventually emerged as part of the Christian canon is a first indication that they achieved their goal: they are *read in the Christian Church*.

The Post-Pauline Letters

2 Thessalonians

Both 1 and 2 Thessalonians deal with the problem of the end of the world and the attitude believers must have as they wait for that final time. Some critics continue to claim that Paul is the author of both letters.[4] However, there are some differences between them. First, 2 Thessalonians 2:1–12 claims that there are some who believe the day of the Lord has already come, and the author responds to this with a description of that time. We do not find this anywhere else in Paul. There are many places where he indicates that this final day may be close at hand (see esp. 1 Cor. 7:25–31 [v. 26, "in view of the impending distress" (AT); v. 31, "For the form of this world is passing away"]), and 1 Thessalonians indicates that there is some anxiety in Thessalonica about the destiny of the faithful who have passed away before the final coming of Jesus (see 1 Thess. 4:13–5:11). But nowhere does Paul have to deal with believers who claim that the day of the Lord has already come.

Second, the author goes out of his way to insist that he is "Paul." He seems to protest too much! He says it twice (1:1; 3:17) and insists upon his authority (2:1; 3:14–15), unlike the letters accepted as certainly Pauline, where Paul is more self-effacing. In those letters his name always appears at the beginning and sometimes also at the end. In Galatians (e.g., 1:11–2:14), 2 Corinthians (e.g., 11:1–12:13), and Philippians (e.g., 3:3–11), Paul indicates biographical details, his Jewish pedigree, and some unique personal experiences. But the tenor of those interventions is different from the heavy-handedness of 2 Thessalonians. Paul is often self-deprecating in his earlier letters; these moments of self-disclosure show his weakness: "for when I am weak, then I am strong" (2 Cor. 12:10). Those who argue for the Pauline authorship of 2 Thessalonians suggest that it was written very shortly after 1 Thessalonians to the same people in the same situation of anxiety about the final coming of the Lord. It is better explained as a later "imitation" of Paul's 1 Thessalonians, addressing a different situation, probably sometime in the 90s, as the Church faced difficulties in the Roman Empire (see 2 Thess. 2:3, 4, 9). But there is still a

---

4. See, e.g., Spivey, Smith, and Black, *Anatomy of the New Testament*, 279–83.

link with 1 Thessalonians, as the author uses the authority of Paul to address mistaken ideas about the imminent end of time (see 2:15; 3:4, 6–13) and the Lord's ultimate victory over the lawless one (2:7–8).[5]

The Letter to the Colossians

Many scholars continue to claim that Paul wrote the Letter to the Colossians. It contains much that belongs to Paul, but the author has developed a rich theology of creation and of God's saving presence in Jesus Christ, the high point and perfection of all creation, majestically articulated in a hymn found in Colossians 1:15–20. If Paul was the author, it must have been the last of his letters, written from Rome sometime in the 60s. The inspiring theology of salvation and creation arises from the problems the author is addressing, which are most evident in Colossians 2:8–23. The author opposes "philosophy and empty deceit," the result of "human tradition" and the "elemental spirits of the universe" (v. 8). The author seems to be dealing with a false way of understanding the world that puts Christ in a position lower than some system of elemental spirits. This cannot be accepted, as only Christ is the universal and cosmic redeemer.

All commentators accept that the Greco-Roman world provides the setting and background for such teaching. Although Paul had enough background in and experience of that world, the majority of critics suggest that Colossians was written in the 80s from Ephesus to the Christians in the city of Colossae (on the west coast of what was then known as Asia Minor—today's Turkey). Paul's fundamental understanding of Jesus Christ does not change in Colossians; it is being transposed into a later time and place. Similarly, although the situation has changed, the author continues the Pauline tradition that no human system responds to the design of God for the salvation of humankind. In this letter, the author can point to the uselessness of Jewish ceremonial law, taboos, and calendar observances (see Col. 2:16–18, 20–23). Only one thing matters: "holding fast to the Head, from whom the whole body, nourished and knit together through its joints and ligaments, grows with a growth that is from God" (2:19). The importance of oneness in Christ is found throughout the Pauline letters, but Paul never quite says it like this.[6]

---

5. See Powell, *Introducing the New Testament*, 387–95. For a helpful commentary, see Furnish, *1 Thessalonians, 2 Thessalonians*.

6. See Powell, *Introducing the New Testament*, 357–85. Powell offers a very balanced appreciation of the relationship between Colossians and Ephesians and, if they both belong to Paul, of their association with Philemon in the 60s (see p. 360). For a treatment of Colossians and Ephesians as post-Pauline, and of their close relationship, see Brown, *Introduction to the New Testament*, 599–637, and Spivey, Smith, and Black, *Anatomy of the New Testament*, 379–89.

The Letter to the Ephesians

The Letter to the Ephesians also seems to reflect a time later than Paul, and most think that the author's starting point and model for his presentation of Jesus Christ was the Letter to the Colossians.[7] The words "in Ephesus" in Ephesians 1:1—"to the saints in Ephesus"—are not found in some ancient witnesses. This suggests that Ephesians was a "circular letter" written in the 80s or 90s to Christian churches in western Asia Minor. Some of the early Church's most moving reflections on Christ are found in this letter: reflections on the riches of God's mercy and love, available to all who believe (Eph. 2:1–10).[8] The anguish that Paul reveals in his concern over the final salvation of the Jews in Romans 9–11 has disappeared. The author develops a magnificent theology of the unity of the Church. The hostility between Jew and Greek has come to an end because of Jesus' death (Eph. 2:11–22). The author looks back: "Remember that you were at that time separated from Christ, alienated from the commonwealth of Israel" (v. 12). But that situation has been transformed by the gracious act of God in and through Jesus Christ: "Now in Christ Jesus you who once were far off have been brought near in the blood of Christ" (v. 13). It is not as if this subject is non-Pauline. Indeed, it is a continuation of Paul's understanding of Jesus' death (see Rom. 15:5–6). However, he has never before approached this subject in this way. Paul offers his imprisonment and prayers so that the believing hearers of this circular letter will comprehend the love of Christ and thus be filled with the fullness of God (Eph. 3:13–19). The author asks for a quality of Christian living (see 4:4–6:20) because God "has blessed us in Christ with every spiritual blessing in the heavenly places, even as he chose us in him before the foundation of the world, that we should be holy and blameless before him" (1:3–4).

A feature of both Colossians and Ephesians that is not found in the earlier Pauline letters is a concern for the right order of the Christian household (see Col. 3:18–4:1; Eph. 5:21–6:9). Family members and their households are given instructions on the way they should behave and relate, inspired by the death and resurrection of Jesus Christ. These instructions reflect a time of deeper insertion of Christian communities into Greco-Roman society. Christian

7. See Powell, *Introducing the New Testament*, 323–41. On Colossians and Ephesians, see the chart on p. 330. For helpful commentaries, see Charles H. Talbert, *Ephesians and Colossians*, Paideia Commentaries on the New Testament (Grand Rapids: Baker Academic, 2007); Margaret Y. MacDonald, *Colossians and Ephesians* (Collegeville, MN: Liturgical Press, 2008).

8. Brown, *Introduction to the New Testament*, 621, rightly cites C. H. Dodd's description of Ephesians as the "crown of Paulinism" and joins many who regard the author of Ephesians as "Paul's best disciple."

uniqueness needed to be addressed, but in a way that made sense in this society. None of this *betrays* Paul. It renders more practical Paul's never-failing insistence on love (see esp. 1 Cor. 13; and Rom. 13:10, "love is the fulfilling of the law"). Behind the authors' use of the name of Paul (Col. 1:1; Eph. 1:1) lies the authority of Paul and the further development of the Pauline understanding of God, the Christ, what God has done for humankind in and through Jesus Christ, and how we are to relate to one another. As such, 2 Thessalonians, Colossians, and Ephesians continue to play a questioning and creative role as they are *read in the Church*.

The Pastoral Epistles: To Timothy and Titus

The Letter to Titus and 1 and 2 Timothy also claim to come from Paul (see Titus 1:1; 1 Tim. 1:1; 2 Tim. 1:1), and they are directed to known and important Pauline disciples (for Titus, see 2 Cor. 2:13; 7:6–16; 8:6, 16, 23; 12:17–18; for Timothy, see 1 Thess. 1:1; 3:2; 1 Cor. 4:17; 16:10–11; 2 Cor. 1:19; Phil. 2:19–23).[9] Given the close relationship that existed between Paul and Titus and Timothy, there would have been good reason for Paul to write to them concerning their mission and pastoral responsibilities. Precisely because these three letters, on the whole, deal with matters that touch on the day-to-day pastoral responsibilities of leaders of churches in Crete (Titus) and Ephesus (1 and 2 Timothy), they have been classified since the eighteenth century as Paul's "Pastoral Epistles." They were written at a time when the churches addressed by these documents were well-established communities beginning to feel the strain that always emerges as a developing group must cope with its human frailty. In a number of places the author, writing as the person of Paul, signals that his time of charismatic leadership is at an end: "The time of my departure has come. I have fought the good fight, I have finished the race, I have kept the faith" (2 Tim. 4:6–7; see also 1 Tim. 1:12–17).

The communities are now in a more stable position, and attention must be given to what today we would call "church order" (see Titus 1:5–9; 1 Tim. 2:1–15; 3:1–16; 5:3–6:2), the right regulation of Christian households (Titus 2:1–3:11; 1 Tim. 5:3–6:2). Warnings against the dangers of false teachings

9. See Brown, *Introduction to the New Testament*, 638–80; Powell, *Introducing the New Testament*, 397–413; Spivey, Smith, and Black, *Anatomy of the New Testament*, 390–99. For helpful commentaries, see Judith M. Bassler, *1 Timothy, 2 Timothy, Titus*, Abingdon New Testament Commentaries (Nashville: Abingdon, 1996); Raymond F. Collins, *I and II Timothy and Titus*, New Testament Library (Louisville: Westminster John Knox, 2002).

and improper living are issued (Titus 1:10–16; 1 Tim. 1:3–11; 4:1–5; 6:3–10; 2 Tim. 2:14–3:9). The tone of 2 Timothy is particularly touching, with the author writing as Paul faces death, speaking of his own suffering and sense of being abandoned (2 Tim. 1:6–18); the author encourages Timothy to look to Paul as a model of faith, patience, love, and steadfastness (2 Tim. 3:10–4:8).[10] As a group of post-Pauline letters, however, the Pastoral Epistles show a concern for the behavior of Christian community leaders and elders, for the treatment of widows and slaves, and for distinguishing between heresy and right teaching. These matters, which are sometimes present in the major Pauline letters, play a larger role in the Pastoral Epistles than they did in the days of Paul. Nevertheless, Paul's thought is present throughout the more theological reflections. First and Second Timothy use hymns that emulate Paul's writing (see 1 Tim. 1:12–17; 2:3–5; 3:16; 6:11–16; 2 Tim. 1:8–14; 2:8–13). The author states two fundamental and perennially important Pauline truths in 1 Timothy 2:3–6: God wishes to save all humankind, and the only mediator between God and human beings is Jesus Christ (1 Tim. 2:3–6).

The Pastoral Epistles carry Paulinism into the second Christian century. Paul had been dead for some forty years, but his message still had to be passed on to a new and different generation of Christians. Whoever the authors were, they made the Pauline understanding of God, Christ, the Christian, and the community of the Christian Church their own. They did not betray Paul; they had taken Paul's message to heart. They applied it to later times and later situations. Tensions within different groups in the community were felt; problems were emerging concerning correct or false interpretation and teaching of what God had done in Jesus and how they were to live as a consequence. Christian communities were facing strange but sometimes fascinating religious teaching and practices as they became more settled and established in the Greco-Roman world.

Paul's letters were written to specific groups in the earliest Church (remember Paul had been martyred by the mid-60s). He did not have to face the internal and external problems that Christians faced later in the first century and in the first decades of the second century. Paul certainly wrote 1 Thessalonians, Galatians, 1 Corinthians, 2 Corinthians, Philemon, Philippians, and Romans. Inspired by that heritage, the later letters claim the authority of

10. A case has been made for a large amount of genuine "Pauline" material in this touching communication, collected from genuine Pauline writings and assembled in 2 Timothy. See Michael P. Prior, *Paul the Letter-Writer and the Second Letter to Timothy*, Journal for the Study of the New Testament Supplement Series 23 (Sheffield, UK: JSOT Press, 1989); Jerome Murphy-O'Connor, "2 Timothy Contrasted with 1 Timothy and Titus," *Revue Biblique* 98 (1991): 403–18.

Paul by their steady reference to him as "author." He is their author insofar as he is their *author*-ity.

Letters of Apostles: James, Peter, John, and Jude

The number "seven," which is significant in many cultures and has its own biblical background (see, e.g., Gen. 2:1–3; 4:24; 41:2–36; Deut. 7:1; Judg. 16:14; Ruth 4:15; Josh. 6:1–21), contributed to the presence of seven letters, known as the Catholic Epistles.[11] There are twice seven (fourteen) letters accepted by tradition as Pauline. There is a sense in which the number "seven" indicates perfection or completion. Within the Apocalypse there are seven "letters to the churches" (Rev. 2:1–3:22).[12] The need for "seven" may be one of the reasons for the acceptance of brief documents like 2 and 3 John and Jude into the Christian canon. There was a sense in the second and third centuries that this final "seven" *completed* the collection.

Some very early writers had already called 1 John a "Catholic Epistle" because the letter was not directed to a particular church. The expression characterized the wide focus of the letter's address, especially when compared to the very specific focus of 2 and 3 John (see 2 John 1, "to the elect lady"; 3 John 1, "to Gaius"). First Peter addresses "the exiles of the Dispersion in Pontus, Galatia, Cappadocia, Asia, and Bithynia" (1 Pet. 1:1). The recipients of James are not identified, and Jude and 2 Peter are addressed to all Christians. These letters, especially the Letter of James and 1 Peter, contain teaching that is both moving and fundamental to Christian life and practice. Our reflection on these letters will follow the order in which they appear in the New Testament, with one exception. The brief Letter of Jude normally appears before the final book, the Apocalypse. However, as there is a close relationship between Jude and 2 Peter, I will present them in that order.

The Letter of James

The Letter of James is a striking document.[13] The author addresses urgent issues: caring for the poor, controlling one's tongue, unjust discrimination, the

11. See esp. Francis J. Moloney, *From James to Jude: A Bible Commentary for Every Day* (Abingdon, UK: Bible Reading Fellowship, 1999); Spivey, Smith, and Black, *Anatomy of the New Testament*, 403–4.

12. The author of the Apocalypse uses "seven" as one of the structural elements in his book: seven letters (Rev. 1:9–3:22), seven seals (4:1–8:1), seven trumpets (8:2–11:19), and seven bowls (12:1–22:5). See pp. 183–84 below.

13. See Powell, *Introducing the New Testament*, 445–61; Spivey, Smith, and Black, *Anatomy of the New Testament*, 405–8. What follows also depends on Luke T. Johnson, *The Letter of*

need to put one's deeds where one's words are. Christians are reminded of their vocation to live their call in God-directed practical lives reflecting "the perfect law, the law of liberty" (James 1:25). There is little in the letter about the life and teaching or the death and resurrection of Jesus, whose name appears only twice (1:1; 2:1). Yet James is an outspoken early Christian demanding that we live the Christian life and not just talk about it—that we be doers, not just hearers, of the Word (see 1:19–25). The author has a very Jewish mind-set. He speaks to "the twelve tribes in the Dispersion" (1:1), and the assembly of the community is called by the Greek name *synagōgē* (2:2). He is very devoted to God's law (see 1:25; 2:8–13; 4:11–12) and quotes it as an authority that cannot be questioned (see 2:8, 11, 23; 4:6; 5:11). Old Testament figures appear in the letter more regularly than Jesus: Abraham, Rahab, Job, and Elijah (see 2:21–25; 5:11, 17–18). But the letter is a fine example of the way the earliest Church fused its Jewish roots with the newness of Jesus Christ. Although mentioned only twice, Jesus is called the "Lord Jesus Christ" (1:1) and "our glorious Lord Jesus Christ" (2:1 NRSV). The risen and glorified Christ lies behind the author's teaching on the hope of his second coming (5:7–9) and the description of the Christian community as "the Church" (5:14).

The Letter of James is best described as a "paranesis." This word comes from a Greek word meaning "advice" or "counsel." Most of the letters of Paul end with practical recommendations that are also "paranesis," although they respond to earlier and different problems (see, e.g., Rom. 12–15; 1 Cor. 16; Phil. 4:2–23; Col. 4:2–18; 1 Thess. 5:12–24). The Letter of James is made up entirely of such recommendations, but the author appears to discuss in succession a number of apparently independent issues. He can shift from a discussion of faith without works in 2:14–26 to seemingly unrelated, very frank statements on the misuse of speech in 3:1–12. Perhaps the most troublesome section of the letter has always been its beginning, 1:1–27. Across the letter itself we are able to focus our attention on extended treatments of single issues, but in 1:1–27 the author appears to move rapidly from one theme to another. This is disconcerting to modern readers, who are used to a well-written first page.

Our increased knowledge of ancient literature has taught us that this practice is found not only in the Letter of James. When we open a modern book we often find on the very first page a list of what is "contained" in the book: the book's "contents." The ancients did not always produce such lists on a stand-alone first page, independent of the writing itself. They included their "contents page" as the first section of the document. In ancient rhetoric this

---

James, Anchor Bible 37A (New York: Doubleday, 1995). See also Patrick J. Hartin, *James* (Collegeville, MN: Liturgical Press, 2009).

first page was called the *epitome*, which, loosely translated, was the preface or the contents of the work that followed. The themes mentioned in 1:1–27 of the Letter of James include perseverance in trial (vv. 2–4, 12), prayer (vv. 5–7), the reversal of the situations of the rich and the poor (vv. 9–10), friendship with the world versus friendship with God (vv. 12–18), use of the tongue (vv. 19–20), and the need to act out of religious conviction (vv. 22–27). At first sight, these themes gathered haphazardly on the first page provide the contents of the fuller discussions of the body of the letter. The author does not follow the order of his *epitome*, but all these themes receive extended treatment.

2:1–11	The reversal of the situations of the rich and the poor (see 1:9–10)
2:14–26	The need to act out of religious conviction (see 1:22–27)
3:1–12	The use of the tongue (see 1:19–20)
3:13–4:10	Friendship with the world versus friendship with God (see 1:12–18)
4:13–5:6	The reversal of the situations of the rich and the poor (see 1:9–10)
5:7–11	Perseverance in trial (see 1:2–4, 12)
5:13–18	Prayer (see 1:5–7)

Central to the letter and its overarching theme is friendship with the world versus friendship with God (3:13–4:10). In a world where "friendship" was the most discussed and esteemed relationship, a question of "one soul," involving a sharing of attitudes, values, and perceptions, seeing things the same way, friendship with God was of major concern to the author. Smaller sections of the letter, not listed above (2:12–13; 4:11–12; 5:12), serve the author in moving from one theme to another and creating "bridges" between discussions of major concern. The letter comes to a close in 5:19–20, where the author, who has written so much to exhort his fellow Christians to better behavior, tells his readers that they should do for others what he has done for them.

The First Letter of Peter

First Peter is possibly a genuine letter from the Simon Peter of the Gospels, a significant figure in the earliest years of Christianity.[14] He died a martyr in

---

14. See Powell, *Introducing the New Testament*, 463–79; Spivey, Smith, and Black, *Anatomy of the New Testament*, 409–13. For helpful commentaries, see Reinhard Feldmeier, *The First Letter of Peter*, trans. Peter H. Davids (Waco: Baylor University Press, 2008), and the more

Rome during the Neronian persecutions (probably around 65 AD). But it may come from a slightly later period, written in elegant Greek, looking back to the authority of Peter. It is the source of some favorite Christian themes:

- "Although you have not seen him, you love him" (1 Pet. 1:8 NRSV).
- "You are a chosen race, a royal priesthood, a holy nation, God's own people" (2:9).
- "Love covers a multitude of sins" (4:8).
- "I exhort the elders among you to tend the flock of God that is in your charge, exercising the oversight, not under compulsion but willingly, as God would have you do it—not for sordid gain but eagerly" (5:1–2 NRSV).
- "Like a roaring lion your adversary the devil prowls around, looking for someone to devour" (5:8 NRSV).

God has given Christians their "home" (2:5; 4:17), after they had been so long "homeless" (2:11). The letter is dominated by the theme of "once . . . now": "Once you were not a people, but now you are God's people; once you had not received mercy, but now you have received mercy" (2:10 NRSV). The transformation from a situation of lostness into "living stones . . . a spiritual house . . . a holy priesthood" (2:4–5) through Jesus' saving death is the other main thrust of the letter (see esp. 2:18–25; 3:18–4:6). First Peter is perhaps the New Testament writing that is most heavily influenced by the figure of the Suffering Servant from the prophet Isaiah. The heart of 1 Peter's understanding of Jesus is found in the use made of Isaiah 53 in 2:21–25: "He committed no sin, and no deceit was found in his mouth" (1 Pet. 2:22 NRSV; see Isa. 53:9); "He himself bore our sins in his body" (1 Pet. 2:24; see Isa. 53:4); "By his wounds you have been healed. For you were going astray like sheep" (1 Pet. 2:24–25 NRSV; see Isa. 53:5–6).

With this understanding of Jesus, Peter addresses Christian communities that are suffering some form of persecution (see 1:6; 3:13–17; 4:12–19). It is difficult to determine the exact nature of this persecution, but there is no need to situate this letter within the context of the great persecutions that emerged late in the first century and became more widespread in the second. The formal language associated with those persecutions, found in Roman documents and perhaps reflected in such passages as Mark 8:34–35; 10:35–36; 13:9; and John 16:2, is notably absent from 1 Peter. The letter may come from a period and a

---

scholarly (but outstanding) Paul J. Achtemeier, *1 Peter: A Commentary on the First Epistle of Peter*, Hermeneia (Minneapolis: Fortress, 1996). For a balanced assessment of the authorship question, see Feldmeier, *First Letter of Peter*, 32–39.

situation in which small, emerging Christian communities were experiencing hostility and mistrust.[15]

The letter is introduced with an address and greeting (1:1–2), after which Peter describes the dignity and responsibilities of the Christian vocation (1:3–2:10). He first describes the salvation that comes from the Father, through the Son, revealed by the Spirit (1:3–12), and then exhorts his readers to holiness (vv. 13–25). The vocation to be a follower of Jesus Christ brings its responsibilities. Christians are to live as God's children (2:1–3), as a new household of God (vv. 4–10). Once the situation of the Christian has been described, the second part of the letter turns to a presentation of the witness of the Christian life (2:11–3:12). Christians are to live in a pagan world (2:11–12), an integral part of life in the larger world (2:13–3:7). This calls for specific instructions on behavior toward civil authority (2:13–17) and behavior in the family (2:18–3:7). Above all, the life of the Christian is to feature love and humility (3:8–12).

The third major section of the letter deals with persecution (3:13–5:11). There is a uniquely Christian approach to persecution (3:13–4:11), marked by confidence (3:13–17) and based on the person of Christ (3:18–4:6). Christ's victory over sin is applied to Christians by baptism (3:18–22), and the Christian, through suffering, renounces sin (4:1–6) and looks toward the end of time (vv. 7–11). Peter realistically faces the rejection and persecution of the Christians (4:12–5:11), instructing them to rejoice as they share in Christ's suffering in the face of very real persecution (4:12–19), exhorting both elders and the faithful on the importance of Christian leadership (5:1–5). This section on persecution closes with a call for trust in God, who brings glory through suffering (vv. 6–11). The letter concludes by insisting that what Peter has taught is the true grace of God. Peter bids farewell and exhorts his readers to stand firm in this truth (vv. 12–14). The letter moves from introduction (1:1–2), to the beauty of the Christian vocation (1:3–2:10), to the need to be living witnesses to that form of life (2:11–3:12) and the suffering that may flow from such witness (3:13–5:11). Christian life and its challenges are precious gifts of God (5:12–14).

The Letter of Jude and the Second Letter of Peter

Jude and 2 Peter come from a very different time and situation than 1 Peter.[16] It is likely that 2 Peter used the Letter of Jude as the author composed his

---

15. On the background to the suffering of the community, see Achtemeier, *1 Peter*, 23–36.

16. See Powell, *Introducing the New Testament*, 481–91, 509–17; on the parallels between Jude and 2 Peter, see the chart on p. 483. See also Spivey, Smith, and Black, *Anatomy of the New Testament*, 435–37. For helpful commentaries, see Richard J. Bauckham, *Jude, 2 Peter*, Word

attack on the errors that were creeping into the Christian community. Both letters are dealing with the same challenges, and they share many ideas and words. Reading Jude 4–16 alongside 2 Peter 2:1–8, and reading Jude 17–25 alongside 2 Peter 3:1–18, shows an undeniable dependence. We cannot be certain that 2 Peter depends upon Jude, as the sharing of ideas might have gone in the other direction: Jude may have borrowed from 2 Peter. However, Jude is a more general letter, denouncing opponents with very little recognition of the situation of the Christians receiving the document. Second Peter is carefully descriptive of a specific attack on the Christian understanding of God as the Lord of all history, and it gives more attention to the uniqueness of the Christian message and the Christian vocation. Given the detailed focus of 2 Peter, it is widely accepted that the author of this brief letter used the more general Jude to compose his attack on specific dangerous currents of thought and practice.

Some scholars attribute the authorship of Jude to "Judas, the son of James," one of the apostles according to Luke 6:16, and maintain that the letter was directed to a Jewish-Christian community. But details in the document indicate that it belongs to the latest of the New Testament documents.[17] The close relationship between Jude and 2 Peter is important for these considerations. Jude speaks of "the apostles of our Lord" in verse 17 as if they were figures of the distant past. Second Peter is aware of a chain of tradition, from Gospel traditions and Paul's "letters," and of the need to establish a correct and unified interpretation of these traditions (see 2 Pet. 1:12–15). Both letters show a familiarity with both the Jewish world and the Greco-Roman world, and they are written in elegant Greek, not common in the earliest Christian writings. The Letter of Jude cites from both Jewish and pagan authors (see vv. 6, 9, 11, 14–15, 17–18). Arguments about God's just judgment in 2 Peter have parallels in classical literature as well as in Jewish sources.

Although not a perfect model of an ancient letter, the Letter of Jude displays many features of the genre. It has an opening, in which the author introduces himself, addresses a general audience, and asks that they be blessed (vv. 1–2). The letter is written because of the urgent need for those receiving it to "contend for the faith" in the face of dangerous perversions (vv. 3–4). The author then attacks the dangers faced by the Christian community: the inevitable judgment of God will fall upon the heretics (vv. 5–15), who are sinners compared to the ideal members of Jude's church, described as saints

---

Biblical Commentary 50 (Waco: Word, 1983); Jerome H. Neyrey, *2 Peter, Jude*, Anchor Bible 37C (New York: Doubleday, 1993).

17. See Brown, *Introduction to the New Testament*, 756–59.

(vv. 16–23). The letter closes with a memorable proclamation of the goodness and grandeur of God (vv. 24–25). The author is a skilled writer who uses Christian and non-Christian traditions to warn of dangers to faith and practice. Despite its brevity and its rare use in Christian tradition, prayers, and liturgy, the Letter of Jude contains valuable and eloquent Christian teaching.

Second Peter also follows the overall structure of an ancient letter. After the traditional form of introduction and greeting (2 Pet. 1:1–2), the author points to the power of God's action in giving good gifts to believers to defend them from sinfulness (vv. 3–4). He reflects on a good life that guarantees entry into the kingdom (vv. 5–11) and then indicates he is leaving this document so that readers might be rightly instructed after his oncoming death (vv. 12–15). The author, using material also found in the Letter of Jude, presents six issues.

1. The tradition about the end of time is not mythmaking, but based on authentic prophecy (2 Pet. 1:16–21).
2. The heretics are attacked (2:1–22).
3. The certainty of the coming of the end time is again presented (3:1–7).
4. There will be a delay, as a gracious gift of God (3:8–9).
5. We must live a good life during the in-between time, waiting for the day of the Lord (3:10–13).
6. The author (Peter) and Paul agree (3:14–16).

The author concludes his letter by issuing some final warnings and by praising God (3:17–18). Second Peter insists on the tradition of God as Lord of all creation. It will be revealed in a dramatic "day of the Lord." All who teach differently are to be shunned, as the Christian lives under God's lordship, made known in and through Jesus Christ.

The Letters of John

The letters of John show that early in the second Christian century, Christians looked back to their story of Jesus.[18] Although recent Johannine scholars

18. See Brown, *Introduction to the New Testament*, 383–485. See also Powell, *Introducing the New Testament*, 493–507; on the similarities between the Gospel of John and the Letters of John, see the chart on p. 497. See also Spivey, Smith, and Black, *Anatomy of the New Testament*, 414–21; on house churches, see p. 421. For helpful commentaries, see Judith M. Lieu, *I, II, and III John: A Commentary*, New Testament Library (Louisville: Westminster John Knox, 2008); John Painter, *1, 2 and 3 John*, Sacra Pagina 18 (Collegeville, MN: Liturgical Press, 2002); David Rensberger, *1 John, 2 John, 3 John*, Abingdon New Testament Commentaries (Nashville: Abingdon, 1997).

have suggested otherwise, it appears that they looked to the Gospel of John for their inspiration. However, problems emerged because, as in our own time, different people and groups of people can look back to the same event or story and interpret it in different ways. The most important evidence indicating that the letters were written later than the Gospel is the strong conflict between Jesus and "the Jews," which is found in the Gospel (see, e.g., John 2:13–25; 5:10–18; 7:1–9, 14–31, 40–44; 8:12–20, 39–47, 48–59; 10:31–39; 11:45–52) but not in the letters. The Gospel reflects a period when those who confessed that Jesus was the Christ had been thrown out of the synagogue (see 9:22; 12:42; 16:2). The final separation of the communities from their Jewish roots, reflected in the letters of John, must have been long since past, as the letters show no interest in the relationship between the members of the Christian community and their Jewish neighbors. The problem with people "outside" these Christian communities had been resolved, for better or for worse. The Johannine letters face an inevitable further stage in the story of the people for whom they were written: problems emerging "within" the communities. There had been a breakdown between members of the Johannine communities, and a number of different, conflicting "Johannine" communities existed. The author can write: "They went out from us, but they were not of us; for if they had been of us, they would have continued with us; but they went out, that it might be plain that they all are not of us" (1 John 2:19; see also 2 John 7).[19]

The Gospel and the letters come from the same background, even though the letters reflect a situation of conflict different from the Gospel; the original group is gradually spreading (and dividing). This is evident in all the letters of John, as one Christian leader addresses his fellow Christians in an attempt to dissuade them from following the behavior and beliefs of others who, in his opinion, are in error. The presence of different communities is especially clear in 3 John, where the author pleads with the leader of another community, Gaius, to disregard the thought and behavior of a third party, Diotrephes (3 John 9–10).

The churches that looked back to the Gospel of John for their inspiration were divided, and there are hints that the division led the parties in the argument into different forms of Christianity during the second century. The author of the letters and the Christians whom he represented may have become members of the larger established Church, while Diotrephes and his friends may have adopted another form of early Christianity. But we cannot

19. For a survey of current thought on this matter and its importance for understanding the Johannine letters, see Moloney, *Love in the Gospel of John*, 192–98.

be sure of this. In the letters we have only one side of the argument. No doubt Diotrephes and his community would have had some hard things to say about the author of the letters. The term "antichrist" (see 1 John 2:18, 22; 4:3; 2 John 7) may have also been used about him! We only have one end of the conversation, and we can only guess what was being said or not said at the other end.

THE FIRST LETTER OF JOHN

Throughout 1 John, the elder writes negatively of the group who "went out" (see 1 John 2:19). The first part of the letter is dedicated to an attack upon some who do not share the ideas of the elder. The language used by the author is a thinly veiled reference to errors of others. He is obviously attacking others as he accuses: "If we say that we have fellowship with him while we are walking in darkness, we lie and do not do what is true" (1:6 NRSV). The same spirit lies behind a series of further accusations (see 1:8, 10). Another accusation is phrased differently: "The one who says 'I know him' but disobeys his commandments is a liar, and the truth is not in that person" (2:4 AT; see also 2:6). The list could go on, as the writer continually attacks "whoever says . . ." (2:4, 9 NRSV; see also 2:11) or "everyone who . . ." (2:23; 3:4, 8 NRSV). This sort of polemic is directed against people with views different from the author.

However, behind this polemic we trace not only anger; there is also pain. From the first pages of the letter we sense separation. Soon this will be shown to be the case (see 1 John 2:9). A fundamental belief of the Christian tradition that has its origin in the Gospel of John is that God is love (see 1 John 4:8, 16). This belief comes from the Gospel's insistence that the presence of Jesus in the human story is the result of God's love: "God so loved the world that he gave his only Son" (John 3:16). The mission of the Son was to make the Father known (see John 4:34; 5:36; 15:13; 17:3–4). This takes place in the loving self-gift of Jesus on the cross. There the love of God can be seen as generations of believers gaze upon the one whom they have pierced (John 19:37). But the mission of Jesus has consequences for all who would regard themselves as his disciples. They are called to a unity of love (see John 13:34–35; 15:12, 17; 17:11, 20–23). At the heart of John's Gospel, the initiative of God is made clear. A loving God has called disciples who are to love one another as he has loved them: "You did not choose me, but I chose you and appointed you that you should go and bear fruit and that your fruit should abide" (John 15:16).[20]

---

20. On the centrality of love in the Gospel, see Moloney, *Love in the Gospel of John*.

This central feature of John's Gospel had not become a reality in the lives of the subsequent members of those communities who looked back to the story of Jesus as it had been passed down to them in the Gospel. The author looks around himself, seeking the fruits that should be visible. According to the author, the abiding fruits that should flow from the initiative of God in choosing his disciples are hard to find among some. He writes to share his concern and to instruct all who look back to the story of the Gospel of John for their guidance and inspiration (see 1 John 1:1–4).

But the letters are not all anger and pain. The early Church found its faith reflected in these letters. They tell of the incarnation of the Son of God, the genuine human experience of that Son, the centrality of love, God as light and love, the gift of the Spirit, and the abiding of the Father and the Son in the believer. Rightly, the letters continuing this tradition form part of the Christian Scriptures, a treasure house that continues to support and inspire believers through all ages and in all situations. The author writes to members of the communities, all of whom regarded the Gospel of John as their founding story of Jesus, and restates fundamental principles of that Gospel. He faces the inevitable difficulty of looking to a document from the past as he tries to make it relevant to his present situation. He presupposes that the recipients of this letter are on his side, but he may have some doubts. They may be wavering, and this could explain the harshness of his stance against all who have a different understanding of the Gospel of John.

Through the anger and harshness, central themes from that Gospel return: the appearance of the Word (1 John 1:1–4), Jesus' self-giving love for his own (3:1–3), God is light (1:5), God is love (4:8, 16), the abiding of the Son (3:24), the gift of the Spirit (4:13), true believers are children of God (5:1–5), and the mutual indwelling that can exist between the Son and the believers (3:24). From the writings of Christianity, only John's Gospel could have provided this understanding of God, God's Son, and the believer. For his message, the author of the letter looks back to the tradition in the Christian Church created by the story of the Gospel of John. But the tone of the document indicates that one of the central elements in the Gospel's teaching on discipleship is not being lived. No doubt he writes in the hope of restoring the mutuality of love demanded by the teaching of Jesus. However, he risks the establishment of a community where like-minded people love one another but have little affection or concern for those outside the boundaries of their community.

The readers receive a document restating in a letter-tract form the major theological arguments of the Gospel of John. To make this clear, the author has modeled 1 John upon the structure of the Gospel, with a prologue (1:1–4;

see John 1:1–18), a two-part body (1:5–3:10 [see John 1:19–12:50]; 3:11–5:12 [see John 13:1–20:19]), and a conclusion (5:13–21; see John 20:30–31). The prologue (1:1–4) recalls John 1:1–18. It too tells of the "beginnings" of the Christian story: Jesus who revealed the word of life. But it also looks back to another "beginning," to the original community that lived in fellowship with the Father and the Son. In the first part of the Gospel's account of the ministry of Jesus (John 1:19–12:50), Jesus lived and proclaimed his message within the context of hostile rejection. So also the first central section of the letter (1 John 1:5–3:10), which could be given the description, "God is light and we must walk in the light as Jesus walked," is at times hostile. It insists that the Christian live as Jesus lived and attacks the false ideas and way of life of some who have left the community. In the second central section (3:11–5:12), to which we could give the title "We must love one another as God has loved us in Jesus Christ," the hostility softens but does not disappear. Recalling John 13:1–17:26, the author develops the themes of the centrality of true love and true faith as the basis for Christian confidence. The letter concludes (5:13–21) with an assurance that true believers can pray with confidence in the midst of difficulties and conflicts and rest in God's unfailing protection.

As is obvious from this presentation of the First Letter of John, the pain and anger generated by the division behind the writing of this letter have not impoverished the power and comfort of the Christian message. The power of the presentation of God, Jesus, and the Christian response to the action of God in his Son is not dissipated. The Christian tradition, which first found expression in the unforgettable story of Jesus in the Gospel of John, remains strongly present in the First Letter of John. The very way in which the author has organized his letter, following the overall shape of the Gospel, is an indication of his loyalty to that tradition.

The Second and Third Letters of John

A close relationship exists between 1 John and the letters known as 2 and 3 John. They were most likely all written by the same person ("the elder" of 2 John 1 and 3 John 1). They were addressed to a local situation in an attempt to deal with real-life situations in early Christian communities, but they were quickly associated with the figure of John, the author of the Fourth Gospel. They were rightly seen to continue a Christian tradition and thus deserve to stand as companion pieces to 1 John.

The way 2 and 3 John were written corresponds with the widely attested form of a first-century Hellenistic letter. The following scheme indicates how the three basic elements of these letters appear in 2 and 3 John:

2 John	3 John
Opening formula (vv. 1–3) Sender, addressee, greeting (vv. 1–3)	*Opening formula (vv. 1–2)* Sender, addressee, greeting (vv. 1–2)
Body of the letter (vv. 4–12)	*Body of the letter (vv. 3–14)*
• Expression of joy—transition to the body of the letter (v. 3)	• Expression of joy—transition to the body of the letter (vv. 3–4)
• Request concerning the commandment to love (vv. 5–6)	• Request for hospitality and support (vv. 5–8)
• Warning against the antichrists and their teaching (vv. 7–11)	• The hostility of Diotrephes (vv. 9–10)
	• An appeal to do good and a recommendation for Demetrius (vv. 11–12)
• Promise of a visit, closing the body of the letter (v. 12)	• Promise of a visit, closing the body of the letter (vv. 13–14)
Concluding formula (v. 13)	*Concluding formula (v. 15)*

Although we hear only one side of the argument, these documents allow us to eavesdrop on a conversation between a significant figure within the communities ("the elder") and a community (2 John: the elect lady and her children) or the leader of one of the communities, another "elder" (3 John: Gaius). These documents are not theological tracts but are the communication of matters regarded by the elder as crucial for the ongoing faith of an early Christian community. They thus afford us privileged access to the sometimes difficult experiences of an emerging Christian Church.

The author of 2 John, in a way reminiscent of 1 John 2:19, warns the community of those who have left them. Not only have they departed from a once-unified community; they have also departed from the teachings the author would regard as true Christian belief. Such dangerous deceivers and antichrists must be shunned if they approach the community to which 2 John is written. For the moment that is all the author wishes to tell his fellow believers. He will explain the situation when he comes to visit them in the near future. The situation in 3 John is more local, more personal, and more bitter, written to Gaius, a senior figure in a community (also an "elder"). He deserves praise for the way he has welcomed wandering fellow Christians. His acceptance of itinerant believers is to be contrasted, however, with the attitude and arrogance of a certain Diotrephes who has refused to welcome the emissaries of the letter writer and has refused to accept his authority. But all is not lost, as the author can recommend another Christian, Demetrius, who is true. Divisions are hardening, and some are "in" and others are "out." But this arrogance is not to be laid only at the door of Diotrephes. It was also the position advocated by the author of 2 John as he instructed his "beloved lady and her children" to avoid the dangerous influence of the deceivers and the antichrists.

Scholars rightly discuss the situation that occasioned these letters and how the letters relate to the Fourth Gospel and 1 John.[21] But that is not our task. The Bible is not simply a book we use to excavate *the world behind the text*, the life and practice of the Jewish people or the early Church. It also raises questions to *the world in front of the text*, its contemporary readers. Do the experiences of the different groups of early Christians whose story is reflected in 2 and 3 John, as well as the Gospel of John and 1 John, say anything to practicing Christians today? The agonizing task of maintaining a balance between purity of thought and action and the call to welcome all—even sinners—into our communities is already faced in these brief but important letters.

Hebrews

Critics have long regarded Hebrews as one of the most elegant and passionate documents in the New Testament. Contemporary scholars are unanimous in accepting that it was not written by Paul. Much about the date and place of origin of Hebrews and its original author cannot be determined. There is very little reference to people, places, or time in the document itself. The mention of Timothy and Italy in Hebrews 13:23–24 is the only exception. A working hypothesis is that Hebrews was written by a cultivated Jew during the 80s. The author was familiar with philosophical currents of the day (especially Philo, a Jew working in Alexandria who was influenced by Plato) but was ultimately dependent upon the Old Testament. It was written, in the most eloquent Greek in the New Testament, to Christians in Rome (see Heb. 13:22–24). Hebrews affirms the superiority of Jesus Christ subsequent to the trials they have experienced under Nero (see 10:32–34) and prior to those that might lie ahead, exhorting them to accept suffering as Jesus did (see 12:3–4). Hebrews most likely appeared before the Roman persecutions of the emperor Domitian in the 90s.[22] It is difficult to identify the precise literary

---

21. For a fascinating study of this question, reading something like a detective novel, see Raymond E. Brown, *The Community of the Beloved Disciple* (New York: Paulist Press, 1979). See also Moloney, *Love in the Gospel of John*, 191–203.

22. For a very good survey of this unresolved discussion, coming to the conclusions adopted above, see Brown, *Introduction to the New Testament*, 691–701. On Hebrews, see again the introductions of Powell, *Introducing the New Testament*, 427–43; Spivey, Smith, and Black, *Anatomy of the New Testament*, 427–35. For helpful commentaries, see Luke T. Johnson, *Hebrews: A Commentary*, New Testament Library (Louisville: Westminster John Knox, 2006); Andrew T. Lincoln, *Hebrews: A Guide* (London: T&T Clark, 2006).

form of Hebrews, as it contains exhortation to faithfulness and perseverance and a passionate theological treatise arguing for the superiority of Christ over every other possible authority and power, but also bears the signs of a letter, especially in the instructions and the conclusion in 13:1–25. Raymond Brown helpfully gathers these elements together, suggesting that "perhaps we should settle for the relatively simple description of Hebrews as a written sermon or homily with an epistolary ending."[23]

In a subtle fashion, Hebrews argues that all the institutions and means of communication between God and humankind as they are portrayed in the Old Testament have been perfected in Jesus Christ. The author does this by arguing for the superiority of Christ. There is widespread agreement that the argument of Hebrews has been very carefully and elegantly argued.[24]

1:1–4	Introduction: The definitive and unique revelation has been spoken by God through his Son, now at the right hand of God, superior to the angels.
1:5–2:18	Superior to the angels, the Son has experienced the trials, sufferings, and temptations of the human condition. But even though for a short while lower than the angels in his humanity, he has been established as the final judge. This section can be seen as dealing with Jesus Christ as Lord and judge. In technical language, it deals with *eschatology*, "the end things."
3:1–5:10	Jesus' faithfulness and compassionate sharing of everything we have experienced "in the days of his flesh" makes him superior to Moses. He forms a new people of God and brings them eternal salvation as their High Priest. His word surpasses the law of Moses "piercing to the division of soul and spirit." Across this section the author claims that Jesus Christ has established a people of God, perfecting the old, now governed by his Word. It deals with a new vision of the *new community of Jesus Christ*, the Church.
5:11–10:39	Superior to Abraham, to Moses, and especially to the priests who offered continual sacrifice for sin, Jesus Christ is an eternal priest of the order of Melchizedek, establishing a new and eternal covenant. He "entered once for all into the Holy Place, taking not the blood of goats and calves but his own blood,

---

23. Brown, *Introduction to the New Testament*, 690.

24. The following literary and theological structure is from Albert Vanhoye, *Structure and Message of the Epistle to the Hebrews* (Rome: Pontifical Biblical Institute, 1989). For this summary and further suggestions see Brown, *Introduction to the New Testament*, 690–91.

thus securing an eternal redemption" (9:12). This centerpiece of Hebrews addresses the perfection of all that God has done for Israel in the "once and for all" sacrifice of Jesus. His second appearance will be to save all who are eagerly waiting for him. The saving sacrifice of Jesus Christ and his ultimate lordship lie at the heart of this central section of Hebrews, both theologically and structurally.

11:1–12:13   The author then turns to outline a new way of life that is to be lived by the members of the community. He points to the faith and endurance of the great figures who went before them: Abel, Noah, Abraham, Joseph, Moses, the people who crossed the Red Sea, Rahab, Gideon, Barak, Samson, Jephthah, David, Samuel, and the prophets. "We are surrounded by so great a cloud of witnesses" (12:1). The virtues of faith and endurance are to mark the lives of all who form the *new community of Jesus Christ.*

12:14–13:19   As Hebrews draws to a close, the author writes of more practical matters. He calls for peace that must be the fruit of justice and of love for one another and for their leaders. This form of life shows that "this life" is no eternal city and directs the believer toward "the city that is yet to come." Themes that touch upon final hopes—*eschatology*, the end things—reappear.

13:20–25   Conclusion: Only at the end of Hebrews does the author adopt a tone and a literary form that is common in letters. He wishes his readers and listeners peace and grace, mentions the recent release of Timothy, and sends greetings from Italy.

This "structure" should not be regarded as a straitjacket for the interpretation of Hebrews. The theological, christological, and ecclesial instructions outlined above run back and forth across the whole document. As the preexistent Son of God, the Christ is superior to Wisdom. As Son, he is superior to the angels, having experienced both lowliness and exaltation. There can be no exaltation without suffering, and Jesus, who has been made perfect through his suffering, is the pioneer of salvation. Perhaps more than any other document in the New Testament, Hebrews states the unconditionally human status of Jesus Christ (see 2:14–18; 4:14–5:10), beautifully summed up by two memorable passages that have spoken to the Church for two thousand years: "For we have not a high priest who is unable to sympathize with our weaknesses, but one who in every respect has been tempted as we are, yet without sin" (4:15). And "in the days of his flesh, Jesus offered up prayers and supplications, with loud cries and tears, to him who was able to save him from death, and he was heard for his godly fear. Although he was a Son, he learned obedience through what he suffered" (5:7–8). The new covenant was foreshadowed in the law of Moses and came to reality in the person and work of Jesus. Jesus is thus superior to Moses (3:1–4:13). The superiority of the word of the Son perfects all that has gone before (1:1–4). Unlike the law, "the word of God is living and active, sharper than any two-edged sword, piercing to the division of soul and spirit, of joints and marrow, and discerning the thoughts and intentions of the heart" (4:12).

Only in Hebrews is the theme of the priesthood of Jesus developed, to show that the mediation and the expiatory sacrifice of Jesus' death and resurrection are superior to the sacrificial ministry of the former high priesthood exercised in the Jerusalem temple. This is again rooted in his human condition (see 5:1–10). There is now only one sacrifice, offered once and for all in Jesus' death (10:11–12). The effects of this sacrifice last forever. There is no longer a need for daily sacrifice offered in the temple (7:23–25, 26–27). Jesus' sacrifice establishes a heavenly tabernacle and a new and eternal covenant between God and the believer (8:1–10:18).

Hebrews also exhorts believers who have been through recent suffering to faith and endurance (10:19–12:29). They are to look to the witnesses by whom they are surrounded (12:1–2), but courage and commitment to their own discipleship are called for (12:3–13), and there are warnings about the consequences that flow from a rejection of "him who warns from heaven" (12:25). The work closes with early Christian recommendations on ethical matters: hospitality, care for prisoners, marriage, possessions, obedience to authorities, and mutual care. But moral exhortation is based on the theological/christological argument of Hebrews: "So Jesus also suffered outside the gate in order to sanctify the people through his own blood" (13:12). Before ending with traditional letter-like formulae (13:20–25), another memorable word from Hebrews draws the document to closure: "Here we have no lasting city, but we seek the city which is to come" (v. 14).

Within the literary confines of the introduction (1:1–4) and the letter-like conclusion (13:20–25), there appears to be a deliberate unfolding of several themes: Jesus Christ as the end-time judge (1:5–2:18), the new community (3:1–5:10), the sacrificial role of Jesus Christ in bringing eternal salvation (5:11–10:39), a way of life for the new community (11:1–12:13), and a return to Jesus Christ as the end-time judge of a community of peace, justice, and love (12:14–13:19). Hebrews is bold in its presentation of the uniqueness and superiority of Jesus, over against every other institution. Yet Jesus Christ has shared unconditionally in every human experience, even temptation; but he never sinned (4:15). His crucial role as the one who saves us by means of the "once and for all" sacrifice of himself depends on his oneness with us. A critical reading of the Letter to the Hebrews *within the Church* exhorts us: "Let us then with confidence draw near to the throne of grace, that we may receive mercy and find grace to help in time of need" (4:16).

Conclusion

The books of the New Testament that this chapter has situated in the unfolding historical, literary, and theological life of the Church do not play a major role in the faith experience of many practicing Christians. We are mostly in touch with the Jesus of the Gospels and with the message of Saint Paul. Yet there is much to learn from what we have traced together. From the significant theological tract, the Letter to the Hebrews, to the pastorally oriented pseudepigraphic letters associated with the authority of one of the founding apostles, the process of "writing" continued over the second half of the first Christian century and into the earliest decades of the second century. The sole reason for the existence of this literature was to address the life of the Church. The Letter to the Hebrews, although sparsely used in the contemporary liturgical life of the Church, continues to proclaim, in sometimes unforgettable ways (see, e.g., Heb. 4:14–5:10), the uniqueness, superiority, and centrality of Jesus Christ. It summons hearers and readers to face the many challenges associated with the vocation to live within the community of Jesus Christ and the promise of a final "rest."

But we also have apparently lesser documents, amounting to only a few verses (2 and 3 John and the Letter of Jude).[25] Between the extremes of the Letter to the Hebrews and these brief early Christian letters, we have seen other documents, presented in a variety of literary forms, sometimes using the practice of pseudonymity, that maintain a perennial freshness and theological relevance, even within today's Church. This is especially the case with James, 1 Peter, and 1 John. What Reinhard Feldmeier writes of 1 Peter could be said of the whole corpus: these letters "endeavour *to make plausible the eschatological existence of the Christians in a new context.*"[26] Although the Pastoral Epistles (Titus, 1–2 Timothy) are very concerned to address the issues

---

25. There are good reasons for the presence of these slight documents in the New Testament, which have been suggested above (see pp. 60–63 above) and in the relevant sections of Brown, *Introduction to the New Testament*, 395–504, 748–72; Powell, *Introducing the New Testament*, 481–91, 494–507, 509–17; and Spivey, Smith, and Black, *Anatomy of the New Testament*, 418–22, 435–37.

26. Feldmeier, *First Letter of Peter*, 23. Emphasis in original.

of Church order and internal discipline, they are rooted in the Pauline tradition. They look back to fundamental beliefs of the earliest Church so that what has been and is being *taught* might also be *lived* in the early Christian communities (see 1 Tim. 1:3–7, 15; 3:16; 4:9–10; 6:14–16; 2 Tim. 1:8–14; 2:8–13; Titus 2:11–14; 3:3–8).[27]

Even the lesser documents (2–3 John, Jude, 1 Peter) have their relevance, once one is aware of why they came into existence and why the early Church eventually decided to make them part of its Sacred Scripture.

27. Some of these statements reflecting sound Christian (Pauline) tradition are either introduced or concluded with an indication that the "saying is sure" (Greek: *pistos ho logos*; see 1 Tim. 1:15; 3:1; 4:9; 2 Tim. 2:11; Titus 3:8). In other words, the authors are not "inventing" the traditions they are using to demand discipline within their communities.

9

The Revelation to John

Apocalypse Now

The subtitle of this final chapter obviously comes from a significant 1979 Hollywood movie by Francis Ford Coppola, using the central theme of Joseph Conrad's *Heart of Darkness*. Continuing Conrad's wondering about what constitutes a barbarian over against a civilized society, Coppola dealt starkly with a drama set during the war in Vietnam. The movie traces the grim attempt of Captain Benjamin L. Willard (played by Martin Sheen) to hunt down and kill the renegade and supposedly insane Colonel Walter E. Kurtz (played by Marlon Brando). One of the messages of this many-layered movie is that there is no need to wait until the end of all time for an "apocalypse." Coppola took the name for his film from the final book in the New Testament, which has the Greek name *apokalypsis* and is generally regarded as a book that deals with events that will take place at the end of time.[1] It is sometimes rendered as "Revelation," or sometimes as the English word that comes directly from the Greek: the "Apocalypse." The biblical book is different in every way from

1. Although not widely used in English, reference to an "apocalyptic" moment or event indicates something final and all-determining. Many who use the expression would not be aware that it comes from an ancient literary form (apocalyptic) or that it is the name given to a book in the New Testament that uses this form.

the movie, except for the fact that—as I will argue in this chapter—the New Testament Apocalypse also argues that we do not have to wait for the "apocalypse" (the revelation) of God's victory. It is with us *now*.

Most readers regard this book as the most obscure text in the New Testament. The complexity comes from the literary form of the document. Borrowing from a way of writing that was common in Judaism in pre- and post-Christian times, John tells of the action of God in and through Jesus Christ.[2] However, as God is the active agent intervening in the history and affairs of the world, this can be no ordinary story. To convey a message of the victory of God over evil by means of the death and resurrection of Jesus, and to convey the subsequent confidence this must give to Christians no matter how difficult their situation, no ordinary story can be told. Powerful, graphic, and sometimes confusing symbols are regularly used. Day-to-day language and imagery are abandoned to tell a tale of God's intervention in the world. The reader encounters a slain lamb, a sealed scroll, good and fallen angels, various riders on different-colored horses, souls under an altar, robes cleansed by blood, trumpets, flaming mountains, stars, bowls, a woman clothed with the sun and adorned with stars, a serpent, a monster with the name 666, a great harlot, the city of Babylon, and a new Jerusalem.

Taking their cue from the setting, thought, and literary techniques of the Jewish apocalypses, almost all interpreters of the Apocalypse take it to be addressed to Christians suffering under Roman imperial persecution under Domitian (emperor from 81 to 96 CE). In the light of what God has done by means of his victory in and through the death and resurrection of Jesus, the suffering Christians are told that they must be patient, as in the end God will be victorious over all evil and suffering. A new Jerusalem, the spouse of the Lamb and a blessed symbol of peace and oneness with God, lies in the future.[3]

There are two problems that can be associated with this reading, which I would like to challenge. One is practical: the "end-time" interpretation can lead to uncontrolled uses of the symbols and images found in the book. The

2. The apocalyptic literary form of these documents is generally written in situations of human suffering where no foreseeable escape from impending destruction and disaster is available. There are many Jewish apocalypses. In addition to the New Testament book of the Apocalypse, the best known Jewish apocalypse is the Old Testament book of Daniel. Daniel 7, which contains the vision of "one like a son of man" (vv. 13–14), is regularly used in Christian lectionaries. See Larry R. Helyer, "Apocalypticism," in Green and McDonald, *World of the New Testament*, 252–71.

3. This almost universally accepted position is adopted in the fine introductions to the New Testament I have used throughout to guide interested readers. See, e.g., Brown, *Introduction to the New Testament*, 773–813; Powell, *Introducing the New Testament*, 519–37; Spivey, Smith, and Black, *Anatomy of the New Testament*, 438–50. What follows questions this interpretation.

enemies of persecuted Christians are found not only in the first Christian century. As this book asks Christians to continue to wait in hope for God's final resolution of sin and suffering, some interpreters read the symbols as prophecies of organizations and people they despise and judge as opposed to God's way in the world. For example, the whore of Babylon in Revelation 17 has been identified as the Catholic Church, and the number 666 in Revelation 13:18, representing the Antichrist, has been variously applied to a number of Roman emperors, the popes, Adolf Hitler, Saddam Hussein, and Ronald Reagan. These examples could be multiplied, and they seriously distract us from reading this document in the Church.

The second problem is more theological and seriously affects the use of the Apocalypse in the Church, especially in comfortable Western society. If interpreters are correct in assuming that the determining theme of the Apocalypse is the exhortation of Christians suffering Roman persecution to retain their hope and faith until God's final intervention brings this to an end, what is the *current significance* of Jesus' death and resurrection for its author? Are we experiencing only pain and persecution as we await the Lord? Can this interpretation of the Apocalypse be regarded as a *genuinely Christian* book, or is it simply a Christian use of a Jewish literary form and message—urging patience in the midst of suffering, promising God's ultimate victory?[4]

A provocative *different* reading of the Apocalypse, proposed forty years ago, is adopted here. What follows will suggest that the Apocalypse is dedicated not to generating hope for the future but to affirming that God's victory over evil has already been won in the death and resurrection of Jesus, and that victory has *always* been present.[5] It will present a literary structure and an interpretation that suggest that an early Christian author chose to use an apocalyptic literary form but abandoned the traditional association of that form with a

4. The use of the apocalyptic literary form within Judaism was always associated with suffering and disappointment. A great deal of this literature appeared after the fall of Jerusalem, as the Jewish thinkers and theologians wondered what God was doing with them. However, the use of apocalyptic literature gradually disappeared within Judaism as rabbis directed their people to God's saving grace as found in the Torah. This chapter suggests that the Christian Apocalypse continues the literary form (still widely used within Judaism at the end of the first Christian century) but no longer looks to the end of the world, as is traditional in such literature.

5. What follows depends on Eugenio Corsini, who published *Apocalisse prima e dopo* [The Apocalypse Before and After] in 1980, available in English as *The Apocalypse: The Perennial Revelation of Jesus Christ*, trans. Francis J. Moloney, Good News Studies 5 (Wilmington, DE: Michael Glazier, 1983). Almost completely ignored by English-speaking interpreters since then, Corsini has returned to this argument, enlarging his study and responding to the difficulties that his interpretation may generate, in *Apocalisse di Gesù Cristo secondo Giovanni* (Turin: Società Editrice Internazionale, 2002). This more complete volume is not available in English. Readers will find the following argument already clearly expounded in my 1983 translation.

promise of hope for the future. The closing book of the New Testament, I will suggest, is about the presence of the crucified and resurrected victorious Lamb *now*. The use of Coppola's title, *Apocalypse Now*, corresponds with the message of the New Testament Apocalypse. Readers who do not find the sketch that follows helpful or convincing can easily have recourse to one of the many good commentaries that read the Apocalypse as looking forward to the end time: "Apocalypse—eventually!"[6]

The literary structure of the book is determined by the regular use of "seven." There are seven letters to churches (Rev. 1:9–3:22), seven seals on the scroll (4:1–8:1), seven trumpets (8:2–11:19), and seven bowls (12:1–22:5). The "events" within the septets are similar, but each septet, after an introduction, proclaims the same truth: the fulfillment of God's salvific intervention in the coming, death, and resurrection of the Messiah Jesus. Each septet is thus self-contained, leading to this proclamation, but presents the mystery from a different perspective.[7] Almost half of the Apocalypse is dedicated to the pouring out of the seven bowls. The "action" of this pouring out recapitulates all that went before. Given the crucial role of the septets, the document is structured as follows:

1:1–8	Prologue
1:9–3:22	The seven messages to the churches
4:1–8:1	The seven seals to the scroll
8:2–11:19	The seven trumpets
12:1–22:5	The seven bowls
	Recapitulation and deepening of the previous septets (12:1–14:20)
	Introduction of the bowl angels (15:1–8)
	Pouring out of the bowls (16:1–21)

6. Readers of this book will find helpful, among commentaries that take a traditional "end-time" approach, the following: M. Eugene Boring, *Revelation* (Louisville: John Knox, 1989); Wilfred J. Harrington, *Revelation*, Sacra Pagina 16 (Collegeville, MN: Liturgical Press, 1993); James L. Resseguie, *The Revelation of John: A Narrative Commentary* (Grand Rapids: Baker Academic, 2009).

7. End-time interpretations of the Apocalypse read across the septets an accumulating development that reaches a climax only in the septet of the bowls. On the basis of 1:19—"Now write what you see, what is and what is to take place hereafter"—commentators divide the book into a presentation of past, present, and future: prologue (1:1–20); introduction: messages to the seven churches (2:1–3:22: "what you see"); prophetic visions (4:1–22:5: "what is and what is to take place hereafter"); and an epilogue (22:6–21). But *each* septet reaches a christological climax. There is no need to wait for the conclusion to the septet of the bowls for such a climax.

> Description of the effects of the events accompanying the
> pouring out of the bowls (17:1–22:5)

22:6–21   Epilogue

John opens his prologue with the word "apocalypse" to introduce the reader/
listener to a book that is dedicated to the "revelation" of Jesus as Messiah.
The "servants" to whom the revelation has been made known are the prophets
of Israel (see Rev. 10:7: "his servants the prophets"). The fact that it must
"soon take place" is not chronological but is an indication of the urgency
and inexorability of God's plan. John's book (see 1:4; 22:8) is a symbolic
compendium of the Law and the Prophets witnessing to the coming of the
Messiah and a demonstration that Jesus fulfills that expectation. The words
"the time [Greek: *kairos*] is near" (1:3) refer to the decisive moment of the
coming of the Messiah. The cry of victory with which the prologue closes
(vv. 5b–8) makes it clear that the coming of Jesus has *already* brought about
eschatological effects: believers are released by his blood *already*, and they
belong to a kingdom where they are priests, serving the God and Father of
Jesus, the Alpha and the Omega.

The septet of the letters is introduced by two "voices" (Rev. 1:9–20). The
trumpet-like voice from behind is an angelic voice, associated with the old
covenant (vv. 9–11; see 4:1). Turning around, he finds himself confronted with
the glorified "son of man," whose description is unsurpassed elsewhere in the
Apocalypse: he holds angels/stars in his hands and is described in ways otherwise only applicable to God. He is the one who lives forever and who *already*
holds the keys of death and Hades (vv. 12–20).

The messages to the churches recapitulate the history of God's dealings
with Israel. Ephesus: the fall from original love and the promise of eating
from the tree of life recalls the creation accounts from Genesis (Rev. 2:1–7;
see Gen. 3:1–24). Smyrna: persecution recalls the persecution of the Hebrews
in Egypt, and the ten days may be an allusion to the ten plagues (vv. 8–11; see
Exod. 7:1–11:10). Pergamum: references to Balaam and Balak recall Israel in
the desert, as does the promise of the hidden manna (vv. 12–17; see Exod.
4:16–31; Num. 22:1–30). Thyatira: the use of Jezebel recalls the apostasy of
the kings of Israel (vv. 18–29; see 1 Kings 16:29–22:40 [Ahab and Jezebel]).
Sardis: being on the point of death recalls the destruction of Israel and Judah
(3:1–6; see 2 Kings 17:19–28 [Israel]; 25:1–21 [Judah]). Philadelphia: reference
to the temple alludes to the return from exile and the rebuilding of Jerusalem
(vv. 7–13; see Ezra and Nehemiah). Laodicea: the threatening tone of the
letter, with its image of the Son of Man standing at the door, represents the
final preparatory stage of salvation history prior to the coming of the Messiah

(vv. 14–22). With an outline of the biblical history of salvation in place, John turns to the septet of the scrolls.

The introduction to the opening of the seals is John's vision of the throne and the Lamb. In a reworking of Daniel 7:9–14, the throne represents God's creative activity, and the Lamb portrays God's redemptive activity. Instead of presenting the Son of Man to the one on the throne, the slain Lamb takes this place. The Lamb's opening of the seals takes place in a 4 + 3 scheme, and the message of creation and redemption (4:1–5:14) affects all of them.

The first four seals focus on the human world. The first horseman represents human nature in all its splendid potential (Rev. 6:1–2), while the next three portray the fall into sin, along with its effects, already adumbrated in Genesis: violence (vv. 3–4, the second horseman; see Gen. 3:14–16), need for toil (vv. 5–6, the third horseman; see Gen. 3:17–18), and death (vv. 7–8, the fourth horseman; see Gen. 3:19). The remaining three seals address the divine response to the disaster of the first four. The souls under the heavenly altar—"the souls of those who had been slain for the word of God and for the witness they had borne" (6:9)—are those who have received the covenant of God offered to fallen humanity, and the testimony is the prophetic testimony to the expectation of the Messiah, now revealed as Jesus. The souls are those killed for their fidelity to the old covenant and for their prophetic mission. They are not consigned to Hades but given a white robe. As violence against God's faithful mounts, there is a prophetic cry for divine judgment (vv. 9–11). This is rendered by means of the extensive description of the effects of opening the sixth seal. It depicts the death of the Christ-Lamb (accompanied by cosmic phenomena)[8] and brings about the redemption of Israelites faithful to the covenant (the 144,000) and the gentiles (the innumerable multitude). The great ordeal is the death of the Lamb, whose blood cleanses the robes of the slain faithful (6:12–7:17). The silence in heaven that accompanies the opening of the seventh seal marks the end of the cry for judgment and the cessation of the angelic liturgical and mediatory functions that mark the death of Christ (8:1).[9]

After an introduction that puts the angels at center stage (8:2–5), the trumpet septet also follows a 4 + 3 scheme. But John's focus is now on events in the angelic world that necessarily have dramatic effects on the physical world. The

8. The earthquake, the darkening of the sun, and other cosmic phenomena recall the Markan and especially the Matthean accounts of Jesus' death (see Mark 15:33, 37; Matt. 26:51–54). This is still present, though more muted, in Luke (see 23:41–42).

9. This "silence" is reminiscent of the Markan portrayal of Jesus' presence in Jerusalem in Mark 11:1–13:36. He brings temple worship to an end (11:1–25), silences the leaders of Israel (11:26–12:44; see 12:34: "After that no one dared to ask him any question"), and tells of the end of Jerusalem (13:1–23) and the end of the world (vv. 24–37). See Moloney, *Gospel of Mark*, 215–73.

theme of the first four trumpet visions is that of warfare between the faithful angels and the rebellious angels (see also 12:7–12). The symbols of the flaming mountain (8:8) and the star (v. 10) are clear references to angelic beings. At each trumpet blast the fall or casting down of the evil angels wreaks havoc on earth (vv. 7, 8–9, 10–11, 13): "Woe, woe, woe to those who dwell on the earth" (v. 13). The three further trumpet blasts show the effects of the fallen angels upon the human world, described as "woes." A rebellious angel, identified with Satan (9:1: "a star fallen from heaven to earth"), possesses the key to the abyss. This is not a vision of the future, as the risen Christ holds the keys of death and Hades (see 1:18), and it is impossible to suggest that he handed them over to Satan. As with the seals, the sixth trumpet vision, the second "woe," is more highly developed (9:13–11:14) and (again, as with the sixth seal) indicates the salvific intervention of God. The old economy is represented by a little scroll, borne by a mighty angel. It contains the promise to the prophets of the imminent fulfillment of the mystery of God (10:7). This vision is amplified in 11:1–14 by virtue of the true worship of God in the temple cult and the two witnesses, the Law and the Prophets. The death and resurrection of the witnesses repeats a theme from the sixth seal, that those killed for their faithful witness are rewarded with the privilege of an intermediate state: "Come up hither" (11:12; see 6:9: "I saw under the altar the souls of those who had been slain for the word of God and for the witness they had borne"). With the seventh trumpet comes the promised "fulfillment of the mystery of God" (see 10:7). The death of the Messiah and his enthronement open the temple, and the old economy and its cult come to an end (11:15–19).[10]

The long septet of the bowls (12:1–22:5) focuses most intensely upon the fulfillment of the mystery of God in the death of Christ (see esp. 16:17: "It is done!").[11] Chapters 12–14 serve as an extended introduction. John again presents a symbolic narrative of the old economy. Genesis 3 is essential background for an understanding of the woman, of humankind in its created innocence, fallen and pursued by "that ancient serpent, who is called the Devil and Satan, the deceiver of the whole world" (12:9), yet protected by God (12:1–6, 13–17). Satanic incarnation is described in the forms of the beast from the sea (corrupt political power) and the beast from the land (corrupt religious power)

10. The theme of the opening of the temple at the death of Jesus is also found across the Synoptic tradition (see Mark 15:38; Matt. 27:51; Luke 23:45).

11. Although the verbs are different, this cry of the voice from the throne in the temple as the seventh bowl is poured matches Jesus' final word from the cross in the Gospel of John: "It is finished" (John 19:30). Apocalypse 16:17 has *gegonen*, while John 19:30 has *tetelestai*. Despite the different verbs, relationships continue between the Gospel traditions that surround the death of Jesus and the presentation of the salvific death of the Christ in the Apocalypse.

(13:1–18).[12] In the midst of satanic persecution, the Messiah is promised, as the salvific power of his death is in action since the foundation of the world (13:8). Satan is expelled from heaven, while the 144,000 (14:1–5; see also 7:1–8) are the firstfruits of the exercise of that power. Their "virginity" is a symbol of their rejection of the idolatrous worship of the beast from the sea. The final destruction of the satanic power and its adherents, however, occurs after the death of Christ (14:6–20).

The description of the seven angels pouring out the bowls follows (15:1–16:21). The sequence is clearly modeled on the plagues of Exodus (Exod. 7:1–11:10). The vision of the seventh bowl with its violent earthquake represents the death of Christ: "It is done!" (16:17).[13] Chapter 17 through verse 5 of chapter 22 presents the principal effects of the death of Christ: the end of Babylon (corrupt Jerusalem and its cult), described in 17:1–19:4, and the descent of the new Jerusalem (the Church), described in 19:5–11 and 21:1–22:5. These chapters are the continuation of the seventh bowl, interrupted in 19:11–20:15 with a reprise of a symbolic presentation of the old economy and its end in the death of Christ, present from the beginning of the section as the Word of God whose robe is dipped in his own blood (see 19:11–14). The thousand-year reign of 20:4–6 does not look forward to some future anticipation of the final coming but represents the heavenly reign of the martyrs of the old economy. In 20:7–15 Satan's reign finally comes to an end.

The epilogue (22:6–21) shows signs of an original liturgical context. "The prophecy of this book" (v. 7) is not a prediction but a proclamation of the Word of God, as with the prophets of Israel. The order given by John not to seal up the prophecy distinguishes the Apocalypse from other "apocalyptic" literature: nothing is to be "hidden," but all is to be "revealed" (see 1:1). The "coming" of Jesus Christ on which the epilogue centers is a "perennial" coming: it is past, present, and future. It could be said that the Apocalypse is a summing up of the biblical writings, a triumphal climax in an apocalyptic key. At its heart lies an understanding of what God has done in Christ, articulated in 2 Timothy 1:9: "[God] saved us and called us to be holy, not in virtue of our works, but in virtue of his own purpose and the grace which he gave us in Christ Jesus, before the beginning of time" (AT).

12. There is no call to identify a historical figure behind the 666 of 13:18. It is best understood as the perfection of imperfection: three times one short of the number "seven" representing totality and perfection, heavily used by John. This is consummate corruption. Corsini follows the suggestion of Irenaeus from the end of the second century (who reads the Greek word *Teitan* in 666): it represents the mythical Titans, the giants who challenged the divinity. For his survey of the discussion in 1980, see Corsini, *Apocalypse*, 237–40.

13. The Synoptic Gospel images of the earthquake and the Johannine idea of completion combine in this final statement.

This extended explanation of the structure and interpretation of the Apocalypse is offered as a guide for an appreciation of this difficult document as genuinely Christian. The Apocalypse does not ask us to wait patiently—in the midst of suffering and persecution—until the Christ comes at the end of time. The death and resurrection of Jesus, whose fruits are perennial, have overcome evil. They were already present in the old covenant but are now universally available: "The grace of the Lord Jesus be with all the saints" (22:21). The Apocalypse, like all the other books of the New Testament, is not about a future for the saints, who must wait patiently in the midst of suffering. It is a proclamation, in an apocalyptic form, of the presence of the grace won by the death and resurrection of the Lord Jesus and found perennially *in the Church*.

Conclusion

The reading of the Apocalypse outlined above is little known, but it suggests a confident Christian community, facing all the terrors that the powers of this world might produce, confident that the death and resurrection of Jesus have *already* given victory to the believer. I first encountered the above interpretation of Eugenio Corsini in April 1978 at a conference in Rome on the use of the Scriptures in the early Church. I was so struck by it that I was eventually responsible for the translation of Professor Corsini's book on the Apocalypse in 1983.[14] I was motivated to produce that translation by my awareness that few English-speaking or even European scholars would pay attention to a book published in Italian. Aware of the immense scholarship that has surrounded the study of the Apocalypse over the centuries, I tentatively placed this translation on the market in the hope that it might generate some interest and perhaps suggest to interpreters that there may be something to Corsini's interpretation they had overlooked. After all, if he was correct in his reading of early Christian literature, it was not until the fourth century that the "end-time" interpretation of the Apocalypse became the dominant approach.

But these considerations, and my reading of the Apocalypse through this interpretative lens, are not the most important issues for the reader of this book. The use of this obscure New Testament document in contemporary society, as well as in the Church, calls for a strong appreciation of one approach or another that makes sense of the document as it has come down to us as part of our Sacred Scriptures. Passages and images from the Apocalypse are widely used in various forms of popular piety, in the explanation of heavenly

14. For details, see n. 5 above.

visions, and in the Roman Catholic liturgy, especially the use of the figure of the "woman clothed with the sun" from Apocalypse 12 for the celebration of some Marian feasts. Although used differently in various Christian traditions, the Apocalypse provides some optional readings for funeral liturgies. I have already mentioned the widespread application of some of the imagery to explain post-Christian and contemporary personalities and phenomena. Many of these contemporary uses of the Apocalypse in popular culture—occult speculations, threats of the imminence of God's impending (and violent) justice, and outrageous attacks on people and institutions—have nothing to do with what an early Christian author was trying to communicate.

It is not crucial that the above interpretation of the Apocalypse be used by a reader of this book for guidance through the issues just mentioned. But it is important that *some* interpretative key be adopted by a Christian reader that makes sense of a text that had its origins and purpose within the life of early Christianity and should continue to address Christians in a relevant fashion. Despite my role in making the work of Corsini available in English, I have also had occasion to adopt the more widespread interpretation of the Apocalypse as pointing the suffering Christian toward an "end time."[15] Given the popularity of the Apocalypse in so many settings and applications in today's society, it is perhaps the text that most urgently calls for a readership that is both catholic and critical, no matter what interpretive lens one uses to make this possible.

My personal preferences are just that—personal. However, they are grounded in my reading of the text of the Apocalypse. I find that when read in the light of Easter it is not a wild-eyed apocalyptic exhortation to suffering Christians of the late first century that one day they would eventually overcome all suffering.[16] The book insists, from its opening verses until its closure—like Francis Ford Coppola, although in a different key because the victory of the death and resurrection of Jesus lies at its heart—that the apocalypse is *now*.

15. See, e.g., Francis J. Moloney, *A Friendly Guide to the New Testament* (Mulgrave, Australia: John Garratt Publications, 2010), 20–21. See notes 3 and 6 above for suggested further reading that could guide a reader through this more commonly accepted interpretation of the book.

16. It is important to note that the Apocalypse is read in its entirety in the Office of Readings in the Catholic *Prayer of the Church* in the period immediately after Easter. This liturgical setting makes sense of the interpretation offered above, as one possible interpretation among many.

Epilogue

I opened this study sharing the concern of such differently oriented scholars as Ernst Käsemann and Joseph Ratzinger on the importance of the Word of God in the life of the Church. My particular concern throughout the pages of this book has been to bring to life the faith-filled pages of the New Testament for Catholic clergy and laity, including religious educators, but also to reach beyond them to believing Christians of all denominations. Despite lip service that is given to the importance of the Word, and despite Vatican II and subsequent directives from the Church's leadership, a massive program of biblical education is still a dream. The problem is not limited to the Catholic tradition. All Christian traditions face challenges from an increasingly secularized world and, in consequence, a deepening awareness of our own fragility and sometimes poor performance, which make it increasingly difficult for consistent attention to be devoted to the role of the Word of God in the life of the Church. At best we attend to the correct ritual use of the lectionary, but decisive action has not been taken to resolve the widespread inability of believers to understand and thus appreciate more fully what is actually read and heard from the lectionary.

The recent study by David Crump, *Encountering Jesus, Encountering Scripture*, is one of several appeals from a Protestant perspective to restore the Word of God to its rightful place in the faith life of the believer. A growing intellectualization has led to an increased number of erudite biblical scholars but not to greater numbers of genuine believers.[1] His response, strongly supported by a well-informed use of Søren Kierkegaard, is to draw attention

---

1. David Crump, *Encountering Jesus, Encountering Scripture: Reading the Bible Critically in Faith* (Grand Rapids: Eerdmans, 2013). On the practical dangers of overintellectualizing the Scriptures, see pp. 1–6, 12–13.

to the need for a prior commitment of a faith that comes from a personal encounter with Jesus. That will impel a leap into the uncertainty of faith. This kind of faith must precede any critical reading of the New Testament.

An encouraging new initiative has emerged from a collaborative publishing initiative by the Roman Catholic Vatican Press and the mainstream Protestant American Bible Society. Both share a common concern about a fading interest in the Bible. Together they worked to produce a volume dedicated to the ancient practice of *lectio divina*, a way of prayerfully reflecting on the Bible that developed largely in Christian monastic traditions. The book is available in English, Italian, and Spanish.[2] Clearly, the Catholic tradition is not alone, nor am I, in hoping to promote more awareness of the role of the New Testament in the life and practice of the Church.[3]

The Word and the Christian Community

In his recent provocative book, David Crump states a traditional and courageous understanding of what it means to believe.

> Christian faith is an either-or, an all or nothing, a yes or no to God right now. It is based on a decision that can only be rendered by the single individual and is not a collective act. Such passionate, individualized commitment to Jesus does not flourish under the homogenized regimen of popular opinion. Rather, such passion is typically drowned out by the monotonous voice of the crowd.[4]

This act of faith, then, is prior to any appreciation of the Word of God as we find it in our Sacred Scriptures. Only a personal encounter with Jesus can generate a leap of faith—and this has no support except in the act of faith itself: "ultimately every individual stands alone."[5] There is a great deal to be said for this position, an exciting and eloquent restatement of the Reformation insistence upon faith alone, Christ alone, Scripture alone. Crump is also

2. See Gabriel Mestre, *Pray with the Bible, Meditate with the Word* (Rome: Editrice Libreria Vaticana; Tulsa: American Bible Society, 2013). For a recent endorsement of the practice of *lectio divina* in the Catholic tradition, see Joseph Ratzinger (Pope Benedict XVI), *Verbum Domini*, paras. 86–87 (pp. 140–46).

3. See, among several others, Marc Zvi Brettler, Peter Enns, and Daniel J. Harrington, *The Bible and the Believer: How to Read the Bible Critically and Religiously* (Oxford: Oxford University Press, 2012), for a discussion of this issue by a Jewish, a Protestant, and a Roman Catholic scholar. For a recent Catholic reflection, based on the recent Roman Synod on the Word of God in the Church, see Okoye, *Scripture in the Church*.

4. Crump, *Encountering Jesus*, 59.

5. Ibid., 14.

correct in his claim that a critical approach to the Scriptures without a prior commitment of faith can be at best only informative, and at worst destructive of a burgeoning faith. We do not come to faith because of what we learn from the Scriptures; we go to the Scriptures as believing individuals and communities. As Crump puts it: "Reason is educated by Christian faith."[6]

But does this "existentialist" understanding of the act of faith, this unique and transforming result of a personal encounter with Jesus Christ, reflect what has generated faith across the centuries? The further question that arises is: *Where* does the individual have this personal encounter with Christ? I have lived as a believing Christian for more than seventy years, but the birth of my faith was within the context of my mother and father, my brothers and sisters, in a loving and believing family that took Jesus and the Church seriously. They did their best to live generous, joyful, and hope-filled lives that produced moving and beautiful deaths.[7] I find it hard to accept Crump's assertion: "External factors such as history, community, culture, and family may determine the environmental factors that influence our choices, but ultimately every individual must stand alone before God to give an account of the sum total of his or her personal decisions."[8] I agree that I am responsible for my personal decisions and that the act of faith is mine alone, but my personal encounter with Jesus Christ has always been *mediated*, and this mediation is not only an "external factor," despite my own responsibility for my Christian faith. I do not stand alone; I stand with others in the presence of the crucified, risen, and exalted Jesus Christ.

I have no recollection of a moment in my life when I was transformed by a personal encounter with Jesus Christ, even if my first communion and later confirmation, religious profession, and ordination were deeply formative. I first encountered Jesus Christ in the people who loved me and to whom I gave myself in love. I continue to encounter Jesus Christ there, as I also do in a community that shares my faith, and through my participation in two thousand years of Christian witness, experience, and "memory." This memory is rendered actual within the celebration of the Eucharist, which is not only a ritual but above all a way of life: "For as often as you eat this bread and drink the cup, you proclaim the Lord's death until he comes" (1 Cor. 11:26).[9] Paul is aware that an encounter with Jesus Christ is essential for the

6. Ibid., 132. See also: "The claim that an individual has had a firsthand encounter with Jesus Christ is completely beyond the horizon of enquiry" (123).

7. On this personal detail, see Moloney, *Love in the Gospel of John*, 213–14 and 214n12.

8. Crump, *Encountering Jesus*, 14.

9. On the eucharistic life of the Christian community, see Moloney, *Body Broken*, 174–77. In my Catholic tradition, the same could be said for the complex of the sacramental life of the

leap of faith. Nevertheless he presents himself as the one who has represented Jesus Christ in every community that knew him physically: "Be imitators *of me*, as I am *of Christ*" (1 Cor. 11:1, emphasis added; see further 1 Thess. 1:6; 1 Cor. 4:16–17; Gal. 4:12; Phil. 4:9). He states this most eloquently in Philippians 1:24–26: "But to remain in the flesh is more necessary on your account. Convinced of this, I know that I shall remain and continue with you all, for your progress and joy in the faith, so that *in me* you may have ample cause to glory *in Christ Jesus*, because of my coming to you again" (emphasis added). Paul could not write this to the Romans who had never laid eyes on him. They had never had the opportunity to experience the flesh and blood of Paul, so that *in him* they might glory *in Christ Jesus*.[10] This has nothing to do with "homogenized popular opinion" but lies, rather, at the very heart of the mystery of Christianity focused in the incarnation of the divine in the person of Jesus of Nazareth. As God's Word has scandalously become flesh and dwelt among us, and we have gazed upon his glory (see John 1:1–2, 14), our personal encounter with Jesus Christ underlying the decision for faith is not purely spiritual; it depends upon "flesh"—in a uniquely Christian sense.[11]

Living Christian communities were united from the beginning because they believed the God of Israel had intervened in the human story in a unique and once-for-all fashion. They came to understand and confess that Jesus, "Son of Man," was the Christ, the Lord, and the Son of God. Such believing individuals and communities existed well before there was ever a written "word" of Scripture. However, apart from the Pauline "Damascus road" experience (recorded only in Acts, never in Paul's own writings), there is little biblical evidence that the origin of Christian faith involved a personal and highly individual encounter with Jesus Christ that called for an existential decision.[12]

---

community. For all traditions, the communitarian nature of baptism (not the rite of reception but the subsequent living of a baptized life) is hardly an "external factor."

10. See Murphy-O'Connor, *Becoming Human Together*, 187–212, for a detailed examination of this material.

11. Theologically, more needs to be said about the nature of an act of faith that may not be quite the scandal that Crump and Kierkegaard suggest. This is not the place for a lengthy reflection, but see Moloney, *Resurrection of the Messiah*, 148–49, for a summary of discussion with Roger Haight by Philip Gleeson and Joel Hodge. Haight calls faith "a universal human phenomenon." As Haight puts it: "The ultimate issue in the question of faith does not deal with yes or no, faith or unfaith. Rather, the point at issue is which faith to choose: which faith makes most sense? . . . The pluralism of the objects of faith shows that faith is not demonstrable knowing, and that it is universal and inescapable" (*Dynamics of Theology*, 2nd ed. [Maryknoll, NY: Orbis, 2001], 18).

12. It is incorrect to interpret the resurrection narratives in this way. See, among many, Moloney, *Resurrection of the Messiah*, 137–82.

This fundamental statement is not a hypothesis, for it is grounded in historical evidence, as we saw above in chapter 3.[13] In the chapters on Jesus, Paul, the development of a narrative tradition in the Gospels and Acts, and the further documents of the New Testament, especially Hebrews and the Apocalypse, we traced the explosion of "writings" that depended *entirely* on the belief that Jesus of Nazareth, who was crucified, had been raised from the dead and exalted as Lord. All the *writing* was subsequent to the developing *traditions* in the various communities, born of the belief in Jesus' death, resurrection, and exaltation—a scandal for the Jews, stupidity to the Greeks, but for those who believe, the power and wisdom of God (see 1 Cor. 1:23–24).[14]

Although there are scholarly debates surrounding some New Testament books, most likely there is not a single book in the New Testament explicitly written to "generate" faith in Jesus.[15] The books themselves do not provide first "encounters" with Jesus Christ that call people to decision. That encounter had already taken place in the experience of the individuals and the communities that produced the books. As has been often said, the New Testament was written *by* people who believed *for* people who believed. Our survey of all the New Testament literature has attempted to show the faith and passion that generated the books of the New Testament intended that others might share that same faith and passion. The goal was to draw others more closely into the circle of faith—the Christian community as we know it, then and now. Although Christian faith was certainly born in the founding community through encounter with the risen Jesus, it did not presuppose the documents of the New Testament, in whole or in part.[16]

Numerous Christian communities emerged from that foundational experience of the risen Lord. Some, but not all, eventually left a witness to their

---

13. See pp. 45–63 above.

14. For a most helpful reflection on this reality, see Edith M. Humphrey, *Scripture and Tradition: What the Bible Really Says*, Acadia Studies in Bible and Theology (Grand Rapids: Baker Academic, 2013). As indicated in the title, the major focus of this book is the way in which the Bible itself is the result of the process of "traditioning" and the appropriation (or rejection) of *traditions*. However, as a Christian who has journeyed from the Salvation Army, through Anglicanism, into Eastern Orthodoxy (see pp. 17–24), Humphrey offers a broad ecumenical perspective on the relationship between Scripture and Tradition.

15. Because of the nature of book production and circulation in antiquity, more limited audiences are a given. A hefty debate surrounds the motivation for the writing of the Gospel of John. Some have claimed that this is an "evangelical" text, written to convert nonbelievers (most likely a Jewish readership). For the discussion, and a rejection of this position, see Francis J. Moloney, "The Gospel of John and Evangelization," in *The Gospel of John: Text and Context*, Biblical Interpretation Series 72 (Boston/Leiden: Brill, 2005), 3–19.

16. See Moloney, *Resurrection of the Messiah*, for the experience communicated to the post-Easter communities of Mark, Matthew, Luke, and John. See especially pp. 137–82 on what actually took place and what it means in the life of the Church today.

ongoing experience of Jesus Christ in their writings. Believing individuals and communities produced texts that could be read, proclaimed, and performed in order to challenge, to chide, to encourage, and to bless those who received them, to mention but a few of the reasons such "writings" emerged.[17] Many such texts were written in the early centuries of the Christian tradition. However, only twenty-seven of them were eventually regarded as "Sacred Scripture," a New Testament to be read and interpreted side by side with the Old Testament, the sacred writing of Israel that had come to the early Church from its Jewish roots. But, as we have seen, the decision about which books were "in" and which were "out" did not come from an external authority. It emerged from the inner dynamic of the faith experience of the Christian Church itself.[18] It can therefore be said that *Tradition* preceded and formed *the Word*, and that *Tradition* determined what books eventually formed the Sacred Scripture of the New Testament. Not only did Tradition give birth to the Word, but it continues to nourish it and keep it alive. The practice of reading the Sacred Scriptures in the Christian Church, in whatever form that takes, whether liturgical, communal, familial, or personal Bible reading, takes place *because we have always done this*, following the practice that comes to us from our Jewish heritage and its respect for a Sacred Text. It is this generative Tradition that not only gave birth to the scriptural Word but that also maintains the lively presence of that Word *within the Church*. This biblical Word was born in the Church and is nourished by the life of the Church. It comes into its own when it nourishes the faith-filled life and practice of believers.[19]

Scripture and Tradition

In some ways this book finishes where it began. If the Tradition of the Christian community gave birth to the Scriptures, nourishes them, and keeps them alive in the community, then what is the relationship between the Tradition and Scripture, and how does this relationship play into Christian life and practice?

---

17. Other possible motivations for such "writing" are mentioned above, as each New Testament book is presented. Recently, Richard Bauckham, *The Gospels for All Christians: Rethinking the Gospel Audiences* (Grand Rapids: Eerdmans, 1998), 9–48, has argued that the Gospels were not written to address or challenge specific communities. Bauckham claims that, from the beginning, the New Testament documents addressed the broader Christian community. The evidence indicates that specific communities *initially* were addressed but that those books were *subsequently* received by the Church as a whole. This is what led to their acceptance into a Christian canon.

18. See pp. 57–63 above.

19. See the fine reflections of Humphrey, *Scripture and Tradition*, 91–131.

As we have seen in our reflections on Vatican II, especially *Dei Verbum*, the council's 1965 document on Revelation, this is a matter of some concern. One of the several causes of the sixteenth-century Reformation was the importance of some beliefs and practices in the Roman Catholic Tradition that had no roots in the biblical Word of God. At the Council of Trent and at Vatican I, the Catholic response was that there were two sources of Revelation, namely, Scripture and Tradition. Although it never became an article of Roman Catholic belief, both councils maintained that the Tradition had a certain priority. It did not matter whether aspects of Catholic faith and practice were not found in the Scriptures. Insofar as they were part of the Tradition, they were part of the divine communication with humankind. This stance, although nuanced now in ways that are different from the period of the Council of Trent, remains an essential aspect of the use of the Scriptures in the Catholic Church. To make a play on catchphrases from the time of the Reformation, Catholics are committed not to *sola Scriptura* (only Scripture) but to *prima Scriptura* (the primacy of Scripture).

After a hefty debate at Vatican II, there emerged something entirely new: Scripture and Tradition are intimately linked. Both contribute "to make the people of God live their lives in holiness and increase their faith" and "converse with the spouse [i.e., the Church] of His beloved Son" (*DV* 8). The two different sources for Revelation are now regarded as one: "Sacred tradition and sacred scripture, then, are bound closely together, and communicate one with the other. Flowing from the same divine wellspring, both of them merge, in a sense, and move towards the same goal" (*DV* 9). This is a major contribution to the history of Roman Catholic thought. Fortunately, in that same statement, the council does not attempt to eliminate a healthy tension that might exist between Scripture and Tradition. This tension is found in the words "both of them merge, in a sense [Latin: *in unum quodammodo coalescunt*], and move towards the same goal." The fathers of the council wisely decided not to attempt a description of *how* the two merge into one. They recognized that by means of an interaction between Scripture and Tradition we encounter divine communication with the human. The initiative in this communicative act lies with God, and thus we do not know *how* this functions, but the highest form of the Church's Magisterium stated in *Dei Verbum* 9 *that* it happens.

It is within this "uncomfortable" relationship between Scripture and Tradition that Christian faith is lived, even though there must be an awareness of the great richness of *both* Tradition and Scripture. All Christian traditions believe that the New Testament is an inspired Word of God. At Vatican II the Catholic Church taught that "the books of the Old and the New Testaments [are] whole and entire, with all their parts, on the grounds that, written under the inspiration of the Holy Spirit (cf. Jn 20:31; 2 Tim 3:16; 2 Pet 1:19–21; 3:15–16), they have God as their author, and have been handed on as such to the Church itself" (*DV* 11). These statements call for further elaboration. Traditionally, inspiration was regarded as the direct action of God in the production of the book, often represented artistically with an angel guiding the hand of the biblical author.[20] Inspiration was, therefore, regarded as a "one-off," single charismatic experience of a sacred author. Such a point of view does not take into account the obvious fact that these books developed over long periods of time. Some of the Old Testament books were composed over hundreds of years, and many people were involved in speaking them, hearing them, remembering them, writing them, and canonizing them.[21] A case can be made, for example, that 2 Corinthians was the compilation of several letters and that John 1–20 and John 21 came from different times and perhaps different hands.[22]

Critical biblical scholarship has provided a deeper appreciation of the presence of the inspiring Spirit through the manifold formative process of reading, especially the discernment of the active presence of God within the experience of a people or a community. Some have argued that the experience of "inspiration" belonged to certain early Christian communities. That possibility need not imply that such inspiration was a "community" experience, although different community experiences have affected the character of each of the four Gospels. Inspiration, therefore, entails a long history of interaction between human beings, individuals, and communities, under the direction and inspiration of the Holy Spirit. The inspired text as we have it today resulted. A major contributor to the development of a contemporary theory of inspiration, Pierre Benoit, has written:

> Those who would be pastors, prophets, apostles and writers, are always privileged individuals whom the Spirit has seized and made use of. Carrying the argument a bit further, we could show that these individuals were numerous, more numerous than we might ever guess: a good many hands contributed to the shaping of the Pentateuch and the Gospels. But the number and anonymity

20. See for example, Caravaggio's splendid painting of Matthew getting some help from an angel (dictating to him), reproduced on the frontispiece of Spivey, Smith, and Black, *Anatomy of the New Testament*, and another portrait of an angel, this one whispering in Matthew's ear, reproduced in Powell, *Introducing the New Testament*, 96.

21. For example, the Psalms reflect many periods of Israel's history, from the time of David (to whom all the Psalms are traditionally attributed) to the exile and possibly to periods after that time. There are clearly three stages in the writing of the book that we know as Isaiah, representing periods prior to the exile in Babylon (Isa. 1–39), during the exile (Isa. 40–55), and rejoicing in the return from the exile (Isa. 56–65).

22. On 2 Corinthians, see the summary of Brown, *Introduction to the New Testament*, 548–51. On John, see Moloney, *Gospel of John*, 545–68.

of these biblical workers does not gainsay the fact that they were individuals, moved by the Spirit to carry their stone, big or small, and contribute it to building up the monument of Revelation.[23]

Whatever we make of these theoretical discussions, the Word of God is received into the life of the Church as inspired and God-given. Ignorance of Scripture is ignorance of Christ (Saint Jerome). Such ignorance has consequences, because it means that an essential element in the dynamic relationship between Tradition and Scripture is lacking. The formation and nourishment of Christian faith and practice inevitably suffers.[24]

Conclusion

The biblical Word of God is inspired. It flows from the same wellspring as Tradition, so that each interacts with the other in God's self-revelation to humankind. What, then, is the role of Sacred Scripture within God's self-revelation?[25] There are always, of course, the great truths that come to us directly from Jesus, Paul, and the early witnesses to the Christian tradition, and the relationship between Tradition and Scripture is itself a life-giving synergy. As we have seen, the Tradition gave birth to the scriptural Word, even as it nourishes it and keeps it alive within the life and practice of the community. But Tradition always runs the danger of being manipulated by historically conditioned practices, however unwittingly this might happen. In other words, sometimes "traditions" can be the products of human imagination responding to a human need or to a given pastoral problem that may have come and gone in the Church's history.[26] The

23. Pierre Benoit, "Inspiration and Revelation," *Concilium* 10 (1965): 9. See his more comprehensive *Inspiration and the Bible*, Stagbooks (London: Sheed & Ward, 1965). Another important contributor to this ongoing discussion is Karl Rahner, *Inspiration in the Bible*, 2nd rev. ed. (London: Burns & Oates, 1964). He bases his suggestions on his theological anthropology that every human being is fundamentally constituted as potentially obedient to the life of the Spirit. See also the more literary response to the question in Luis Alonso-Schökel, "Inspiration," in *Encyclopedia of Theology: A Concise Sacramentum Mundi*, ed. Karl Rahner (London: Burns & Oates, 1975), 717–26. For a very recent important study of the role of "reception" in inspiration, see Rush, *Eyes of Faith*, 153–72.

24. Most practicing Catholics would claim to be well versed in the Church's traditions, but they would also admit to very little familiarity with the Church's Scriptures. This may also be true of some Protestant traditions.

25. For what follows, see the original suggestion by Ratzinger, "Transmission of Divine Revelation," in Vorgrimler, *Commentary*, 3:192–93; and idem, "Sacred Scripture in the Life of the Church," in Vorgrimler, *Commentary*, 3:268. See pp. x–xii above.

26. See Humphrey, *Scripture and Tradition*, 45–68, a reflection on the way the biblical authors received and transmitted seemingly uncreative traditions, and 133–57, a balanced treatment of

need or the pastoral problem may no longer exist, but the once-very-important "traditions" may have merged so deeply into a community's life and practice that they come to be regarded as Tradition itself.[27]

Examples of this in the contemporary Catholic Church are the alteration of the General Roman Catholic liturgical calendar immediately after Easter to make way for a Sunday dedicated to the celebration of devotion to Divine Mercy;[28] the universal imposition of clerical celibacy; degrees of honor and hierarchy taken for granted within the administration of the Catholic community, with their associated decorative clothing and rituals; and certain misguided Marian devotions and practices that sideline the centrality of God and Jesus Christ.[29] None of this is without its value and role in the life of the Church, and no doubt every Christian church has developed its own "traditions" that run the risk of being regarded as authentic Tradition.[30] This is perfectly understandable, for as Edith Humphrey has rightly said, "Each generation has its blind spots, and we need each other, through the ages, for complete understanding."[31] I do not wish to ignore the importance of many such "traditions." Some of them reside deeply within the believers' national ethos and have sustained Christian faith and practice in times of great hardship and persecution. Religious orders and congregations of women and men have developed many important traditions that enable members to be aware of their particular charism. Many traditions generate quality religious practice, although there are some exceptions where an overzealous commitment to a devotion may prove to be detrimental to the local church. It is here

the contemporary challenge to discern the difference between "Holy Tradition" and "human traditions." Her major concern is with the use of Scripture (see 138–49), but the chapter closes (149–56) with reflections on four crucial contemporary issues: head covering for women, celibacy, the use of exclusively male terminology to refer to the triune God, and the neutralization of gender in biblical prayers (i.e., the Psalms).

27. See pp. 8–9n8 above.

28. Divine Mercy Sunday was recently introduced into the General Roman Catholic liturgical calendar to be celebrated on the first Sunday after Easter. A much older tradition, reaching back to the fourth century CE, was lost. That Sunday (*Domenica in Albis*) celebrated those who had been newly baptized at the Easter Vigil. The end of the Easter Octave was marked by the newly baptized dressing in white and undergoing mystagogy. The devotion to Jesus as "Divine Mercy" and its association with the first Sunday after Easter had its origins in the revelations of the twentieth-century mystic Sister (Saint) Faustina Kowalska (1905–38). It became part of the Roman Catholic liturgical calendar on April 22, 2001.

29. For a brief but rich reflection on the requirement of celibacy, see Humphrey, *Scripture and Tradition*, 150–52.

30. Across all religious traditions (not only Christian), such "popular devotions" can be the most important access many have to religious life and practice. What follows suggests a way to "test" the enduring value of these devotions.

31. Humphrey, *Scripture and Tradition*, 166.

that the Word of God can raise a questioning finger. The New Testament's single-minded focus—on the centrality and lordship of God; on the unique revelation of God in and through his Son, Jesus Christ, in his life, teaching, death, and resurrection; and on the lifestyle that is urged upon all who wish to follow him—can be disruptive to "Church life as usual." On the other hand, particular traditions can narrow the sense of the great generative Tradition and even distract from it, obscuring the need for reform and conversion.

This book is an attempt to summon Christians, especially Catholics, to recognize the treasure we have in Scripture, making God and God's ways known to us, running side by side with the Tradition—indeed, flowing from the same wellspring.[32] "Scripture and tradition . . . are at every step interwoven—in their prehistory in the process of writing and compiling, and in the ongoing acts of reading and interpreting."[33] The revelation of God and the ways of God through Scripture and Tradition necessarily question "traditions." The Christian Tradition gave birth to the Word of God and nourishes and maintains its presence in the life of the Church. But the Word of God "is living and active, sharper than any two-edged sword, piercing to the division of soul and spirit, of joints and marrow, and discerning the thoughts and intentions of the heart" (Heb. 4:12). It has been given to the Christian Church *to keep the Tradition honest.*

In the preface to this book I introduced some personal reflections. I close with a similar note to indicate what I mean by "keeping the Tradition honest." In doing this, I am following the lead of all the Gospels, creating a literary "inclusion" between my preface and my epilogue (see Mark 1:1–13; 16:1–8; Matt. 1:23; 28:20; Luke 1:8–25; 24:52–53; John 1:1–18; 20:30–31). As an ordained minister of the Catholic Church, whatever success I may have had nationally and internationally as a New Testament scholar, however eloquent I may or may not be as a teacher or a preacher, the words of Jesus that first appeared in Mark 10:42–45 ring daily in my mind and heart, *to keep me honest:*

> You know that those who are supposed to rule over the Gentiles lord it over them, and their great men exercise authority over them. But it shall not be so among you; but whoever would be great among you must be your servant, and whoever would be first among you must be slave of all. For the Son of man also came not to be served but to serve, and to give his life as a ransom for many.[34]

---

32. Medieval writers called Scripture a treasure, a forest, a banquet, an ocean, a torrent, an abyss. See Alonso-Schökel, "Inspiration," 724.

33. Humphrey, *Scripture and Tradition*, 134.

34. See also Matt. 20:24–28; Luke 22:25–27; and in a different key, Phil. 2:5–11.

Bibliography

Commentaries

The Gospel of Mark

Byrne, Brendan. *A Costly Freedom: A Theological Reading of Mark's Gospel.* Collegeville, MN: Liturgical Press, 2008.

Culpepper, R. Alan. *Mark.* Smyth & Helwys Bible Commentary. Macon, GA: Smyth & Helwys, 2007.

Donahue, John, and Daniel J. Harrington. *The Gospel of Mark.* Sacra Pagina 2. Collegeville, MN: Liturgical Press, 2003.

Dowd, Sharon. *Reading Mark: A Literary and Theological Commentary on the Second Gospel.* Reading the New Testament. Macon, GA: Smyth & Helwys, 2000.

Hooker, Morna D. *The Gospel according to St. Mark.* Black's New Testament Commentaries. Grand Rapids: Baker Academic, 1991.

Moloney, Francis J. *The Gospel of Mark: A Commentary.* Grand Rapids: Baker Academic, 2012.

The Gospel of Matthew

Byrne, Brendan. *Lifting the Burden: Reading Matthew's Gospel in the Church Today.* Collegeville, MN: Liturgical Press, 2004.

Garland, David E. *Reading Matthew: A Literary and Theological Commentary.* Macon, GA: Smyth & Helwys, 2001.

Keener, Craig S. *A Commentary on the Gospel of Matthew.* Grand Rapids: Eerdmans, 1998.

Meier, John P. *Matthew.* New Testament Message 3. Wilmington, DE: Michael Glazier, 1980.

Nolland, John. *The Gospel of Matthew.* New International Greek Testament Commentary. Grand Rapids: Eerdmans, 2005.

Senior, Donald. *Matthew.* Abingdon New Testament Commentaries. Nashville: Abingdon, 1998.

The Gospel of Luke

Byrne, Brendan. *The Hospitality of God: A Reading of Luke's Gospel.* Collegeville, MN: Liturgical Press, 2000.

Carroll, John T. *Luke: A Commentary.* New Testament Library. Louisville: Westminster John Knox, 2012.

Johnson, Luke T. *The Gospel of Luke.* Sacra Pagina 3. Collegeville, MN: Liturgical Press, 1991.

Tannehill, Robert C. *Luke.* Abingdon New Testament Commentaries. Nashville: Abingdon, 1996.

The Gospel of John

Byrne, Brendan. *Life Abounding: A Reading of John's Gospel.* Collegeville, MN: Liturgical Press, 2014.

Culpepper, R. Alan. *The Gospel and Letters of John.* Interpreting Biblical Texts. Nashville: Abingdon, 1998.

Hoskyns, Edwyn C. *The Fourth Gospel.* Edited by Francis N. Davey. London: Faber & Faber, 1947.

Lincoln, Andrew T. *The Gospel according to Saint John.* Black's New Testament Commentaries. Grand Rapids: Baker Academic, 2005.

Moloney, Francis J. *The Gospel of John.* Sacra Pagina 4. Collegeville, MN: Liturgical Press, 1998.

Stibbe, Mark W. G. *John.* Readings: A New Biblical Commentary. Sheffield, UK: JSOT Press, 1993.

Special Gospel Commentaries

Brown, Raymond E. *The Birth of the Messiah: A Commentary on the Infancy Narratives in Matthew and Luke.* New York: Doubleday, 1977.

———. *The Death of the Messiah: From Gethsemane to the Grave; A Commentary on the Passion Narratives in the Four Gospels.* 2 vols. Anchor Bible Reference Library. New York: Doubleday, 1993.

Moloney, Francis J. *The Resurrection of the Messiah: A Narrative Commentary on the Resurrection Accounts in the Four Gospels.* Mahwah, NJ: Paulist Press, 2013.

The Acts of the Apostles

Gaventa, Beverly R. *Acts.* Abingdon New Testament Commentaries. Nashville: Abingdon, 2003.

Johnson, Luke T. *The Acts of the Apostles.* Sacra Pagina 5. Collegeville, MN: Liturgical Press, 2006.

Parsons, Mikael C. *Acts.* Paideia Commentaries on the New Testament. Grand Rapids: Baker Academic, 2008.

The Letters of Paul

Barrett, C. Kingsley. *The First Epistle to the Corinthians.* 2nd ed. Black's New Testament Commentaries. Grand Rapids: Baker Academic, 1971.

———. *The Second Epistle to the Corinthians.* Black's New Testament Commentaries. Grand Rapids: Baker Academic, 1973.

Byrne, Brendan. *Galatians and Romans.* Collegeville, MN: Liturgical Press, 2010.

———. "The Letter to the Philippians." In *The New Jerome Biblical Commentary*, edited by Raymond E. Brown, Joseph A. Fitzmyer, and Roland E. Murphy, 791–97. Englewood Cliffs, NJ: Prentice Hall, 1990.

———. *Reckoning with Romans: A Contemporary Reading of Paul's Gospel.* Good News Studies 18. Wilmington, DE: Michael Glazier, 1986.

———. *Romans.* Sacra Pagina 6. Collegeville, MN: Liturgical Press, 1996.

Collange, Jean-François. *The Epistle of Saint Paul to the Philippians.* Translated by A. W. Heathcote. London: Epworth, 1979.

Furnish, Victor P. *1 Thessalonians, 2 Thessalonians.* Abingdon New Testament Commentaries. Nashville: Abingdon, 2004.

Lambrecht, Jan. *Second Corinthians.* Sacra Pagina 8. Collegeville, MN: Liturgical Press, 1999.

Lightfoot, J. B. *St. Paul's Epistle to the Philippians.* London: Macmillan, 1913.

Matera, Frank. *Galatians.* Sacra Pagina 9. Collegeville, MN: Liturgical Press, 1992.

———. *Romans.* Paideia Commentaries on the New Testament. Grand Rapids: Baker Academic, 2010.

Perkins, Pheme. *First Corinthians*. Paideia Commentaries on the New Testament. Grand Rapids: Baker Academic, 2012.

Reumann, John. *Philippians*. Anchor Yale Bible 33B. New Haven: Yale University Press, 2008.

Thurston, Bonnie, and Judith Ryan. *Philippians and Philemon*. Sacra Pagina 10. Collegeville, MN: Liturgical Press, 2005.

Ephesians and Colossians

MacDonald, Margaret Y. *Colossians and Ephesians*. Collegeville, MN: Liturgical Press, 2008.

Talbert, Charles H. *Ephesians and Colossians*. Paideia Commentaries on the New Testament. Grand Rapids: Baker Academic, 2007.

The Pastoral Epistles

Bassler, Judith M. *1 Timothy, 2 Timothy, Titus*. Abingdon New Testament Commentaries. Nashville: Abingdon, 1996.

Collins, Raymond F. *I and II Timothy and Titus*. New Testament Library. Louisville: Westminster John Knox, 2002.

Hebrews

Johnson, Luke T. *Hebrews: A Commentary*. New Testament Library. Louisville: Westminster John Knox, 2006.

Lincoln, Andrew T. *Hebrews: A Guide*. London: T&T Clark, 2006.

The Catholic Epistles

Achtemeier, Paul J. *1 Peter: A Commentary on the First Epistle of Peter*. Hermeneia. Minneapolis: Fortress, 1996.

Bauckham, Richard J. *Jude, 2 Peter*. Word Biblical Commentary 50. Waco: Word, 1983.

Feldmeier, Reinhard. *The First Letter of Peter*. Translated by Peter H. Davids. Waco: Baylor University Press, 2008.

Hartin, Patrick J. *James*. Collegeville, MN: Liturgical Press, 2009.

Johnson, Luke T. *The Letter of James*. Anchor Bible 37A. New York: Doubleday, 1995.

Lieu, Judith M. *I, II, and III John: A Commentary*. New Testament Library. Louisville: Westminster John Knox, 2008.

Moloney, Francis J. *From James to Jude: A Bible Commentary for Every Day.* Abingdon, UK: Bible Reading Fellowship, 1999.

Neyrey, Jerome H. *2 Peter, Jude.* Anchor Bible 37C. New York: Doubleday, 1993.

Painter, John. *1, 2 and 3 John.* Sacra Pagina 18. Collegeville, MN: Liturgical Press, 2002.

Rensberger, David. *1 John, 2 John, 3 John.* Abingdon New Testament Commentaries. Nashville: Abingdon, 1997.

The Apocalypse

Boring, Eugene. *Revelation.* Louisville: John Knox, 1989.

Corsini, Eugenio. *Apocalisse de Gesù Cristo secondo Giovanni.* Turin: Società Editrice Internazionale, 2002.

———. *The Apocalypse: The Perennial Revelation of Jesus Christ.* Translated by Francis J. Moloney. Good News Studies 5. Wilmington, DE: Michael Glazier, 1983.

Harrington, Wilfred J. *Revelation.* Sacra Pagina 16. Collegeville, MN: Liturgical Press, 1993.

Resseguie, James L. *The Revelation of John: A Narrative Commentary.* Grand Rapids: Baker Academic, 2009.

Introductions to the New Testament

Brown, Raymond E. *An Introduction to the New Testament.* Anchor Bible Reference Library. New York: Doubleday, 1996.

Moloney, Francis J. *The Living Voice of the Gospel: The Gospels Today.* Peabody, MA: Hendrickson, 2006.

Powell, Mark Allan. *Introducing the New Testament: A Historical, Literary, and Theological Survey.* Grand Rapids: Baker Academic, 2009.

Spivey, Robert A., D. Moody Smith, and C. Clifton Black. *Anatomy of the New Testament: A Guide to Its Structure and Meaning.* 7th ed. Minneapolis: Fortress, 2013.

Other Works Cited

Allison, Dale C., Jr. *Constructing Jesus: Memory, Imagination, and History.* Grand Rapids: Baker Academic, 2010.

———. *The Historical Christ and the Theological Jesus*. Grand Rapids: Eerdmans, 2009.

Alonso-Schökel, Luis. "Inspiration." In *Encyclopedia of Theology*, edited by Karl Rahner, 717–26. London: Burns & Oates, 1975.

Augustine, Saint. *Confessions*. Translated by Henry Chadwick. Oxford: Oxford University Press, 1991.

Barrett, C. Kingsley. *Paul: An Introduction to His Thought*. London: Geoffrey Chapman, 1994.

Barton, John, and Michael Wolter, eds. *Die Einheit der Schrift und die Vielfalt des Kanons* [The Unity of Scripture and the Diversity of the Canon]. Beihefte zur Zeitschrift für die Neutestamentliche Wissenschaft 118. Berlin/New York: Walter de Gruyter, 2003.

Bauckham, Richard. *The Gospels for All Christians: Rethinking the Gospel Audiences*. Grand Rapids: Eerdmans, 1998.

Becker, Jürgen. *Paul: Apostle to the Gentiles*. Translated by O. C. Dean Jr. Louisville: Westminster John Knox, 1993.

Beker, J. Christiaan. *Paul the Apostle: The Triumph of God in Life and Thought*. Philadelphia: Fortress, 1980.

Benoit, Pierre. "Inspiration and Revelation." *Concilium* 10 (1965): 5–14.

———. *Inspiration and the Bible*. Stagbooks. London: Sheed & Ward, 1965.

Bloom, Harold. *The Shadow of a Great Rock: A Literary Appreciation of the King James Bible*. New Haven: Yale University Press, 2011.

Botha, Pieter J. J. *Orality and Literacy in Early Christianity*. Biblical Performance Criticism 5. Eugene, OR: Cascade, 2012.

Brakke, David. *The Gnostics: Myth, Ritual and Diversity in Early Christianity*. Cambridge, MA: Harvard University Press, 2010.

Brettler, Marc Zvi, Peter Enns, and Daniel J. Harrington. *The Bible and the Believer: How to Read the Bible Critically and Religiously*. Oxford: Oxford University Press, 2012.

Brodd, Jeffrey, and Jonathan L. Reed, eds. *Rome and Religion: A Cross-Disciplinary Dialogue on the Imperial Cult*. Writings from the Greco-Roman World Supplement Series 5. Atlanta: SBL, 2011.

Brown, Dan. *The Da Vinci Code*. New York: Random House, 2003.

Brown, Raymond E. *The Community of the Beloved Disciple*. New York: Paulist Press, 1979.

Brown, Sherri. "Faith, Christ, and Paul's Theology of Salvation History." In Skinner and Iverson, *Unity and Diversity in the Gospels and Paul*, 249–71.

Burridge, Richard A. *What Are the Gospels? A Comparison with Graeco-Roman Biography*. 2nd ed. Grand Rapids: Eerdmans, 2004.

Byrne, Brendan. "Christ's Pre-Existence in Pauline Soteriology." *Theological Studies* 58 (1997): 308–30.

———. *Inheriting the Earth: The Pauline Basis of a Spirituality for Our Time*. Homebush, Australia: St. Paul Publications, 1990.

———. "The Problem of *Nomos* and the Relationship with Judaism in Romans." *Catholic Biblical Quarterly* 62 (2000): 294–309.

Callor, Callie. "*Adulescentes* and *Meretrices*: The Correlation between Squandered Patrimony and Prostitutes in the Parable of the Prodigal Son." *Catholic Biblical Quarterly* 75 (2013): 259–78.

Campbell, Constantine R. *Paul and Union with Christ: An Exegetical and Theological Study*. Grand Rapids: Zondervan, 2012.

Casey, Maurice. *Son of Man: The Interpretation and Influence of Daniel 7*. London: SPCK, 1979.

Charlesworth, James H., ed. *The Old Testament Pseudepigrapha*. 2 vols. New York: Doubleday, 1983–85.

Collins, John J. *The Scepter and the Star: Messianism in Light of the Dead Sea Scrolls*. 2nd ed. Grand Rapids: Eerdmans, 2010.

Crossan, John Dominic. *The Dark Interval: Towards a Theology of Story*. Niles, IL: Argus Communications, 1975.

Crump, David. *Encountering Jesus, Encountering the Scriptures: Reading the Bible Critically in Faith*. Grand Rapids: Eerdmans, 2013.

Danker, Frederick W. *A Greek-English Lexicon of the New Testament and Other Early Christian Literature*. 3rd ed. Chicago: University of Chicago Press, 2000.

Dodd, Charles H. *About the Gospels*. Cambridge: Cambridge University Press, 1952.

———. *Historical Tradition in the Fourth Gospel*. Cambridge: Cambridge University Press, 1965.

Dodds, Eric Robertson. *Pagans and Christians in an Age of Anxiety: Some Aspects of Religious Experience from Marcus Aurelius to Constantine*. Cambridge: Cambridge University Press, 1965.

Dunn, James D. G. *Jesus and the Spirit: A Study of the Religious and Charismatic Experience of Jesus and the First Christians as Reflected in the New Testament*. London: SCM, 1975.

———. *The New Perspective on Paul*. Rev. ed. Grand Rapids: Eerdmans, 2008.

———. "Prophetic Movements and Zealots." In Green and McDonald, *World of the New Testament*, 242–51.

———. *The Theology of Paul the Apostle*. Grand Rapids: Eerdmans, 1998.

Edwards, Ruth. *Discovering John: Content, Interpretation, Reception*. 2nd ed. London: SPCK, 2014.

Elledge, C. D. "The Dead Sea Scrolls." In Green and McDonald, *World of the New Testament*, 228–41.

Evans, Nancy. "Embedding Rome in Athens." In Brodd and Reed, *Rome and Religion*, 83–97.

Fitzgerald, John T. "Greco-Roman Philosophical Schools." In Green and McDonald, *World of the New Testament*, 135–48.

Flannery, Austin, ed. *Vatican Council II: Constitutions, Decrees, Declarations; A Completely Revised Translation in Inclusive Language*. Northport, NY: Costello, 1995.

Frye, Northrop. *The Great Code: The Bible and Literature*. London: Routledge & Kegan Paul, 1982.

Furnish, Victor P. *Theology and Ethics in Paul*. 2nd ed. New Testament Library. Louisville: Westminster John Knox, 2009.

Gaillardetz, Richard. *The Church in the Making*. Rediscovering Vatican II. Mahwah, NJ: Paulist Press, 2006.

Galinsky, Karl. "The Cult of the Roman Emperor: Uniter or Divider?" In Brodd and Reed, *Rome and Religion*, 1–21.

———. "In the Shadow (or Not) of the Imperial Cult: A Cooperative Agenda." In Brodd and Reed, *Rome and Religion*, 215–25.

Gamble, Harry Y. "The New Testament Canon: Recent Research and the Status Quaestionis." In McDonald and Sanders, *Canon Debate*, 267–94.

Grant, Frederick C. "A Response." In *The Documents of Vatican II*, edited by Walter M. Abbott, 129–32. New York: Herder & Herder, 1966.

Green, Joel B., and Lee Martin McDonald, eds. *The World of the New Testament: Cultural, Social, and Historical Contexts*. Grand Rapids: Baker Academic, 2013.

Haight, Roger. *Dynamics of Theology*. 2nd ed. Maryknoll, NY: Orbis, 2001.

Hammann, Konrad. *Rudolf Bultmann: A Biography*. Translated by Philip E. Devenish. Salem, OR: Polebridge, 2013.

Helyer, Larry R. "Apocalypticism." In Green and McDonald, *World of the New Testament*, 252–71.

Hengel, Martin. *The Crucifixion in the Ancient World and the Folly of the Message of the Cross*. Translated by John Bowden. Philadelphia: Fortress, 1977.

———. *Judaism and Hellenism: Studies in Their Encounter in Palestine during the Hellenistic Period*. Translated by John Bowden. 2 vols. Philadelphia: Fortress, 1974.

———. "The Titles of the Gospels and the Gospel of Mark." In *Studies in the Gospel of Mark*, 64–84. Philadelphia: Fortress, 1985.

Hooker, Morna D. *Paul: A Short Introduction*. Oxford: Oneworld, 2003.

Horrell, David G. *An Introduction to the Study of Paul*. 2nd ed. T&T Clark Approaches to Biblical Studies. London: T&T Clark, 2006.

Hubbard, Moyer V. "Greek Religion." In Green and McDonald, *World of the New Testament*, 105–23.

Humphrey, Edith M. *Scripture and Tradition: What the Bible Really Says*. Acadia Studies in Bible and Theology. Grand Rapids: Baker Academic, 2013.

Iverson, Kelly R. "Orality and the Gospels: A Survey of Recent Research." *Currents in Biblical Research* 8 (2009): 71–106.

Josephus, Flavius. *The Jewish War*. Translated by Geoffrey A. Williamson. Edited by E. Mary Smallwood. Penguin Classics. London: Penguin Books, 1981.

Käsemann, Ernst. "Thoughts on the Present Controversy about Scriptural Interpretation." In *New Testament Questions of Today*, 260–85. Philadelphia: Fortress, 1969.

Keith, Chris, and Anthony Le Donne, eds. *Jesus, Criteria, and the Demise of Authenticity*. London/New York: T&T Clark, 2012.

Kloppenborg, John S. *Q, the Earliest Gospel: An Introduction to the Original Stories and Sayings of Jesus*. Louisville: Westminster John Knox, 2008.

Kraus, Hans-Joachim. *Psalms*. Translated by Hilton C. Oswald. 2 vols. A Continental Commentary. Minneapolis: Fortress, 1993.

Lambrecht, Jan. *Once More Astonished: The Parables of Jesus*. New York: Crossroad, 1983.

Lee-Barnewall, Michelle. "Pharisees, Scribes, and Essenes." In Green and McDonald, *World of the New Testament*, 217–27.

Lohfink, Gerhard. *Jesus of Nazareth: What He Wanted, Who He Was*. Translated by Linda M. Maloney. Collegeville, MN: Liturgical Press, 2012.

Lüdemann, Gerd. *Paul, Apostle to the Gentiles: Studies in Chronology*. Translated by F. Stanley Jones. Philadelphia: Fortress, 1984.

Ludlow, Morwenna. "'Criteria of Canonicity' and the Early Church." In Barton and Wolter, *Die Einheit der Schrift*, 69–93.

Martin, Ralph P. *Carmen Christi: Philippians ii. 5–11 in Recent Interpretation and in the Setting of Early Christian Worship*. Society for New Testament Studies Monograph Series 4. Cambridge: Cambridge University Press, 1967.

Martyn, J. Louis. *History and Theology in the Fourth Gospel*. Rev. ed. Nashville: Abingdon, 1979.

Matera, Frank. *God's Saving Grace: A Pauline Theology*. Grand Rapids: Eerdmans, 2012.

McDonald, Lee M., and J. A. Sanders, eds. *The Canon Debate*. Peabody, MA: Hendrickson, 2002.

Meier, John P. *A Marginal Jew: Rethinking the Historical Jesus*. 4 vols. Anchor Yale Bible Reference Library. New Haven: Yale University Press, 1991–2009.

Mestre, Gabriel. *Pray with the Bible, Meditate with the Word*. Rome: Editrice Vaticana; Tulsa: American Bible Society, 2013.

Metzger, Bruce M. *The Canon of the New Testament: Its Origin, Development, and Significance*. Oxford: Clarendon, 1987.

Moessner, David P. *Lord of the Banquet: The Literary and Theological Significance of the Lukan Travel Narrative*. Harrisburg, PA: Trinity Press International, 1989.

Moloney, Francis J. *A Body Broken for a Broken People: Eucharist in the New Testament*. Rev. ed. Peabody, MA: Hendrickson, 1997.

———. "*Constructing Jesus* and the Son of Man." *Catholic Biblical Quarterly* 75 (2013): 719–38.

———. *A Friendly Guide to the New Testament*. Mulgrave, Australia: John Garratt Publications, 2010.

———. *Glory Not Dishonor: Reading John 13–21*. Minneapolis: Fortress, 1998.

———. "The Gospel of John and Evangelization." In *The Gospel of John: Text and Context*, 3–19. Biblical Interpretation Series 72. Boston/Leiden: Brill, 2005.

———. *The Johannine Son of Man*. 2nd ed. Eugene, OR: Wipf & Stock, 2007.

———. *Love in the Gospel of John: An Exegetical, Theological, and Literary Study*. Grand Rapids: Baker Academic, 2013.

Moule, Charles F. D. *The Origins of Christology*. Cambridge: Cambridge University Press, 1977.

Müller, Mogens. *The Expression 'Son of Man' and the Development of Christology: A History of Interpretation*. Sheffield, UK: Equinox, 2008.

Murphy-O'Connor, Jerome. *Becoming Human Together: The Pastoral Anthropology of St. Paul*. Good News Studies 2. Wilmington, DE: Michael Glazier, 1982.

———. *Paul: His Story*. Oxford: Oxford University Press, 2004.

———. *St. Paul's Corinth: Texts and Archaeology*. Good News Studies 6. Wilmington, DE: Michael Glazier, 1983.

———. "2 Timothy Contrasted with 1 Timothy and Titus." *Revue Biblique* 98 (1991): 403–18.

Okoye, James Chukwuma. *Scripture in the Church: The Synod on the Word of God and the Post-Synodal Exhortation* Verbum Domini. Collegeville, MN: Liturgical Press, 2011.

O'Malley, John W. *Trent: What Happened at the Council.* Cambridge, MA: Harvard University Press, 2013.

———. *What Happened at Vatican II.* Cambridge, MA: Harvard University Press, 2008.

Pagels, Elaine. *Beyond Belief: The Secret Gospel of Thomas.* New York: Random House, 2003.

Parsons, Mikael C. *Luke: Storyteller, Interpreter, Evangelist.* Peabody, MA: Hendrickson, 2007.

Perrin, Nicholas. "The Imperial Cult." In Green and McDonald, *World of the New Testament,* 124–34.

Pervo, Richard I. *Luke's Story of Paul.* Minneapolis: Augsburg Fortress, 1990.

Pontifical Biblical Commission. *The Interpretation of the Bible in the Church.* Rome: Editrice Vaticana, 1993.

Pope Leo XIII. *Holy Scripture (Providentissimus Deus).* New York: Paulist Press, 1951.

Pope Pius XII. *Foundations of Renewal: Four Great Encyclicals of Pope Pius XII.* Deus Books. New York: Paulist Press, 1961.

Powell, Mark Allan. *Jesus as a Figure in History: How Modern Historians View the Man from Galilee.* Louisville: Westminster John Knox, 1998.

Prior, Michael P. *Paul the Letter-Writer and the Second Letter to Timothy.* Journal for the Study of the New Testament Supplement Series 23. Sheffield, UK: JSOT Press, 1989.

Rahner, Karl. *Inspiration in the Bible.* 2nd rev. ed. London: Burns & Oates, 1964.

Ratzinger, Joseph. *Jesus of Nazareth.* 3 vols. New York/San Francisco: Doubleday/Image/Ignatius Press, 2007–12.

———. "Sacred Scripture in the Life of the Church." In *Commentary on the Documents of Vatican II,* edited by Herbert Vorgrimler, 3:262–72. London: Burns & Oates/Herder & Herder, 1969.

———. "The Transmission of Divine Revelation." In *Commentary on the Documents of Vatican II,* edited by Herbert Vorgrimler, 3:181–98. London: Burns & Oates/Herder & Herder, 1969.

Ratzinger, Joseph (Pope Benedict XVI). *Verbum Domini: The Word of God in the Life and Mission of the Church.* Post-Synodal Apostolic Exhortation. Rome: Editrice Vaticana, 2010.

Renan, Ernest. *Life of Jesus.* Translated by Charles E. Wilbour. New York: Modern Library, 1955.

Riesner, Rainer. *Paul's Early Period: Chronology, Mission Strategy, Theology.* Translated by Doug Stott. Grand Rapids: Eerdmans, 1994.

Rush, Ormond. *The Eyes of Faith: The Sense of the Faithful and the Church's Reception of Revelation.* Washington, DC: Catholic University of America Press, 2009.

Sanders, Ed Parish. *The Historical Figure of Jesus.* London: Penguin Press, 1993.

———. *Paul and Palestinian Judaism: A Comparison of Patterns of Religion.* London: SCM, 1977.

Schäfer, Peter. *The Jewish Jesus: How Judaism and Christianity Shaped Each Other.* Princeton: Princeton University Press, 2012.

Schneemelcher, Wilhelm. *New Testament Apocrypha.* Rev. ed. Translated by R. McL. Wilson. 2 vols. Louisville: Westminster John Knox, 1991.

Schweizer, Eduard. *Luke: A Challenge to Present Theology.* Atlanta: John Knox, 1982.

Scroggs, Robin. *The Last Adam: A Study in Pauline Anthropology.* Oxford: Basil Blackwell, 1966.

Segal, Alan F. *Paul the Convert.* New Haven: Yale University Press, 1990.

Skinner, Christopher S. *What Are They Saying about the Gospel of Thomas?* Mahwah, NJ: Paulist Press, 2012.

Skinner, Christopher S., and Kelly R. Iverson, eds. *Unity and Diversity in the Gospels and Paul: Essays in Honor of Frank J. Matera.* Early Christianity and Its Literature 7. Atlanta: SBL, 2012.

Smith, D. Moody. *John among the Gospels.* 2nd ed. Columbia: University of South Carolina Press, 2001.

———. "When Did the Gospels Become Scripture?" *Journal of Biblical Literature* 119 (2000): 1–18.

Soards, Marion. "The Question of a PreMarcan Passion Narrative." Appendix 9 in Brown, *Death of the Messiah*, 2:1429–1524.

Stark, Rodney. *The Rise of Christianity: A Sociologist Reconsiders History.* Princeton: Princeton University Press, 1996.

Tate, W. Randolph. *Biblical Interpretation: An Integrated Approach.* 3rd ed. Grand Rapids: Baker Academic, 2008.

Taylor, Vincent. *The Gospel according to St. Mark.* 2nd ed. London: Macmillan, 1966.

Thackeray, Henry St. John, Ralph Marcus, and Louis Feldman. *Josephus in Nine Volumes*. Loeb Classical Library. London: William Heinemann; Cambridge, MA: Harvard University Press, 1927–65.

Theissen, Gerd. *The Shadow of the Galilean: The Quest for the Historical Jesus in Narrative Form*. Translated by John Bowden. Minneapolis: Fortress, 2007.

————. *Sociology of Early Palestinian Christianity*. Translated by John Bowden. Philadelphia: Fortress, 1978.

Theissen, Gerd, and Annette Merz. *The Historical Jesus: A Comprehensive Guide*. Translated by John Bowden. Minneapolis: Fortress, 1998.

Thompson, Marianne M. *The God of the Gospel of John*. Grand Rapids: Eerdmans, 2001.

Throckmorton, Burton H., Jr. *Gospel Parallels: A Comparison of the Synoptic Gospels*. Nashville: Thomas Nelson, 1992.

Vanhoye, Albert. *Structure and Message of the Epistle to the Hebrews*. Rome: Pontifical Biblical Institute, 1989.

Vermes, Geza. *The Complete Dead Sea Scrolls in English*. 7th ed. Penguin Classics. Harmondsworth, UK: Penguin, 2012.

Webster, John. "'A Great and Meritorious Act of the Church'? The Dogmatic Location of the Canon." In Barton and Wolter, *Die Einheit der Schrift*, 95–126.

Index of Subjects

Index of Authors

Index of Scripture
and Other Ancient Sources

Printed and bound by CPI Group (UK) Ltd, Croydon, CR0 4YY

13/04/2025

14656459-0002